CHICAGO IN MAPS

1612 to 2002

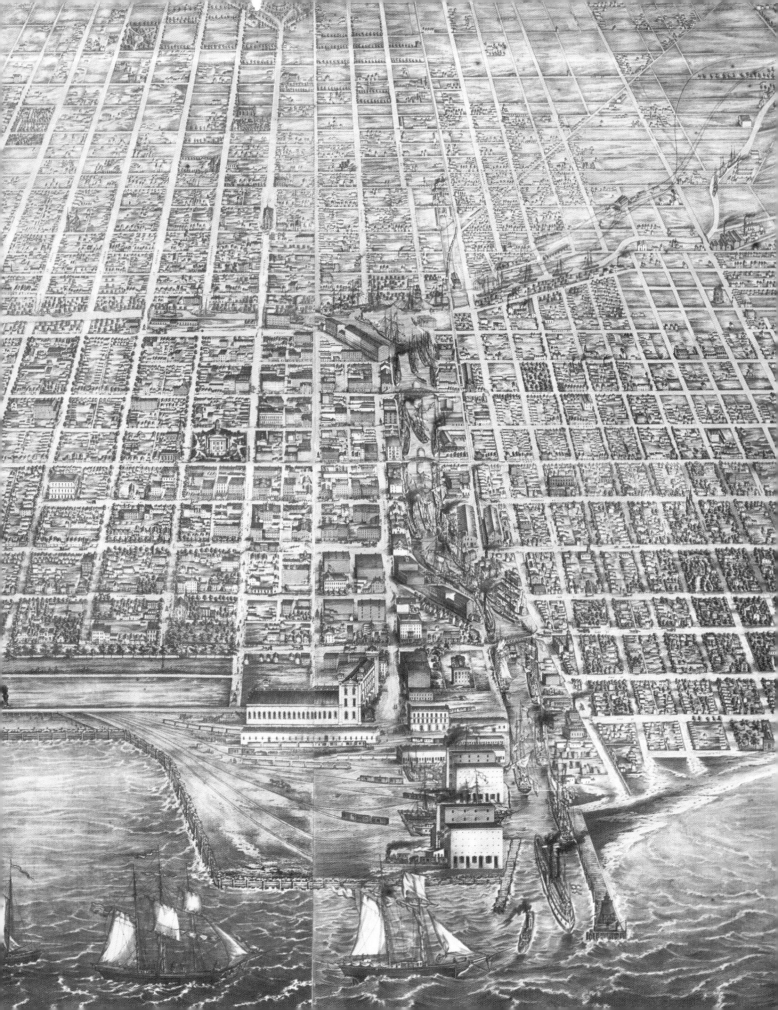

CHICAGO IN MAPS

1612 to 2002

ROBERT A. HOLLAND

Rizzoli
NEW YORK

For Lori

First published in the United States of America in 2005 by
RIZZOLI INTERNATIONAL PUBLICATIONS, INC.
300 Park Avenue South, New York, NY 10010
www.rizzoliusa.com

ISBN: 0-8478-2743-7
LCCN: 2005904551

Page 2: Bird's-Eye View of Chicago from 1857
by J. T. Palmatary (p. 82)

Designed by Aldo Sampieri

Printed and bound in China

2005 2006 2007 2008 2009 / 10 9 8 7 6 5 4 3 2 1

CONTENTS

ACKNOWLEDGMENTS

I can trace my fascination with matters cartographic back to childhood, when I spent many hours drawing and studying maps of all sorts. As an adult, this interest has led to a modest collection of antique maps. I must admit, however, that the idea of writing a book on maps had never really occurred to me. For this, I am obliged to Paul Cohen, who suggested over lunch one day that a book on Chicago maps would be a good project for me to undertake. Paul, who has authored several entries in Rizzoli's series of map books, then introduced me to his (and now my) agent, Asher Jason, to whom I would also like to express my gratitude.

As this project began to take shape, I benefited from the counsel of numerous local map experts. Harry Stern gave me helpful advice on Great Lakes maps. I presented an early outline of the book to Bob Karrow and Jim Akerman of the Newberry Library, who were both enthusiastic about the project. I would like to thank Pat Morris at the Newberry for suggesting a number of additions to my original list of maps. I am especially grateful to George and Mary Ritzlin for their comments on the book's early framework (Mary has also contributed an essay to the book). I have profited from numerous conversations with Carl Kupfer, a private collector with a great knowledge of Chicago area maps (images of several of Carl's maps can be found in this book).

I would also like to thank Gerald Danzer, not only for providing the Foreword to the book, but also for his comments on a draft of the manuscript.

Most of the maps reproduced in this book are housed in two august Chicago institutions, the Newberry Library and the Chicago Historical Society. I am indebted to the staffs at both of these establishments for their help in procuring the images of these maps. I would like to single out Rob Medina at the Historical Society for his help in tracking down several important early Chicago maps. I would also like to thank Tom Huber of the Illinois State Library and John Reinhardt of the Illinois State Archives for their assistance in locating and reproducing several maps for the book. I thank David Rumsey, Susan Danforth, Jo Ann King, Richard Smith, Mary Carroll, Clark Nelson, John Powell, Catherine Gass, John Alderson, and Ron Grossman, all of whom were instrumental in my obtaining images for the book.

Finally, I would like to thank my editor at Rizzoli Publications, Douglas Curran, for his help in putting this book together. Not only did he have to endure an author whose text contained more words than could possibly fit into the book, but one who provided the book's images in a rather piecemeal fashion. I thank him for his patience and understanding.

Map of
CHICAGO
for the Year
1933

Portraying some of its History and indicating the approximate
location of Points of Historical Interest: also a few of the Present Day
Institutions and Civic Improvements.

FOREWORD

Maps and cities go hand in hand. Some of the oldest surviving maps feature cities and every urban place in the modern world has been erected according to a host of plans, blueprints, maps, and views. This cartographic armada has not only given structure to the built environment, it has also helped to define each city's character as well. City builders need urban plans before the start of construction. Then they need promotional maps to sell their structures, followed by street maps to help people find their way around. The finest cartographic efforts are then called upon to celebrate the urban achievement, to review the city's past, inventory its present state, and conjure up visions for its future.

A newcomer seeking to understand a place like Chicago obviously needs a variety of cartographic tools. If this understanding is to be pursued to any depth, it will soon be found necessary to add old maps to the toolbox. Thus it is a great advantage for students of the contemporary city to have at hand a collection of historic maps that surveys Chicago's geographic context and reaches back to times predating the origins of the town. Here we have a selection of over seventy images picturing the environment, documenting the building of the metropolis, and capturing multiple facets of the urban experience.

In most cases Robert A. Holland has arranged his cartographic collection in roughly chronological order, selecting his featured maps so that they cover almost every decade of the city's history and extending to the far reaches of metropolitan influence. Each selection is fitted with an informed commentary encouraging serious readers to strike up a conversation with the map and to consider what it contributes to the collection as a whole. In this way the atlas will appeal to students interested in maps in general, to those studying the urban experience, and to readers focusing on the major theme: the history of Chicago.

Each section of the book collects maps of similar character, pushing the reader to reflect on the ways they fit together, coalescing into an explanatory pattern. The extensive commentary that accompanies each selection answers a fundamental question: "What does the reader need to know about Chicago's history to begin a serious reading of this map?" Sometimes the author supplies information about the cartographer, the sources of information on which the map is based, the style of presentation, the intended audience, or the purpose of the map. But these standard rubrics of cartographic inquiry take a back seat to the historical context. Dr. Holland wants us to follow his story of Chicago as we peruse his maps, tempting us in the process to return to specific selections at the end of our journey.

In most cases, we will need the focus map at full scale to explore it, critique it, and appreciate its richness. If we divert our attention from the general narrative told by the sequence of maps to study particular ones with some intensity, we will, no doubt, begin to see how each example raises questions, makes suggestions, and encourages us to sense tensions in the presentation, to realize, in the end, that each map maker has structured the piece to achieve some specific purpose. Realizing that each map is a rhetorical document, an expression of culture, or an exertion of power need not detract us as we proceed through the collection as a whole, keeping our sights on the major objectives: to understand today's Chicago and to develop an appreciation of the urban experience in general.

Note how the first group of Dr. Holland's maps traces, step by step, the gradual discovery of the North American interior by French cartographers in the seventeenth and eighteenth centuries. Chicago, as a place name on their maps, came to mark a particular spot on the Great Lakes. Ever after Lake Michigan would come first in defining what the future city would be all about. A selection of maps presenting the "Frontier Town" comes next and the images follow a specific sequence from portage settlement to military fort to land division process to town site. The story of Chicago in this respect follows a familiar pattern in the history of the American West. The town quickly became the city, a process documented by a series of classic maps and views in chapter three. Part four employs a dozen maps featuring hydrography to root Chicago's story in its soggy topography. This creative synthesis works the theme of water and waterways to underscore the importance of the natural environment. The next section starts with the Great Fire and cartographically constructs a new untamed city, which the Burnham Plan of 1909 called to order. The following chapter reveals various worlds within the city, reminding us that one image, one map, can never begin to capture the cosmopolitan nature of the living, breathing metropolis. The final section, spanning the twentieth century, suggests some

cartographic resources to help readers bring Chicago's story up to the present.

It is important to see these maps and views as part of a sequence picturing the city in the process of development. Each image records changes that have already taken place and suggests further developments in the process of becoming. The history supplied in the commentaries will help animate the static geography pictured on any particular map. Dr. Holland's compilation totals over seventy images, but the alert student will want to augment the collection by seeking additional frames to add depth to the city's motion picture. Mental maps drawn out of personal experience will also enrich the portrayal for those who know Chicago at first hand. They will go back and forth, from map to memory to reality, fortified to gain new insights from both the images and the commentary. Citizens of Chicago will return to the book again and again.

Along the way this procession of maps will open gates to understanding the modern American city. The first entryway pushes us to envision the city as an artifact, a working machine with a functional design that enables countless transactions of an almost infinite variety to transpire each day. Each part of the metropolis contributes to the whole. It takes an artist with particular talents to help us glimpse the city as an artifact. He or she must stop the animation, catch the entire city at rest, and construct its topographical form from the perspective of a bird flying high above Chicago's spires and towers. The Palmatary (1857) and Poole Brothers (1898) views are classic images in this genre.

A second gate to understanding a city is the geographic character of the place. Scholars distinguish between the elements of site and situation, the former focusing on the physical layout of the immediate environment and latter concentrating on the relationship of the site to the places that surround it. In the final analysis, Chicago's situation extends to the world ocean, that all-encompassing sea connecting each island and continent to all the others by routes for trade, movement, and exchange. Note that Dr. Holland starts his story in the Atlantic Ocean and uses almost seventeen percent of his collection to develop an elaborate prelude to Chicago's story, an overture called the Great Lakes. Later, he interrupts his telling of the city's tale to elaborate on the challenges thrown up by water and waterways, key ingredients in defining Chicago's site as well as its situation.

The third gate, named Nexus, introduces themes of centrality, linkage, and connection and then suggests that any city is more than a crossroads. Urbanity transforms crossroad functions into a great engine of production as well as exchange, multiplying products, generating ideas, and creating new ways of life. Views of the World's Columbian Exposition (1893) and the Elevated Railroad System (ca. 1910), upon close inspection, seem to chant "Nexus, Nexus, Nexus."

Attention to the urban sounds when inspecting individual maps will lead one to the fourth gate to understanding the city. Here we hear the hum of the city as an economic engine, supplying the needs and wants of its citizens, visitors, customers, and dependents spread out into the hinterland and beyond. Depictions of the Union Stock Yards (1891) and the freight tunnel network (1928) provide advantageous listening posts to hear the whir and the thrum, the buzz and the purr, the drone and the murmur, sounds of the city at work.

The fifth gate is often a silent one. This portal reveals the city as a container, a collection of facilities for storing raw materials, finished products, ideas, and memories, becoming a warehouse for everything that expresses our society and culture. The bird's-eye views show us a host of containers neatly arranged along access aisles. Take a close look at Pullman's town (1881) or Graceland Cemetery (1876) with the storage factor in mind and the concept of the city as a container will grow in explanatory power.

The sixth metaphor encourages us to imagine the city as a stage upon which people play out many roles, some scripted and some unscripted, but all brought together into a metropolitan choreography. In spatial terms, the urban fabric is made up of public spaces where the populace can interact and different elements rub shoulders even if they resist mixing very well. Then there are a variety of semi-public places where the populace sorts itself out into groups of every type. Finally the city supports myriads of private places where individuality is nourished and privacy is sustained. The Thompson Plat (1830), the Ethnic Neighborhoods Map (1982), and the Land Use Survey (1942), each in its own way, helps us understand the city as a series of social spatial constructs.

The seventh gateway celebrates the city as an art form. Guerin's picture of Grant Park according to the Burnham Plan (1909) immediately comes to mind, but one can also appreciate aesthetic elements exhibited in the Century of Progress grounds (1933) and the *Pictorial Map and Guide* issued by the Chicago Motor Bus Company in 1926.

But not every portal to urban understanding frames the higher nature of humanity. "The Map of Sin" (1893) by W. T. Stead and the Bruce-Roberts "Gangland Map" forcefully remind us of the city as Anti-Christ. The wage maps compiled by the Hull House workers (1895) lead to a thick report in which the prices for food and shelter often outrun the resources available to many families. Gate eight predicts that its name will be Armageddon.

We do not want to end our discussion on themes of conflict and suffering, darkness and depravity. Instead we should return to Dr. Holland's sequence and notice how he concludes with an expansive satellite image of the metropolitan region, Chicago as viewed from the heavens. It is paired with a topographic sheet showing in detail the Loop Quadrangle in 1963. Reflecting on these final images, and the dynamic between them, pushes us to build a final great gate of cartographic understanding. Here the city will offer many doorways under a great arch. Let us call it "The Measure of the Human Condition" for assessing ourselves, which might be what cities do best. And maps are at their service.

The SPOT Metroview (2001) presents Chicago as a whole, a complete urban system. The U. S. Geological Survey quadrangle (1963) takes one slice of the city to inventory many individual parts of the urban fabric. Here we can trace the footprint of the city as artifact, a retrospective blueprint so to speak, which reveals the orderly arrangement of individual structures on a gridiron plan of streets and public places. Then, note how the forceful presence of lake and river pushes the city into a particular shape. At the same time, discover the routes leading off the map in every direction to mark this as a central place, a nexus for the metropolis and its region. Then we hear the various sounds of the economic machine coming from almost every structure on the page.

Maps by nature encourage us to lift up our eyes. They tend to be positive and optimistic. Urban maps usually show us what the city might be rather than what it actually is. Perhaps that is why maps and cities go hand in hand: they are open-ended. Each one can load us down with information but at the same time can help us frame fundamental questions. As one wise person summed it up, "We are not yet what we shall be, we are in the process of becoming." This book will send us on our way, helping us to appreciate our city, to understand the process of urbanization, and to size up the urban potential. In other words, we will be mapping our way. Bon voyage!

— Gerald A. Danzer

Professor of History Emeritus
University of Illinois at Chicago

THE FIRST SCIENTIFIC CARTOGRAPHY OF THE REGION

Champlain's Map of 1612

Title: Carte Geographique de la Nouvelle France faictte par le Sieur de Champlain Saint Tongois Cappitaine Ordinaire pour Le Roy en La Marine
Date Issued: 1613
Cartographer: Samuel de Champlain
Published: *Les Voyages des Sieur de Champlain* (Paris)
Copperplate Engraving, 44 x 76.5 cm
Newberry Library, Ayer p 121 C6 1613

The site of Chicago was originally a part of "New France"—that part of North America claimed, explored, and colonized by the French between 1534 and 1763. The mapping of Chicago can thus be said to begin with the French explorations of this area, and the Great Lakes region in particular. Since one can make the case that it is the first map to indicate a chain of Great Lakes, this beautiful map is a natural place to start a history of the mapping of Chicago. We do find hints of the fresh water contained by the Great Lakes on earlier maps. Gerard Mercator's famous 1569 world map includes a "Mare Dulce" (a reference to Lake Huron), as does the 1570 world map of Mercator's friend, Abraham Ortelius. The inscription on

Mercator's map states: "Here is a sea of sweet water, the limits of which the Canadians, on the authority of the Saguenay Indians, say they do not know." This description is based on information Jacques Cartier obtained from Native American sources during his explorations of the Gulf of Saint Lawrence and the Saint Lawrence River.

Samuel de Champlain is known as the "Father of New France" for his work exploring, promoting and colonizing the French territories of North America. Most likely born a commoner, Champlain spent several years soldiering in his native Brouage and then acquired a reputation as a first-rate navigator, by taking part in an expedition to the West Indies and Central America. He received an

honorary title (with pension) from Henri IV, and in 1603, accompanied François Gravé, Sieur du Pont, on a voyage to the Rivière de Canada (Saint Lawrence River). The purpose of this trip was to develop the merchant Pontgravé's fur trade. Champlain, who was along as an observer, left Pontgravé to his business at the trading post at Tadoussac, and spent some time studying the natives' customs. He ventured "twelve or fifteen leagues" up the Saguenay River, where he heard descriptions of the whole Saguenay basin and its waterways and learned of a saltwater sea to the north. He concluded that "It is some gulf of this our sea, which overflows in the north into the midst of the continent." Thus, in 1603, seven years before its discovery by the English, Champlain had surmised the existence of Hudson Bay. He went further up the St. Lawrence as far as the rapids at Hochelaga (Montreal), where he learned from native accounts of great lakes to the west, and was also persuaded that the Asian Sea was not far off. Before the summer was out, Champlain made his way back to Tadoussac and returned with Pontgravé to France.

In 1604, Champlain again ventured to New France, this time with Pierre du Gaust, Sieur de Monts, to whom Henri IV had granted a monopoly on trade in the region. Champlain led a group of settlers from the Saint Lawrence region to Acadia, where they chose to spend the winter on an island in the Saint Croix River (at the present-day boundary between New Brunswick and Maine). Scurvy killed nearly half the party this first winter, and in 1605, the settlement was moved across the Bay of Fundy to Port Royal (now Annapolis, Nova Scotia). The next two winters claimed the lives of fewer men, and Champlain spent the summer months exploring the rugged coastlines of Acadia, Québec, and New England, venturing as far south as Cape Cod. The intent was for this colony to become a trading post and a center of settlement, but circumstances both geographic and domestic proved too difficult to overcome. The heavy forests and many inlets, beaches and bays of the area made it impossible to enforce the monopoly of their fur trade, and a lack of support from home led to widespread discouragement among the settlers. In 1607, many of them accompanied Champlain back to France.

While in France, Champlain pleaded with De Monts to return to Canada. He argued that enforcement of the trade monopolies would ensure the success of the lucrative fur trade; that friendly relations with the natives (particularly the Huron) would further bolster their enterprise; and that exploration of the area would lead to a Northwest Passage to China. Champlain's argument won the day, and in 1608, he returned to North America with the Sieur de Monts. Hoping to find more hospitable conditions than those in Acadia, they traveled up the Saint Lawrence River to "the place where the river narrowed" (Québec) and established a small "habitation" or fur-trading fort. Trade with the local natives was slow to develop, and the first winter was particularly harsh—only Champlain and eight of the original thirty-two settlers survived. In the summer of 1609, Champlain made lasting allies of the Algonquin and Huron by fighting alongside them during a raid on a party of Mohawk, the easternmost tribe of the Iroquois Confederacy. After a winter visit to France for supplies and reinforcements, he returned in the spring of 1610, only to be forced to go back upon hearing of the assassination of Henri IV. Securing the backing he needed for his fledgling colony, Champlain returned for the summer season of 1611.

Champlain spent the following year and a half in France, during which time he prepared the map presented here, as well as other illustrations, for the publication of a chronicle of his explorations of 1604–11. This book, *Les Voyages des Sieur de Champlain*, included twenty-two large-scale plans of potential harbors and other features between Cape Cod and the Lachine Rapids, as well as two small-scale maps of New France.

The present map is the larger of these two maps, and it illustrates three excursions Champlain made into the interior. Montreal is marked on the map, and to the west are "Great Lakes." He depicts four intriguingly named lakes: Lac Contenant 15 Journees des Canaux des Sauuages (roughly translated, "Lake Containing Fifteen Days of Canoeing with Indians," and clearly recognizable as Lake Ontario), Lac des Irocois (a misplaced Lake Oneida), Grand Lac Contenant 300 Lieux de Long ("Large Lake that is

Three Hundred Leagues Long") and Lake Champlain. According to Schwartz and Ehrenberg, "Champlain probably bestowed his own name on this last lake by reason both of his battle with the Iroquois near present Crown Point and of the strategic importance he attached to its location." At the western end of Lake Ontario we find "sault de au," which is the first reference to Niagara Falls on a printed map.

This map is a testament to the fact that the scientific exploration and mapping of New France began with Champlain. Gone is the guesswork and copying found on earlier maps of North America. In their place, Champlain relies on his own observations, and (for those regions west of Montreal) native accounts and sketch maps. Where he relied on European sources that he had not verified, he displayed singular honesty: see the note on the northern coast of the Gulf of Saint Lawrence and the Maritimes that "l'auteur n'a point encore recongru cette coast"—the author has not yet seen this coast. Nor did he place Prince Edward Island on the map, even though it could be found on Mercator's map.

Champlain clearly meant to incite the imagination of the French with this map and encourage settlement in New France. He also intended for this map to be used by navigators with uncorrected compasses. Thus, the map is angled so as to make the top of the map correspond with magnetic north, while a slanting latitude bar represents true north. He notes as much in the two legends in the top corners, and states that he "made this map for the greater convenience of those who navigate these coasts, since they sail to that country according to the compasses arranged for the hemisphere of Asia."

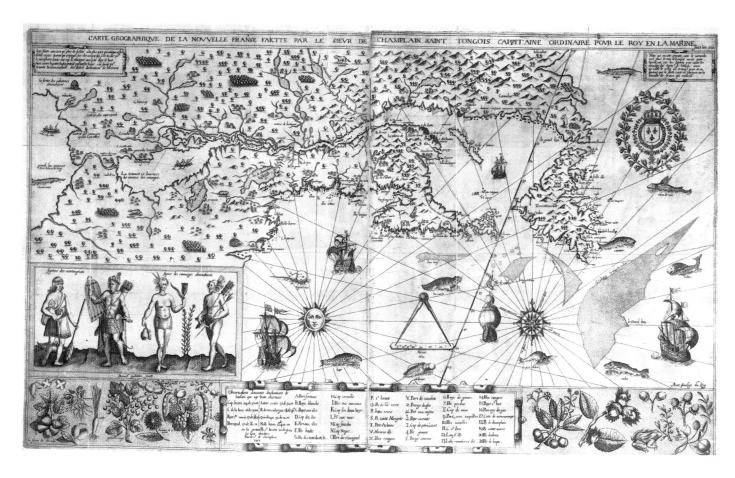

THE FIRST MAP TO DEPICT THE ENTIRE GREAT LAKES NETWORK

Champlain's Final Map

Title: Carte de la nouvelle france, augmentée depuis la derniere, servant a la navigation faicte en son vray Meridien, par le Sr. de Champlain, Capitaine pour le Roy, en la Marine
Date Issued: 1632
Cartographer: Samuel de Champlain
Published: *Les Voyages de la Nouvelle France Occidentale, dicte Canada* (Paris)
Copperplate Engraving, 53 x 87 cm
Library and Archives of Canada, NMC-51970

France's fur trade suffered heavy financial losses in 1611 that prompted Québec's sponsors to abandon the colony. Champlain characteristically worked in a tireless fashion to save the settlement and eventually persuaded Louis XIII to intercede. The king appointed a viceroy of the North American territories who in turn made Champlain commandant of New France.

In 1613, Champlain returned to Québec and set out to restore the ruined fur trade. His first mission took him up the Ottawa River in hope of establishing trade relations with the interior native groups, and in search of a water route to China. He made his way as far as Allumette Island, where he was turned back by Algonquin middlemen trading for furs with the Huron and others, and who wished to retain that trade. Undaunted,

Champlain gained permission to reenter this region by promising to aid the Huron in their campaign against the Iroquois. He again ascended the Ottawa in 1615, and then made his way across to the Georgian Bay on Lake Huron. There he was persuaded by the Hurons to lead a war party against the Iroquois. Working their way down to Lake Ontario and into Iroquois territory, the group launched an unsuccessful raid on a fortified Onondaga village near present day Lake Oneida. Champlain was wounded in the knee, and had to be carried to safety. He writes: "The pain which I suffered in consequence of the wound in my knee was nothing in comparison with that which I endured while I was bound and pinioned on the back of one of our Savages." Champlain spent the winter with the Hurons, continued to explore the southeastern shore of Lake

Huron, and returned to Québec in the summer of 1616.

This courageous journey was perhaps Champlain's crowning achievement in New France. It served to further bolster the French alliance with the northern native tribes and the Huron nation, and, by opening the Ottawa route, secured the mid-continent for the French fur trade. His explorations were recorded on an important, although incomplete and untitled map, which was the first map to depict Lakes Huron and Ontario, and the route of the Ottawa River. (This 1616 map was later finished and published by Pierre Du Val as *Le Canada* in 1653.) A successful fur trading operation was to prove elusive, however, for several reasons. Pressing affairs in Europe often diverted the attention of the French government, and Champlain was repeatedly forced to make trips across the Atlantic to make the case for his beleaguered colony. Moreover, his mandate to both settle the territory and develop a flourishing fur trade often proved contradictory. Indeed, it proved impossible to finance both of these missions from the annual profits, particularly since the French government never saw fit to enforce the fur trading monopoly.

Then warfare erupted between England and France. Although the colony was hardly prosperous, the British deemed Québec worthy of occupation. In 1628, a band of privateers led by David Kirke laid siege to the settlement. By the summer of 1629, the fort's supplies of food and gunpowder were exhausted, and Champlain and his garrison were forced to surrender. Taken into custody, Champlain was detained in England, where he strenuously argued that the surrender of Québec had occurred after the end of French and English hostilities. In 1632, the colony was restored to France, and in 1633, Champlain made his last voyage across the Atlantic Ocean back to Québec. He suffered a stroke in October of 1635, and died on Christmas Day. At the time of his death, his colony extended along both shores of the St. Lawrence River.

The map presented here, Champlain's final map, is an excellent summary of the geography of New France as it was known in 1629. It was to serve as a prototype for later European maps for nearly a century, and thus served as a fitting testament to the

intrepid explorer's brilliant navigational and cartographic skills. The map shows Hudson Bay and many "saults" or falls on the Saint Lawrence between Trois Rivières and Lake Ontario, and Champlain records a number of personal observations on the map: north of Lake Ontario is the "place where there are many deer"; north of Lake

Huron is the "place where Indians dry their berries each year"; just to the west is an "island where there is a copper mine"; and, to the south, is the "nation where there are many buffalo."

Champlain did not travel to the northern and western areas depicted on the map, and here its representation is less accurate. Based on information

received from Native American sources, it is clear that Champlain's knowledge of the Great Lakes was growing, but was still incomplete. Lac St. Louis is clearly Lake Ontario, and for '90' (Niagara Falls), he has the following note: "Waterfall of great height where many kinds of fish are stunned in descending." The two small lakes that form a strait above 'La nation neutre' are Lake Erie, and the lake labeled 'Mer Douce' combines the Georgian Bay and Lake Huron. Champlain notes '34' (Sault St. Marie) flows from "another extremely large lake" that he calls "Grand Lac." He also locates Lake Champlain too far east of Hudson Bay, which he was to never visit.

Despite these inaccuracies, it could be argued this is the first map to depict the entire network of the Great Lakes. To begin, we have Lakes Huron (Mer Douce) and Ontario (Lac St. Louis), both of which were discovered and named by Champlain. Next we find Grand Lac or Lake Superior, a lake that Champlain never saw; rather, his representation here is based on information provided to him by his Native American acquaintances, or perhaps by Etienne Brûlé, one of the first fur traders (*coureurs de bois*). According to Fite and Freeman, Lake Michigan is represented by the river system leading south from Lake Superior, and here is identified as "Grand Rivière qui vient du midy." Finally, an untitled Lake Erie is seen as a strait extending from Lake Huron to the Niagara Falls and Lake Ontario region.

In the words of Heidenrich, "there was no one else who had the personal experience to compile the information for such a map. Posterity is fortunate that in Champlain experience was combined with scientific skill; otherwise the information he gathered would have been lost. With justification this map has become a 'mother map'…" In 1643, Jean Boisseau published a reduced (and therefore more marketable) version of this map as *Description de la Nouvelle France*. On this map, we find that Boisseau has affixed the name 'Lake Derie' to Lake Erie. Thus, according to Burden, it is the first printed map "to illustrate and name all five Great Lakes."

ALL FIVE LAKES IN RECOGNIZABLE FORM

The Sanson Map of 1856

Title: Le Canada, ou Nouvelle Franse, &c.
Date Issued: 1656
Cartographer: Nicolas Sanson
Published: Separately
Copperplate Engraving, 40 x 55 cm
Library and Archives of Canada, NMC-21100

In what became known as "the first English conquest of Canada," the French were expelled from the Saint Lawrence Valley in 1629. The Treaty of Saint-Germain-en-Laye restored the territory to the French in March of 1632 (in return for the payment of a dowry King Louis XIII owed the English crown). Shortly thereafter, the French returned to New France, and a new phase of exploration was to begin. It was not, however, fur-trading or a route to China that provided the impetus for these explorations; rather, it was the redemption of souls—as carried out by the Company of Jesus. The early conversion efforts of the Jesuits were centered near fur-trading centers, but soon penetrated the territory's interior to the region of the Great Lakes.

These missionary expeditions were expensive, and the Jesuits relied on donations from generous benefactors to fund their operations. In an effort to bolster financial and political support from the upper class of French society, the Jesuits began to publish yearly accounts of their missionary work in New France. One might thus consider these publications, known as the *Jesuit Relations*, as promotional material; that is, as attempts to convince the world to contribute to the efforts of the Company of Jesus to convert the aboriginal populations of New France. The *Relations* are, of course, much more than that. They begin where Champlain's writings leave off, and are one of the major sources of information about the early years of French

colonization in North America. They contain a wealth of geographical data, descriptions of wildlife, flora, fauna and other natural resources, as well as information about the native societies encountered by the French, and indeed, information about the consequences of these encounters.

In the *Relation* of 1647–48, Father Paul Regueneau describes the Great Lakes in some detail, and presents the first published description of Niagara Falls. In 1650, Nicolas Sanson incorporated Father Regueneau's account into a landmark map of North America. This map, *Amerique Septenrionale*, was the first printed map to depict all five Great Lakes in recognizable form. (Note that Bouisseau's 1643 map, mentioned earlier, does not portray Lake Erie or

Lake Michigan in a familiar form.) It was also the first printed map to use the names "Ontario" and "Superior," and to present an illustration of (an unnamed) Lake Erie. Lake Huron, also unnamed, is represented in a reasonably accurate manner, although Green Bay is not distinguished from the rest of Lake Michigan. Both Lake Superior and Lake Michigan are depicted as open-ended toward the west, which, in the words of Karpinski, is "a geographical absurdity testifying to the honest ignorance of the cartographer."

The map shown here, first published in 1656, is an enlarged section of Sanson's 1650 map. It covers the French possessions in North America and its neighboring colonies, and improves upon the 1650 map in many ways. We find, for example, the entire drainage basin of the Great Lakes and Saint Lawrence River delineated in greater detail on this map. Hudson Bay is shown in greater detail, Long Island is introduced, and New Amsterdam is accurately located. Perhaps the most important improvement Sanson made was to affix the name 'Erie' to a recognizable lake— the name being that of the native tribe that lived along the shore of the lake. As on his earlier map, Sanson represents the diversity of the native population, as well as the main European settlements and French territorial claims. Both maps contain a line of mountains, the "Apalatcy Montes," or Appalachian Mountains, that run east-west rather than north-south, and which appear to join an extension of the Ozarks. These mountains thus form a barrier between the Great Lakes and the Gulf of Mexico. Although neither map shows a great river, they helped perpetuate the misconception that the Mississippi originates from four rivers hemmed in by mountains that converge at the Gulf of Mexico.

THE COURAGE OF ONE'S FAITH

The Bressani Map

Title: Novæ Fanciæ Accurata / Delineatio 1657
Date Issued: 1657
Cartographer: Francesco Bressani
Published: Separately
Copperplate Engraving, 51 x 75 cm (Western half)
Newberry Library, Novacco 4F 75

Francesco Gioseppe Bressani was born in Rome on May 6, 1612. At the age of fourteen, he became a Jesuit novice. After sixteen years of education and service, he felt drawn to missionary work in New France, having read accounts of these efforts in the *Relations*. Arriving in Canada in 1642, Bressani ministered to the French for a time at Quebec, and the next year to the Algonquins at Three Rivers. In April of 1644, he set out with a young French boy and six converted Hurons on an ill-fated trip to the Jesuit mission in Huron country. On the first day of the journey, the Huron guiding the canoe carrying Father Bressani shot at an eagle, causing the canoe to be overturned. Bressani, who could not swim, was saved from the cold waters, and the drenched party spent the night only a short distance from Three Rivers. Cold and heavy snow hampered their progress the next day, forcing them to set up camp at noon. In the meantime, a group of Mohawk warriors nearby had taken notice of the travelers (perhaps alerted to their presence by the shots fired the earlier day) and ambushed the party the next day. One of the Hurons was slain, scalped, and subsequently eaten; Father Bressani and the others were marched into Iroquois country.

In captivity, Father Bressani was cruelly tortured: he was stabbed, burned, beaten, left exposed to the elements, forced to dance and sing, and had his hair and beard torn out, among other depravities. He was marched to a village where he had his left thumb and several fingers of his right hand cut off, only to be led to another village to face new tortures. He was told that he would be fattened up in order to be eaten, and by June he had accepted this as his fate. Asking his captors for death other than by fire, Bressani was told that he would not be killed; instead, he was given to a woman in the village. Whether through compassion (the woman's daughters could not countenance the sight of his burned and broken body), or because she did not think a man with mangled hands was fit for work, and therefore would be a burden to her, the woman ordered her son to trade Father Bressani to the Dutch at Fort Orange. The Dutch acted generously, paying a ransom and returning Bressani to France in November. Undeterred, the Father's one thought was to return to New France, which he bravely did the following year.

HVRONVM EXPLICATA TABVLA

After a short stay at Three Rivers, he successfully made his way to the Huron mission at Georgian Bay.

About this time, the long and intermittent warfare between the Iroquois and the Huron was drawing to a close. The acquisition of firearms from the Dutch gave the Iroquois a huge advantage in a conflict intensified by fur trading disputes. In 1648, the Iroquois began an invasion of Huron country, intent on annihilating the Huron confederation. This forced Father Bressani, whose mission was destroyed, back to Quebec. The Iroquois confederation's final blow came in March of 1649. In coordinated attacks under winter conditions, Mohawk and Seneca warriors slipped silently across the snow and in two hours destroyed the missions of Saint Ignace and Saint Louis. Hundreds of Hurons were killed or captured, and two Jesuit priests became martyrs to their faiths.

Fathers Jean de Brébeuf and Gabriel Lalemant could have escaped the attack on the Saint Louis mission, but chose to remain with their flock. The two priests were captured and dragged to Saint Ignace, whereupon they were stripped naked, showered with stones, cruelly beaten with clubs, and then tied to posts to be burned to death. Brébeuf is said to have kissed the stake to which he was bound, and, upon seeing the many Christian converts who were also to be tormented, to have consoled them. This infuriated the invaders, who cut off his lips and part of his tongue in order to curtail his preaching. Upon seeing that he did not cease, they tied a collar of red-hot tomahawk-heads around Brébeuf's neck, deriding his faith by saying: "Thou hast told the others that, the more one suffers in this life, the greater his reward in the next; therefore thank us, because we increase thy crown." Brébeuf had scalding water poured on his head several times in a mockery of baptism; a red-hot iron thrust down his throat, and pieces of his flesh cut off, roasted and eaten in front of him. All the while, it was reported, he did not cry out or give the least sign of pain. When he expired, his heart was cut out and divided among the young men so that they might receive a portion of his bravery. Father Lalemant received a similar treatment, and in addition had a resinous bark wrapped around him and set on fire. He survived the night, and the next day one of his captors killed him out of pity.

In the aftermath, Huron resistance to the Iroquois invasion abruptly collapsed. Many retreated to Christian Island in Georgian Bay, swelling the island's population to over six thousand. Father Bressani joined the fugitives, where during the terrible winter of 1649–50, thousands starved. Bressani was sent by his superior back to Québec for aid, but his efforts were futile. The Huron nation had been destroyed, and its members were either adopted into the Iroquois confederation or scattered far to points north or west. The marauding Iroquois prevented Father Bressani from any return to his flock, and he was forced to remain at Québec. In November of 1650, Bressani's failing health and the meager resources of the mission obliged him to return to Italy; there he regained his health and spent many years as a preacher and missionary. He died in Florence in 1672.

Soon after his return to Italy, Bressani wrote *Breve Relatione d'alcune Missioni* (Macerata, 1653), in which he relates his years as a Jesuit missionary in New France. The last sentence of this account reads, "The whole would have been made clearer with the map which I was hoping to add here, but it is not ready. Those who desire it can have it a little while later, in separate form, with pictures of the Barbarians and their cruelties." For many years, the existence of this beautiful map was unknown, until it was discovered in Paris. Another copy was subsequently discovered in Vienna. The map can only be presumed to have been made by Bressani, since his name does not appear anywhere on it. It is in two sheets, and several copies of the western half have appeared recently—apparently modern restrikes from the original plate on old paper.

TRAVELOGUES

The Dablon-Allouez Map of Lake Superior

Title: Lac Svperievr
Date Issued: 1672
Cartographer: Claude Dablon & Claude-Jean Allouez
Published: *Jesuit Relations* (Paris)
Copperplate Engraving, 17 x 23 cm
Newberry Library, Ayer *263 J512 1672 D2

One might consider the *Jesuit Relations* as akin to travelogues—that is, as narrative accounts of the seventeenth-century excursions of the Jesuits in New France. In them, we find geographical descriptions, observations about the local populations, and remarks about the flora, fauna, and natural resources the Jesuits found during their travels. Their readers, then, were invited to join in these journeys, to explore the exotic new territories claimed by the French in North America. And what better way to follow along than with a map? Certainly Father Claude Dablon, the Superior of the Jesuit Missions in New France, realized as much, when he wrote: "By glancing, as one can, at the Map of the lakes, and of the territories on which are settled most of the tribes of these regions, one Will

gain more light upon all these Missions than by long descriptions that might be given of them."

The map that Dablon is referring to here is entitled "Lac Svperievr," and it was included in the *Relation* of 1670–71. Primarily a mission map, its purpose was to chart the westward progress of the Jesuits' evangelical labors among the various Native American nations. It is interesting to note that only the Native American nation mentioned in the title of the map is the "Outaouacs." The explanation given is that this term was "given to all the Savages of these regions, although of different Nations, because the first to appear among the French were the Outaouacs."

By the time of this map's publication in 1672, the Iroquois Confederation had vanquished most

of the native inhabitants that lived along the shores of Lake Huron, the islands of Georgian Bay, and the lower peninsula of Michigan. Many had fled to the southern shores of Lake Superior, and to the dense woods of northwestern Wisconsin, Minnesota, and western Ontario. The French had signed a peace treaty with the western Iroquois nations in 1653, but it did not give them access to the western Great Lakes. As a result, the French found themselves besieged in Quebec and Montreal by the Mohawk and Oneida, and their fur trade began to wither away. What little fur did reach them came by way of the Ottawa, who had replaced the destroyed Huron as middlemen in the French fur trade. This only served to infuriate the Iroquois (who wanted the business for themselves); as a result, they attacked the Ottawa and forced them from the islands they occupied in Lake Huron to what is now Wisconsin and the upper peninsula of Michigan.

The only French who managed to reach the western Great Lakes at this time were two *coureurs des bois* (fur traders), Pierre Radisson and Médard Chouart des Groseilliers. In 1659, they ignored an edict from the French government that required all fur traders to be licensed and set forth from Montreal in search of beaver pelts. Avoiding Iroquois attacks near Lake Huron, they made their way to Lake Superior, where they built a small fort near Chequamegon Bay. They returned to Montreal the following August with sixty canoes full of beaver pelts—the largest such cargo to ever have been brought into New France. The governor, however, was not pleased. He detained des Groseilliers for fur trading without a license, and seized the bulk of the furs as taxes and fines. Furious, des Groseilliers and Radisson left the settlement as soon as des Groseilliers was freed. They later traveled to England to present King James with a new fur-trading plan. They had learned of an abundance of beaver west of Lake Superior, and could establish a trading partnership with the natives in that area. Why not build a trading post on Hudson Bay? Large ships from Europe would have direct access to such a fort, and with their native contacts, des Groseilliers and

Radisson could arrange for furs to be delivered directly to the post. King James was impressed with their proposal and financed a preliminary expedition. Its success led to the establishment of the Hudson's Bay Company.

The natives who had accompanied Radisson and des Groseilliers's return in 1660 to Montreal were anxious to make their way homeward; so it was hurriedly decided that Father René Ménard would return with them to minister to the populous region of which the two businessmen had recounted. The priest reached the area of what is probably Keweenaw Bay along the southern shores of Lake Superior, and spent the mild winter performing his evangelical duties amongst the natives. Moving to Chequamegon Bay, Father Ménard heard of starvation among the fugitive Hurons now living along headwaters of the Black River in the forests of Wisconsin. He was determined to visit these people, but was not to make it; along the way he became separated from his companion during a portage and was never seen again.

In 1663, King Louis XIV decreed that New France should be made a royal colony, and shortly thereafter, a regiment of soldiers was sent to quell the Iroquois. Within a year the French launched a series of attacks on the Iroquois, and in 1665, after receiving the news of Father Ménard's

death, the Jesuits sent Father Claude-Jean Allouez to the mission at Chequamegon Bay. Allouez had dreamed since his youth of the mission fields in New France, and was overjoyed to be assigned to labor amongst the Ottawa and other western tribes along Lake Superior. An account of his trip to this area, and the next two years of his missionary labors, composes the greater part of the *Relations* published in 1668. This report is one of the earliest descriptions of the interior of the continent, particularly of the Sioux and other peoples who lived on the eastern and northern plains. A keen observer, Allouez's graphic writings included descriptions of the geography and natural resources of the area. We read, for example, of the clarity of Lake Superior, of the abundance of copper nodules that could be seen on the lake bottom, and of the native religious beliefs concerning these mineral deposits.

In 1667, Allouez returned to Québec, where he was to pause only two days before embarking west again to Chequamegon Bay. In 1668, he founded a mission at Sault Sainte Marie, which was to serve as the permanent headquarters for the Jesuits working in the western Great Lakes. Here Father Dablon was to take his place as Superior to the Western Missions. By this time, Father Jacques Marquette had replaced Allouez at Chequamegon Bay, and

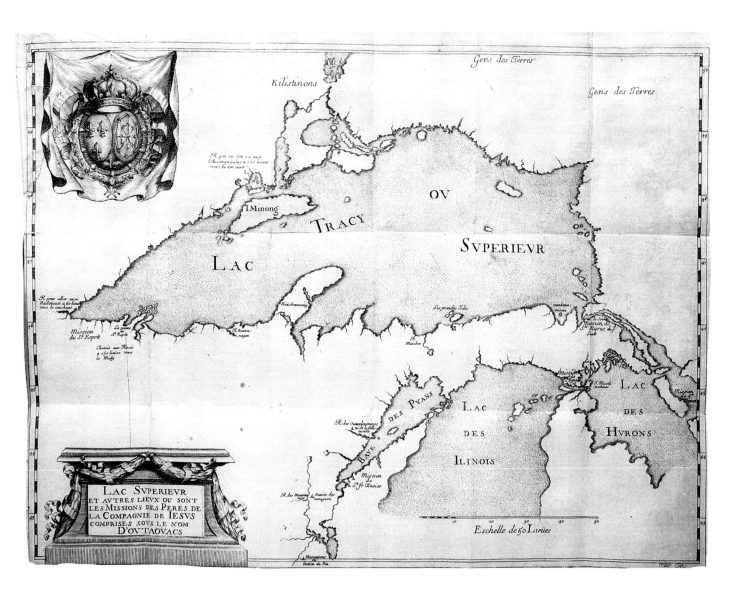

Allouez had set out to work among the tribes found around Green Bay.

Father Dablon had had some training as a geographer, and the map pictured here was probably drafted by him based on information supplied by Allouez, by the local natives, and perhaps also by fur traders, such as Jean Peré, who were active in the area in the late 1660s. The map depicts Lake Superior in amazingly accurate detail, and it is the first map to distinguish Green Bay (Baye des Puans) from Lake Michigan (Lac de Illinois). Note that Lake Superior is also named 'Tracy'. This was to honor Alexander de Prouville de Tracy, who in 1665 was appointed royal lieutenant-general for the French possessions in America. Within two years, with troops made up of career soldiers, militiamen and about one-hundred Huron and Algonquin, Tracy subdued the principal warring Iroquois nations, which were the Onondaga, the Mohawk and the Oneida. The conclusion was a peace that was to last nearly twenty years, and the interior was again open to receive Jesuit missionaries. Thus, notes Father Allouez in his journal, Lake Superior "will henceforth bear Monsieur de Tracy's name in recognition of indebtedness to him on the part of the people of these regions." This alliance of church and state is reinforced by the depiction of the arms of France and of Novasse in the left-hand corner of the map.

MARQUETTE AND JOLIET

The Thévenot Map
The Joliet Map

Title: Carte de las decouverte faite l'an 1673 dans l'Amerique Septentrionale
Date Issued: 1681
Cartographer: Melchisédech Thévenot
Published: *Recueil de Voyages de Mr Thévenot* (Paris)
Copperplate Engraving, 30 x 24.1 cm
Library and Archives of Canada, NMC-15380

Title: Nouvelle Decouverte de plusieurs Nations Dans la Nouuelle France En l'annee 1673 et 1674
Date Issued: 1674
Cartographer: Louis Joliet
Published: Manuscript
Pen, Ink, and Watercolor, 66 x 86 cm
The John Carter Brown Library at Brown University

In 1669, while engaged in missionary labors along the Fox River in modern day Wisconsin, Father Allouez dispatched a note that this "river leads by a six days' voyage to the great river named Messi-Sipi…" His letter, printed in the *Jesuit Relation* of 1669–70, may have been the first mention in print of the Mississippi by its present name. It is also evidence that the French explorers of the seventeenth century were well aware of the existence of this river. The question of who among them was the first to reach the Mississippi is debatable. It may have been Nicolet, Radisson, Perrot, or LaSalle; but, whether any of these men was the first Frenchman to see the

Mississippi, it was Father Jacques Marquette and Louis Joliet who first recorded a voyage on the great river. The purpose of their expedition was dependent on perspective. Certainly for Father Marquette, it was to "visit the nations who dwell along the Mississippi River" in hopes of furthering his evangelical mission. The French government, on the other hand, had more worldly ends in mind. There was some hope that river would lead to the California Sea (and hence, serve as a passage to China); or, at the very least, that the river would lead to the riches found in the gold mines of what is now present day New Mexico.

In May of 1673, the pair of explorers, along with five companions, set out in two canoes from the mission of Saint Ignace, which Marquette himself had founded, on the north shore of the Straits of Mackinac. They proceeded across the northern rim of Lake Michigan to the bottom of the protected Green Bay, and up the Fox River to a settlement of friendly Mascoutins and Miamis. From here they were guided to a portage over to the Wisconsin River, which would lead them directly to the Mississippi. Making their way down river, they came across a village of welcoming Illinois, whose chief was to gift them two items of great portent. The first was a calumet (an ornamental pipe), which the chief told them to display in times of danger, for it would "enable one to walk safely through the midst of enemies, who, in the hottest of the fight, lay down their arms when it is shown." The second was a ten-year-old slave boy, an adopted son of the chief.

Traveling further down the river, they located and mapped the mouths of the Missouri and Ohio Rivers, and began to suffer the hot and mosquito-infested clime. The expedition was then set upon by a group of hostile natives, to whom Marquette anxiously displayed his calumet. Just as the warriors on the shore were about to release their arrows, some of the older men in the group recognized the calumet and checked the ardor of the younger men. The explorers were taken to the village of Akansea, near the mouth of the Arkansas River (and not far from where DeSoto died in 1542). There they

learned that they were but five days from the sea (it was actually seven hundred miles), and that fierce armed warriors would be met along the way. The explorers surmised that these warriors might actually be Spanish soldiers, with whom France was currently at war; so, continuing on now carried the threat of capture by the Spanish. Marquette and Joliet decided that they were satisfied with their great discovery—that the Mississippi flowed into the Gulf of Mexico, not eastward into the Atlantic near Virginia, nor westward into the California Sea—and thus resolved to make their return to Canada.

It was July and the journey back up the river was torturous. They had to battle the river's powerful current in searing heat, and Marquette was suffering the effects of dysentery. Forty days upstream, they reached the mouth of the Illinois River, which their

young native boy told them to enter, assuring them that it would greatly shorten their journey to Lake Michigan. Marquette's journal notes that they "have seen nothing like this river that we enter, as regards its fertility of soil, its prairies and woods; its cattle, elk, deer, wildcats, bustards, swans, ducks, parroquets, and even beaver." They came to a village of the Kaskaskia, and several of these villagers guided the party up the Des Plaines River to a short portage that would take them to the south branch of Chicago River, and on to Lake Michigan. From there they made their way to the Saint Xavier Mission at Green Bay, having traversed over twenty-five hundred miles in four months.

Marquette and Joliet were thus the first to document the land that was to become Chicago. Joliet immediately

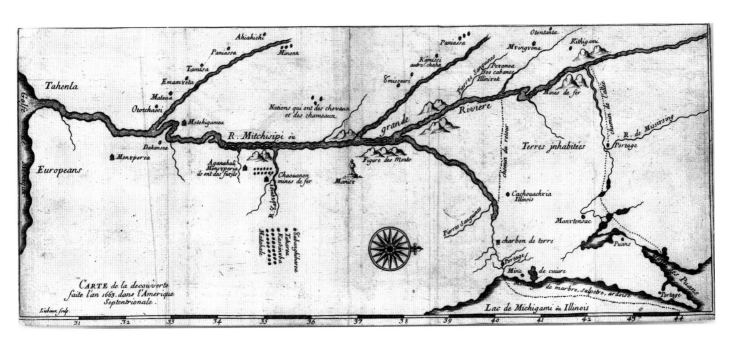

recognized the strategic location of the area, and in his report to Comte de Frontenac, the new governor of Québec, Joliet noted that the area possessed "a very great and important advantage, which perhaps will hardly be believed. It is that we could go with facility to Florida in a bark, and by very easy navigation. It would only be necessary to make a canal by cutting through but half a league of prairie, to pass from the foot of the Lake of Illinois [Lake Michigan] to the river Saint Louis [Illinois River]." Joliet beseeched the governor to create a colony at Chicago, which with its natural harbor and "the excavation of which I have spoken" would provide a gateway to the fertile prairies to the west. Prophetic as Joliet's vision was, the governor did not oblige him. The colony of New France was not populous enough to settle the interior, and the governor was advised that agricultural settlement should focus on the Saint Lawrence Valley; moreover, there was more profit to be had in the fur trade—an enterprise that could potentially be disrupted by interior settlement.

This was not the first of Joliet's setbacks. On the way to make his report to the governor, his canoe had overturned in the churning waters of the Sault Sainte Louis. The young boy who had guided him up the Illinois and two other companions were drowned,

and Joliet lost all his records and maps of the expedition down the Mississippi. He wrote another account and drew a new map from memory, which were forwarded to France by Frontenac, as were copies of Father Marquette's journal and a manuscript map the priest had drawn in 1673–4.

Marquette's map shows the explorers' outbound and homeward routes, and is the first map to show Lake Winnebago, the Wisconsin and Illinois rivers, and the mouths of the Missouri and Ohio rivers. The French court paid scant attention to this map—and indeed, to any of the discoveries of Marquette and Joliet. In fact, it was not until years later (in 1681) that an abridged version of the journal of Marquette was to be published, and then only by a private individual, Melchisédech Thévenot. Thévenot's book, *Recueil de Voyages de Mr Thévenot*, contains the map shown here. This map was probably adapted from maps drafted by Joliet and Dablon of the Marquette and Joliet expedition, and was the first printed map to describe the Marquette-Joliet discoveries. It shows a section of the Mississippi, and the names of the Illinois and other native villages generally correspond to Marquette's map, although there is one glaring omission—the Kaskaskia village on the Illinois River is not shown. There is mention of iron, copper, and coal mines, and the word "bloodstones" appears. The latter term also occurs on

the next map, Joliet's map of 1674, which might lead one to believe that it was used in the drafting of Thévenot's map (although one must still explain the errors on the latter). The map depicts in surprising detail the Chicago River with the south branch, the Des Plaines River, and the Chicago Portage with Mud Lake between them. Although inferior to Marquette's own chart, it is included here because it was the first printed map to apply the name "Lake Michigan" to one of the Great Lakes.

The second map depicts the location of several Native American nations and numerous mineral deposits. Copper (*cuive*), slate (*ardoise*) and saltpeter (*salpestre*) are found just north of Chicago; coal (*carbon de terre*) is shown along the Illinois River, as is the reddish rock along this river's banks. This map was once thought to be one of Joliet's original maps, but closer inspection revealed that the handwriting and signature did not match. It is one of several recreations that were drawn in Quebec at the time (as noted above, Joliet had lost all his maps and papers on the return trip from the Mississippi Valley). This map shows the Mississippi (Rivière de Baude) originating from three lakes and emptying into the Gulf of Mexico (Le Sien de Mexique), and also depicts two rivers entering the Mississippi from the west.

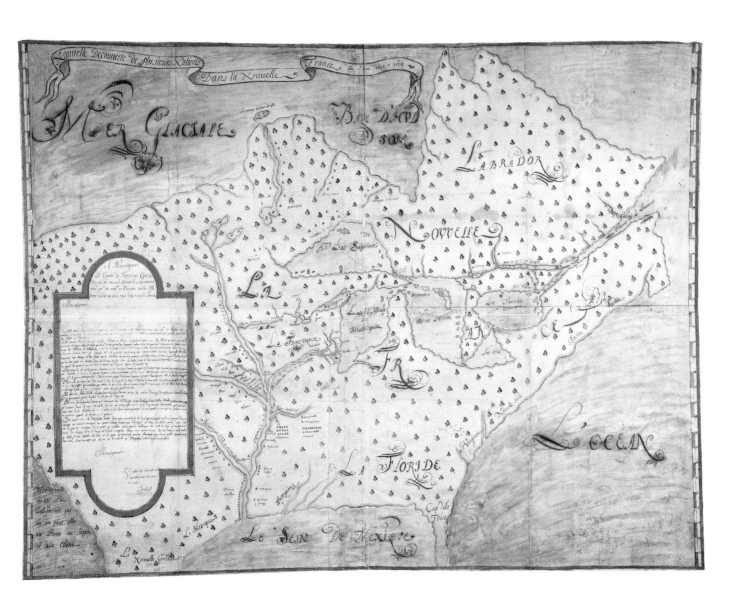

29

'CHECAGOU' ON A MAP

The Franquelin Map of 1688

Title: Carte de l'Amerique Septrionale
Date Issued: 1688
Cartographer: Jean-Baptiste-Louis Franquelin
Published: Manuscript
Pen, Ink, and Watercolor, 146 x 152 cm; copy 103 x 160 cm
Original: *Archives du Dépôt des Cartes et Plans de la Marine, Paris*
Manuscript copy: *Library of Congress, Geography and Map Division,*
G3300 1688 .F7 Vault Oversize

Jean-Baptiste-Louis Franquelin was born in France around 1651, and first came to Canada as a trader in 1671. Toward the end of 1674, Governor Frontenac recruited to him to draw maps of New France, "since he was the only one in the colony equipped for this sort of work." Franquelin thus became the first official cartographer for maps relating to New France. In 1686, Franquelin was appointed by Louis XIV as Canada's first "Royal Hydrographer," which meant that in addition to his regular cartographic duties, he was responsible for teaching navigation and hydrography to young river pilots and others seeking this information.

Franquelin drew some fifty richly illustrated manuscript maps of New France between 1674 and 1708, many produced after his return to France in 1692 (during the years between 1674 and 1684, he concentrated on recording the explorations of Louis Joliet and René-Robert Cavelier de La Salle). None of Franquelin's maps were published in his lifetime, and unfortunately, most of them were unsigned. This makes it difficult to determine just what extent he was responsible for many of these manuscript maps. Although not published, his maps were important sources for French mapmakers, especially Guillaume De L'Isle, Vincenzo Coronelli, and Jacques-Nicolas Bellin.

Franquelin's 1688 map of North America is a beautiful summary of much of his earlier work. It shows the Mississippi Valley in detail, although the Mississippi River is depicted as entering the Gulf of Mexico far west of where it actually does. Indeed, the lower course of the Mississippi is about as far west as the lower Rio Grande ought to be, and its southwesternmost tributary, the Siegnelay (Red River) is placed about where the upper course of the Rio Grande begins.

Many forts are depicted, including a Fort Checagou. This reference can be traced back to La Salle, who by 1681 had begun to use the term *Checagou* to refer to the site of the future city. The word *Checagou* is derived from a Native American word for the wild garlic that grew along the banks of the Chicago River.

THE PINNACLE OF SEVENTEENTH-CENTURY GREAT LAKES MAPS

The Coronelli Map of 1688

Title: Partie Occidentale du Canada ou de la Nouvelle France
Date Issued: 1688
Cartographer: Vincenzo Maria Coronelli
Published: Separately by J. B. Nolin (Paris)
Copperplate Engraving, 44.1 x 56.8 cm
Library and Archives of Canada, NMC-6411

Vincenzo Maria Coronelli was one of Italy's most celebrated cartographers. A Franciscan friar, he rose to become Father General of the order in 1699. By that time, he had already made his name as a mathematician, cartographer and globe-maker. Coronelli drew, engraved and printed over four hundred maps, and produced numerous globes as well. Among the latter was a pair of globes that he constructed for King Louis XIV of France—one terrestrial, one celestial—each over fifteen feet in diameter, and which could be entered by a special door. Coronelli founded the first geographical society, the *Academia Cosmografica degli Argonauti*, and was appointed Cosmographer to the Venetian Republic. He also served as royal geographer to Louis XIV. His major works include a large atlas, *Atlante Veneto*, published in 1690–91, and *Isolario*

dell'Atlante Veneto, which was published in 1696–97. Coronelli's maps maintained the highest standards of engraving, and are often elaborately decorated.

This is Coronelli's 1688 map of western New France, which was the most accurate general portrayal of the Great Lakes (particularly of Lake Superior) on a printed map in the seventeenth century. In drafting this map, Coronelli certainly took advantage of published sources such as Louis Hennepin's widely available book *Description de la Louisiane* (Paris, 1683) and the 1674 map *L'Amerique Septentrionale* by Hubert Jaillot. As official cartographer to Louis XIV, however, he also had access to the many explorers' reports and manuscript maps that were received in Paris. Coronelli benefited the most from the manuscript maps of Joliet and Franquelin, and also from maps

depicting La Salle's work on the Mississippi. This map, then, is an excellent fusion of the most up-to-date sources of the time, although for some reason, Coronelli does not depict Daniel Dulhut's explorations north and west of Lake Superior. Despite its accuracy and its wide availability, this map was not universally adapted by later cartographers.

The title of the map, which in full states, "The western part of Canada, or New France, where the Illinois and Tracy and Iroquois Nations, and many other peoples, are found," is not only found in the cartouche, but also is printed across the face of the map. The intent here is to claim the area depicted for France, a petition that is reiterated by the words "La Louisiane" in the cartouche—this is the area of Louis. This map is also centered on the region between the Great Lakes and the

Mississippi River, unlike earlier maps such as those of Sanson, which are focused on the Saint Lawrence Valley. This depicts a change in French imperial policy, which was now directed toward control of the fur trade and contesting Spanish claims in the Southwest.

The cartouche is highly ornamental, and the map is decorated with small vignettes. In accordance with the cartographic norms of this period, the aim here is to be aesthetically pleasing and instructive at the same time. The cartouche sets up a kind of cultural counterpoint between that of the European fur-traders, two of whom are shown using firearms (one in the act of shooting a beaver, the other a bear) and the indigenous culture of the natives, who are depicted using bows and arrows in the act of shooting what appear to be cows but were probably intended to be buffalo. The scale of miles is decorated in a manner that indicates the bountiful fish available to eat, and, elsewhere on the map, natives are shown hollowing out a canoe by fire, roasting fish, and meting out punishment.

The names and locations of many Indian Nations are found on this map, including the five nations of the Iroquois, and the nations of the Illinois, the Potawatomi, the Mascouten, the Miami, and the Kickapoo. Coronelli also portrays the names of many rivers, including the Illinois and Chicago (Chekagou) rivers, and many place-names, including the Chicago portage (Portages de Chekagou).

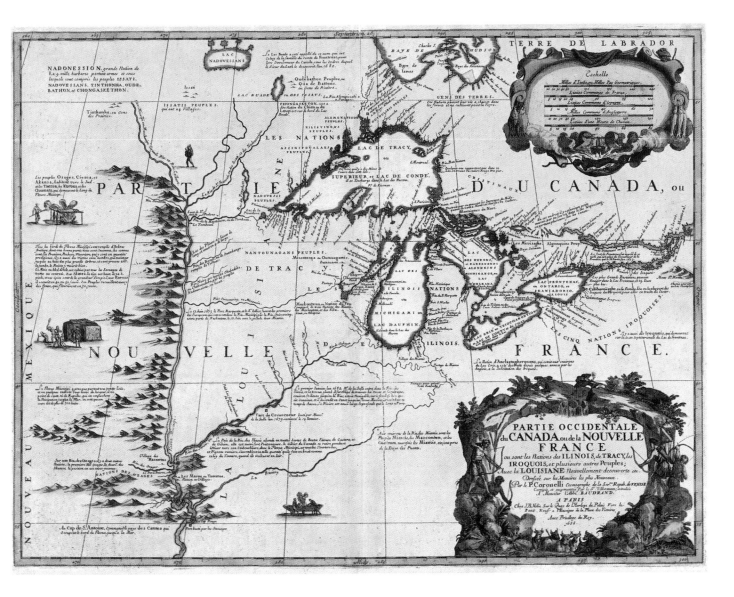

THE DE L'ISLE'S FOUNDATIONAL MAP

The De L'Isle Map of 1703

Title: Carte du Canada ou de la Nouvelle France
Date Issued: 1703
Cartographer: Guillaume De L'Isle
Published: Separately
Copperplate Engraving, 49.5 x 51.8 cm
Newberry Library, Map 4F oG3400 .3

This map is a summation of the seventeenth-century mapping of Canada and the Great Lakes, and was a foundational map for a tradition of mapmakers over the next forty years. It draws on the explorations of Marquette, Joliet, and La Salle, among others, but most especially on the manuscript map of Pierre-Charles Le Sueur, who in 1700–1701, explored and mapped the Mississippi from the Gulf of Mexico to the mouth of the Minnesota River. It is also the first map to use modern measures of longitude. The cartouche, designed by Nicholas Guerard, describes the country with its fauna and customs, depicting missionaries and converts, natives scalping, and a beaver and a wild duck. Although credited to Guillaume, this map was actually drawn by his father, Claude.

By the beginning of the eighteenth century, Claude and his four sons had replaced the Sansons as the preeminent family in the French school of cartography. Guillaume was the most accomplished cartographer in the family. A child prodigy, he purportedly drew his first map at the age of nine; he joined the Académie royale des sciences at age twenty-seven and was later appointed premier géographe du roi. He also studied mathematics and astronomy at the Paris Observatory under Jean Dominique Cassini, an Italian who devised the triangulation method of surveying and a new astronomical method for determining longitude based on the moons of Jupiter. In the annals of cartography, Guillaume is often considered the first modern scientific mapmaker.

The present map depicts a large river, the "Rivière Longue" or "Rivière Morte" that flows into the Mississippi, and which has a western extension that flows into a large salt lake; there is a large river just to the north and west of the salt lake, which, a note relays, the natives report flows to a western sea. The discovery of the "Rivière Longue" is credited on the map to Louis-Armand de Lom d'Arce, Baron de Lahontan.

Lahontan claimed to have come to Canada in 1683 at the age of seventeen as a marine lieutenant. He spent the next ten years in North America, during which he participated in an unsuccessful campaign against the Iroquois in 1684, served a stint as commandant at Fort Saint-Joseph in 1687, and explored territory along the Wisconsin and the Mississippi rivers in 1688–89. During this last excursion, Lahontan reports that he ascended the Mississippi to a river flowing from the west that he came to call the "Rivière Longue" (Long River). His expedition traveled up this river for eight hundred miles, at which point, the story goes, Indians told him that he was about 450 miles from a great salt lake that was near some high mountains. Moreover, Lahontan insists, these Indians had shown him a deerskin map that depicted a large river running to the western sea.

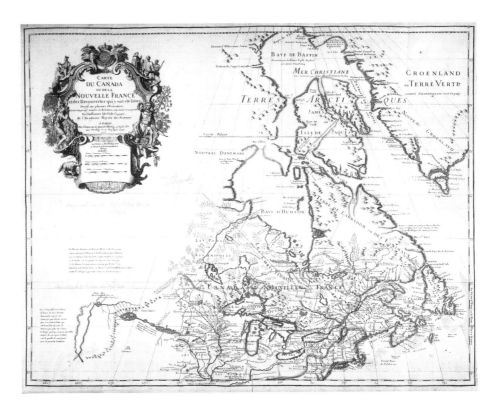

In 1703, Lahontan published an account of his journey on the Rivière Longue, along with his other travels throughout New France, in a book entitled *Nouveaux Voyages de Mr. le Baron de Lahontan dans l'Amérique septentrionale*. At this time, travel narratives were the vogue in Europe, and interest in North America, which had been kindled by the *Jesuit Relations*, and stoked by the explorations of Hennepin and Tonti, was greater than ever. Lahontan's book became immensely popular, and included a map of the Long River. In 1704, Lahontan published another book, *Dialogues de Monsieur le baron de Lahontan et d'un Sauvage, dans l'Amérique*, that contained a series of dialogues between himself and a Native American named Adario (rat).

These dialogues derided the foolishness of superstitions, ridiculed the vices of European society, attacked Christian dogma, espoused the virtues of the "noble savage," and influenced a subsequent growth of primitivism in France and England, as reflected in the works of Diderot, Montesquieu, Rousseau, Voltaire, Jonathan Swift, and others.

The Rivière Longue, of course, was simply a product of Lahontan's fertile imagination. Although it served to arouse old hopes of finding a water route to the Pacific, even the most generous of interpretations does not allow one to identify it with any existing river. Nor can any of the aboriginal nations named along the river (also shown on the De L'Isle map) be identified. The De L'Isles were not, however, the only ones duped by Lahontan. In fact, few cartographers were able to resist the maps in his *Nouveaux Voyages*, and the Rivière Longue continued to appear on maps as late as 1785. Moreover, even though the general map in this book, *Carte Generale / De Canada*, was appallingly inaccurate, it became a popular outline for a line of succeeding mapmakers, and rivaled the mapmaking tradition based on the De L'Isle map.

BELLIN'S MAP OF THE GREAT LAKES

The Bellin Map of 1744

Title: Carte des Lacs du Canada
Date Issued: 1744
Cartographer: Jacques-Nicolas Bellin
Published: *Histoire et Description Générale de la Nouvelle France* (Paris)
Copperplate Engraving, 29 x 46 cm
Newberry Library, Graff 650 3310 1744

Much of the cartographic activity undertaken in New France during the first half of the eighteenth century did not immediately find its way to printed form. This was because the manuscript maps prepared in New France were forwarded to the Dépôt des Cartes et Plans de la Marine in Paris, and were only accessible to qualified personnel at the Dépôt. When the Dépôt decided to release this material to professional mapmakers, Jacques-Nicolas Bellin was one of the first to take advantage of it. He began using this information to construct the maps he provided for a book written by the Jesuit explorer and historian Pierre-François-Xavier de Charlevoix. This book, entitled *Histoire et description générale de la Nouvelle France*, was published in 1744.

Bellin's maps in *Histoire* thus became the first to contain new material on New France since the maps of Guillame D'Isle three decades earlier. The primary source of material for the map presented here was the work of Gaspard-Joseph Chaussegros de Léry and his son of the same name. The elder Chaussegros de Léry arrived in New France in 1716 and served as chief military engineer of the army until his death in 1756. In this capacity, he was responsible for the design and construction of fortifications throughout the country, and also made maps out of the sketches that were sent to Québec from the interior. These maps spanned the territory from Louisbourg to Lake Superior. His son joined him in these activities in the 1730s, and since they both shared the same name, and often either did not sign their maps, or simply signed them with 'de Léry', it is sometimes difficult to determine which of their maps were produced by whom.

Bellin's attractive map of the Great Lakes is particularly notable for the imaginary islands, Philippeaux and Pontchartrain, introduced into Lake Superior. These islands, for which many later explorers searched in vain, originally appeared on a manuscript map drawn by Chaussegros de Léry around 1735. It is likely that these islands, along with the islands named 'Maurepas' (now known as Michipicoten Island) and 'Saint Anne' were intended to honor the French minister of the Marine, Jean Frédéric Phélypeaux, comte de Maurepas, whose father, the comte du

Pontchartrain, had held a similar position, and whose patron saint was Saint Anne. Maurepas and his cousin, Charles de Beauharnois de la Boishe, the Governor of New France at the time, were supportive of the copper mining ventures of Monsieur Louis Denys de La Ronde in the Lake Superior area, and the Chaussegros de Lery map was probably based on information provided by la Ronde. This conclusion is strengthened by the fact that the map also contains an island (Montreal Island), and a river, named after Beauharnois. It is interesting to note that the largest of the fictitious islands, Philippeaux (and often accompanied by other large "false islands"), could

still be found on maps of Lake Superior nearly a century later. This map also shows a curious plateau in the peninsula of Michigan.

Despite these misconceptions, this map was the most accurate portrayal of the Great Lakes in its day, and was one of the most popular models of the Great Lakes for the remainder of the century. Bellin labels the Chicago River as the "R. et Port de Chicagou"—that is, the River and Port of Chicago, and identifies the Chicago Portage as the "Portage aux Chênes"—the Portage of Oaks (the portage also appears to start from the north branch of the Chicago River instead of the south branch). By the time of this map's publication, the Chicago River

and its "port" had been used by the French as a gateway to the Mississippi for at least seventy years. It was not the most reliable of waterways, and during much of the year the Des Plaines River was unnavigable. The better choice would often be to canoe down the St. Joseph River on the southeastern edge of the lake; from there a short portage (also clearly marked on this map) took travelers down the Kankakee and Illinois Rivers to the Mississippi. The actual site of the port of Chicago was a windswept prairie marsh—a place so forbidding that the Native American people of the Miami nation had refused to permanently settle on it. By the end of eighteenth century, it would have its first European settlers.

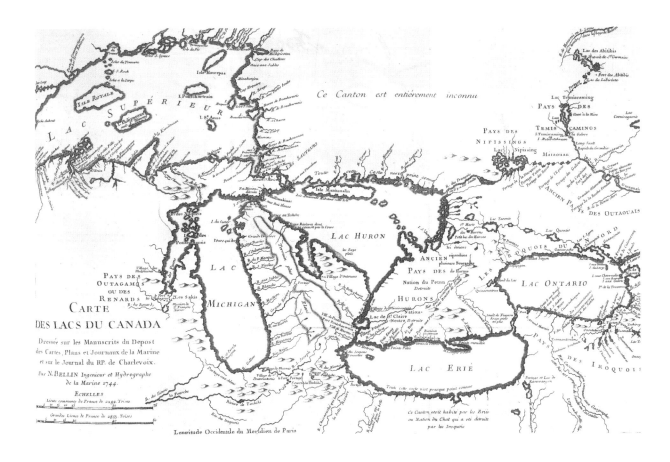

EARLY SETTLERS ON THE PORTAGE

The Site Of Chicago in 1779

Title: Chicago in 1779 (then called Eschikago) showing the cabin of Jean Baptiste Point de Saible (colored), the first permanent settler

Date Issued: 1930

Cartographer: Drawn by E. White, engraved by R. Varin

Published: A. Ackermann & Son (Chicago)

Hand-colored Engraved Aquatint, 40 x 55 cm

Chicago Historical Society, ICHi-05623

Prior to the time of Marquette and Joliet's expedition, the future site of the city of Chicago was probably an important meeting place for Native Americans. As testified by the boy who guided Marquette and Joliet up the Illinois River, the Chicago Portage was part of a well-known highway used by Native Americans to traverse from the Great Lakes to the Mississippi. There is also evidence that wandering *coureurs de bois* and traders were in the region before Marquette and Joliet. We may surmise the last fact from Marquette's account of his return to the portage.

Marquette had promised the Kaskaskia villagers who had accompanied him and Joliet up the Illinois River that he would come again to instruct them in the ways of Christianity. He set out to make good on that promise in late 1674. Marquette and a small party left Green Bay, slowly made their way down a stormy Lake Michigan, and found the Chicago River frozen solid. The party encamped there, and Marquette—suffering again from the illness that had inflicted him on the previous year's expedition—was deemed too sick to travel. Camp was moved closer to the portage, and the decision was made to spend the winter there. Marquette records in his journal that he was visited by two French traders working in the area, as well as villagers of nearby Illinois, all of whom kept the camp well stocked with food. Thus, although Marquette may have recorded the first extended stay of Europeans in the Chicago area, his journal reveals that both Europeans and Native Americans had already established themselves in the region.

Confirmation that Native Americans were frequently camped in the Chicago area may be found in the writings of Marquette's successor at the Immaculate Conception of the Blessed Virgin mission, Father Claude Allouez. Marquette founded this mission in the spring of 1675, by which time he had felt strong enough to leave his winter camp on the portage and make the trip down the Illinois River to the village of the Kaskaskia. He was, according to his superior, received as "an angel from Heaven" by the villagers. He preached to them and founded his mission, all the while suffering great physical torment.

Sensing that he would not live much longer, he asked his companions to return him to the mission at Saint Ignace. He died on the way, near the river that now bears his name on the eastern shores of Lake Michigan. Allouez was selected to succeed Marquette at the mission, and on his first visit, he recounts that upon his arrival at the entrance of "the river which leads to the Illinois," he was greeted by a band of eighty Illinois who had come from their village to welcome him. Allouez tells of traveling to their camp, which was most likely located in the vicinity of the portage. This conclusion is supported by Allouez's remark that it was "shortly after" setting out that they arrived at the village. It is strengthened in light of Marquette's journal, in which he reports that members of the Illinois tribe camped in this vicinity during the winter two years earlier.

In subsequent years, the portage was frequented by French traders and explorers, including La Salle in 1682 on the way to his descent of the Mississippi River, and again in 1683. In 1694, the Native American Wea set up camp in a village where Chicago now is. In 1696, Father Pierre François Pinet, a Jesuit missionary, founded the Mission of the Guardian Angel at Chicago. As described by Saint Cosme, the mission was built "on the bank of a small river, with the lake on one side

and a fine and vast prairie on the other." Saint Cosme notes that a village of the Miami ("with over a one and fifty cabins") was located next to the mission, and that another village, almost as large, was located "a league up river." When the nearby villages were abandoned for the annual winter hunt, Pinet would either follow his flock on their hunt, or would spend time with missionaries on the lower Illinois River. Saint Cosme notes that Pinet's evangelical efforts were wasted on the adult population, who were "hardened in debauchery," but that all the children were baptized, and that even the medicine men, who were the most fervently opposed to Christianity, desired to have their children instructed. The tenure of the mission was brief. In 1698, Governor Frontenac drove Pinet from the mission, but dropped his opposition to its occupation after the clergyman appealed to Bishop Laval. Pinet resumed his work, but closed the mission in 1700 because the migratory habits of the Miami made a permanent establishment impractical.

Trappers and travelers passed through the Chicago area in the eighteenth century, and the region saw a few settlers—mostly traders—establish themselves for various lengths of time. One of these traders, Jean Baptiste Pointe du Sable, is now celebrated as Chicago's first permanent

non-Native American resident. There is little in the way of written records or letters to flesh out Du Sable's life (or even to determine the correct spelling of his name). It is generally thought that he was freeborn to a French father and a Haitian African-American mother. Although he may have been a British subject born in Canada, the British arrested Du Sable in 1779 for his attachment to the French and the Americans. His captors praised his character, and in a 1779 letter a British officer described him as "a handsome negro, well-educated and settled at Eschikagou." From 1780 to 1783 or 1784, his captors had Du Sable manage a trading post called the Pinery on the St. Clair River in present-day Michigan, after which he returned to the future site of Chicago.

By 1790, Du Sable and his Potawatomi wife, Kittihawa, were settled on the shore of Lake Michigan at the mouth of the Chicago River (just east of the present day Michigan Avenue Bridge on the north bank). There Du Sable ran an elaborate trading and farming business, and his establishment became an important link in the region's fur and grain trade. In 1796, Kittihawa delivered Eulalia Pointe du Sable, Chicago's first recorded birth. In 1800, Du Sable sold his property and business, moving south near St. Louis. He died sometime around 1811 or 1812, and it has been reported that in his final years Du Sable lived alone, spending his time hunting and fishing.

The aquatint engraving featured here recreates the site of Chicago in 1779, looking westward from the lake. Engraved by Raoul Varin, it is a facsimile of the frontispiece of A. T. Andreas' pioneering work, *History of Chicago*. The "imaginary view" depicted here shows the flat, grassy plain around Chicago, a geographical feature that was to become a tourist attraction in the nineteenth century. The prairie appeared as an inland sea, its tall grass waving in the breeze as would swells in the ocean. Ablaze with wildflowers, the occasional oak grove would stand out, in the words of Louis Sullivan, "as a solitary island." Charles Weld, an English travel writer who came to Chicago in 1854, was so taken by this vista that he recommended to his readers that it was "worth while going" to Illinois "for the purpose of seeing the prairies near Chicago." The work locates Du Sable's cabin on the north bank of the river, and a Native American encampment on the south bank. The lower right inset contains a likeness of Du Sable, the "Father of Chicago," and the lower left inset pictures his wife sitting outside their cabin.

Chicago in 1779

hen Called Eschikago

of Jean Baptiste Point de Saible (Colored)

First Permanent Settler

41

FORT DEARBORN

The Whistler Plan

Title: Plan of Fort Dearborn

Date Issued: 1808

Cartographer: Captain John Whistler

Published: Manuscript

Pen and Ink, 76.2 x 53.3 cm

Chicago Historical Society, ICHi-37865 ("A True Copy of the Original on file in the War Department")

In 1763, the European rights to possession of the Chicago area had passed from the French to the British as part of the settlement ending the Seven Years' War. Twenty years later, the region became part of the United States by the treaty that secured the independence of the fledgling republic. The British hedged their position by illegally remaining in the area, under the pretext that the posts in the northwestern frontier were being held to guarantee that the Americans fulfilled their treaty obligations. The real reason the British lingered was their desire to shore up their control of the fur trade, and toward this end, they worked to ensure that the Native American tribes in the region retained their lands. The idea here was twofold: first, this land would serve as a buffer between the United States and Canada, and second, the powerful tribes in the territory, properly managed, would help maintain British control of the fur trade. John Jay's 1794 diplomatic trip to Great Britain resulted in a treaty in which the British promised to evacuate the northwestern posts, but by then they had also supplied an army of Native Americans with the necessary provisions to resist sovereignty claims by the United States, and indeed, had encouraged such action.

The inevitable war that followed was ended in August of 1794 with General "Mad Anthony" Wayne's defeat of the local Native American force at the Battle of Fallen Timbers (so named because a tornado had strewn trees all about the ground on which the battle took place). The ensuing treaty was concluded on August 10, 1795, at Fort Greenville in eastern Ohio. The Treaty of Greenville opened most of the present state of Ohio for settlement and named certain tracts in the Northwestern frontier to be used by the United States for forts and portages. One of these was described as "one piece of land six miles square, at the mouth of the Chicago River, emptying into the southwest end of Lake Michigan." Although this tract was never formally surveyed, its approximate boundaries ranged from Fullerton Avenue on the north to Thirty-First Street on the south, and from the lake westward to Cicero Avenue.

In 1803, the War Department ordered the construction of a fort at the mouth of the Chicago River. It would be the first major fort on the western frontier, and from it grew Chicago.

The wave of immigration had not yet reached this point, located as it was in the midst of Native American country. But from here, a garrison could protect the settlements of Indiana and lower Illinois, and would serve to link communication between the latter and the posts of Detroit and Mackinac. Moreover, troops stationed at the fort could conveniently patrol the region between Lake Michigan and the Mississippi River.

Captain John Whistler was appointed the fort's commander, and in August he and his troops arrived at the muddy site near the mouth of the "Chicago creek." There they found four huts or cabins belonging to French Canadian traders. One was occupied by a man named Le Mai, who had bought out Du Sable, another by Antoine Ouilmette, and a third by Louis Pettle. The fourth was owned by John Kinzie and was vacant at the time.

Construction of a stockade and shelters for the troops began immediately, and the fort was christened Fort Dearborn, in honor of Jefferson's Secretary of War, Henry Dearborn. Whistler, who had received artistic and cartographic training in Great Britain, drew a scale plan of the

fort in 1808. As shown here, this pen-and-ink drawing combines an outline map of the site and a plan of the fort with drawings of the military buildings; pictured as well are several of the trader's cabins that line both the river and the road to Detroit. Whistler

included a verbal description of the fort when he submitted this plan to the Department of War, and his plan is apparently the sole surviving graphic record of the settlement around the first Fort Dearborn.

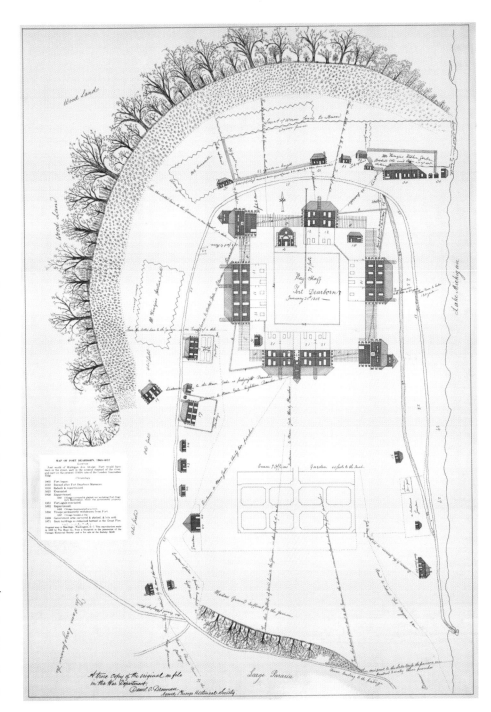

THE MASSACRE OF 1812

The Kinzie Map

Title: Chicago in 1812
Date Issued: 1844
Cartographer: Juliette A. Magill Kinzie
Published: *Narrative of the Massacre at Chicago* (Chicago)
Uncolored Wood Engraving, 11 x 19 cm
Newberry Library, *Case Ruggles 209

To many the War of 1812 might bring to mind General Andy Jackson's victory at the Battle of New Orleans, or the burning of Washington by the British. In Chicago, however, the War of 1812 triggers memories of one of the greatest disasters in the city's early history, the massacre at Fort Dearborn on August 15, 1812.

Even now this seminal event is commemorated by tablets, bas-reliefs or statuary at the Michigan Avenue Bridge and several other places in the city. But in 1844 when Juliette Kinzie published *Narrative of the Massacre at Chicago*, the tragedy was still a living memory for some Chicago residents. Issued as a pamphlet in blue paper covers, the *Narrative* contained the first map of Chicago actually printed in

Chicago. This is a milestone as there is no record of any map whatsoever having been printed in Chicago prior to this example.

Collecting the reminiscences of survivors—including her own mother-in-law—Kinzie recounted the tragedy and the events leading up to it. Acts of kindness by Black Partridge and other Native Americans, incidents of heroism and cowardice, loyalty and treachery, follow one another at a brisk pace. Mrs. Kinzie published anonymously and because few contemporary, first-hand accounts existed, the *Narrative* was presumed for many years to be the memoir of an eyewitness instead of an amalgam. It proved a popular work: in the following year the text was reprinted, along with the map in Norris' Chicago business directory and

again incorporated into *Wau-bun*, Mrs. Kinzie's book on her experiences during the Black Hawk War of 1832. Other authors borrowed freely from the *Narrative*, including Henry Brown for his *History of Illinois*, and by novelists who appropriated dramatic episodes for their books.

Mrs. Kinzie's sketch-map illustrates the march of the evacuees from Fort Dearborn to the site of the attack where a caption reads "Battle Ground 1812." Although there is no distance scale on the map, descriptions from survivors and relics of the battle found later establish the site about a mile-and-a-half south of the fort along the lake front, around present-day Eighteenth Street and Prairie Avenue. The view looks west from the lake, so north is to the right, showing Chicago as a tiny community composed of the fort itself, five civilian/trading company houses huddled nearby, and a farm located near today's Bridgeport neighborhood, along the south branch of the Chicago River. Although simple in format, the map is so detailed even the haystacks at the farm are depicted!

Fort Dearborn was a minor post on the American frontier; with officers and other ranks, the garrison seems never to have consisted of more than 70 men. However, the term "massacre" is not a hyperbolic term used by a Victorian lady to spice up her story. Exact numbers are hard to come by as army records were destroyed at the time of the catastrophe, and initial reports were confused. An early account in a Baltimore newspaper (October 3, 1812, *Niles Weekly Register*) erroneously claims the fort's commander was killed (he was badly wounded but survived) and casualties of 50 soldiers and an unspecified number of women and children with, perhaps, only 10 or 12 survivors. A range of statistics has been used by various writers, but modern scholarship suggests there were around 60 survivors from a combined military and civilian population of approximately 148. Apart from those who died in the initial attack (including twelve women and children) many of the wounded were killed on the field after having surrendered, and a few perished in captivity.

That the isolated Fort Dearborn would be attacked during the War of 1812 seems inevitable. Encroachments by U. S. citizens into Native American areas supposedly protected by treaties added to tensions readily exploited by Britain. Even before the formal declaration of war by Congress in June of 1812, William Clark (of Lewis and Clark fame), the Indian Agent for Upper Louisiana, had received reports of raids by the Potawatomi at Cahokia, Illinois, and across the Mississippi River into Missouri.

The situation was further inflamed by Indian losses at the Battle of Tippecanoe in late 1811, only nine months before the massacre. Early British victories in the War of 1812 in the East and the surrender of Fort Mackinac in July convinced some tribes to ally themselves with British interests.

The fate of the Americans in Chicago was sealed when Captain Nathan Heald, commander of Fort Dearborn, received orders to evacuate to Fort Wayne; he was also instructed to distribute the fort's stores to local Native Americans as he saw fit. Heald recognized the wisdom of destroying his supplies of munitions and liquor, but he decided to formally apportion the remaining goods among the bands of Potawatomi—some five to six hundred in strength—that had gathered outside Fort Dearborn. This was against the advice of Indians

friendly to the Americans as well as experienced frontiersmen who strongly urged Heald to create a diversion. By leaving stores in the fort, the bands would "help themselves" while the garrison marched out. His only other option was to prepare for a siege and await reinforcements, an uncertain proposition given the pressures on other American outposts. Whether these alternatives would have served the purpose is moot, but it is clear some survivors thought Heald exercised poor judgment.

The war went badly for the Americans for some time. Indeed, Detroit surrendered to the British the day following the massacre, August 16, but in that autumn Illinois militia under Colonel William Russell staged a retaliatory raid against a Potawatomi encampment at Lake Peoria. Both Russell's raid and the site of the Fort Dearborn massacre are recorded on Carey & Lea's map of Illinois, published in Philadelphia in 1822 and also on the 1827 edition. By that time Fort Dearborn had been rebuilt, but the defeat of Native Americans in the Black Hawk War of 1832 and their forced move across the Mississippi diminished the need for such an installation. Troops were finally withdrawn in 1836, and the last remnant of the fort was consumed in the Great Fire of 1871.

— *Mary Ritzlin*

CHICA

prairie

Lee's Place

Haystacks?

Battle
Ground
1812

Line   of   Sand Hills

LAKE   MICH

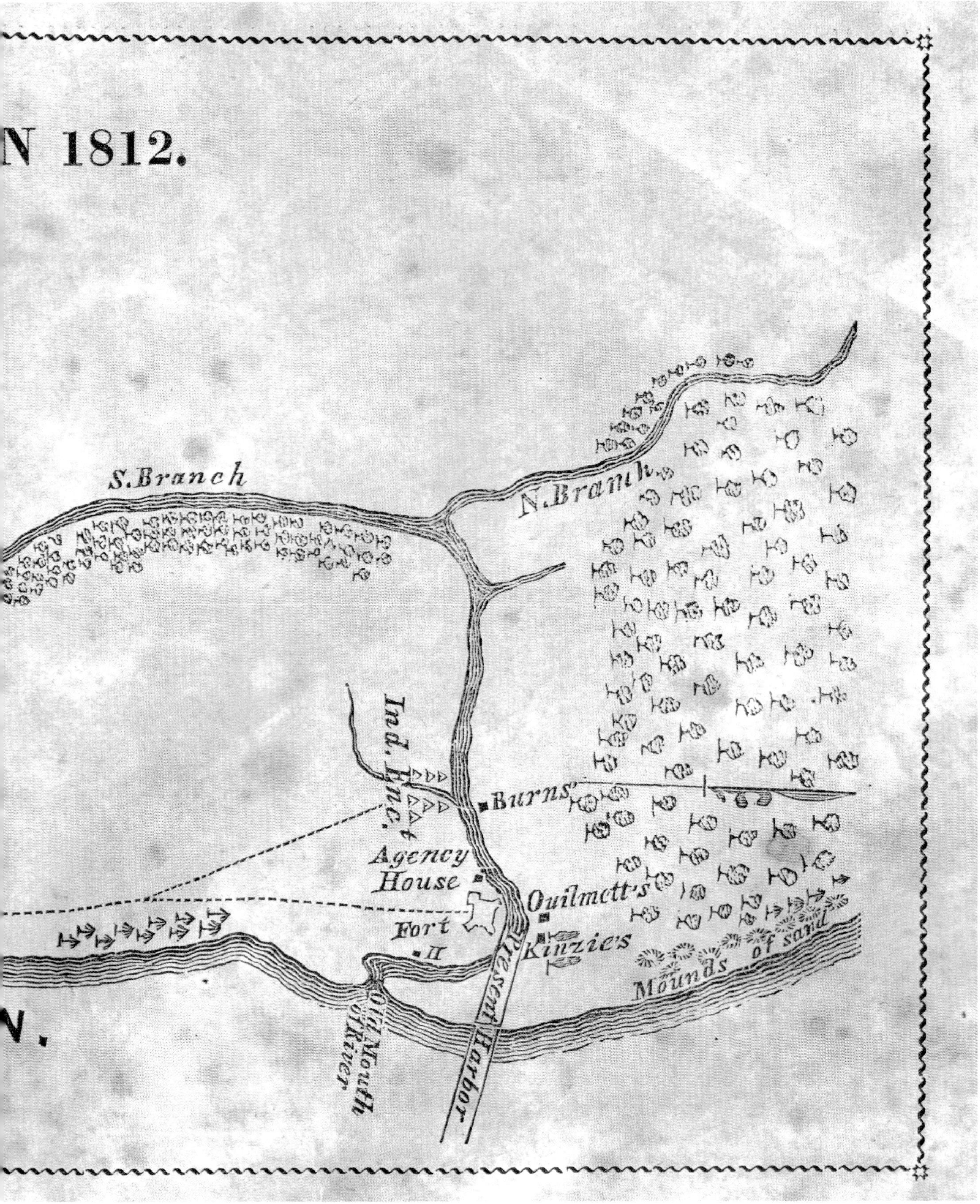

N 1812.

S.Branch

N.Branch

Ind. Enc.

Burns'

Agency
House

Ouilmett's

Fort

Kinzie's

Mounds of sand

Old Mouth of River

Present Harbor

N.

STATE OF ILLINOIS

The Carey and Lea Map

Title: Geographical, statistical, and historical map of Illinois

Date Issued: 1822

Cartographer: Joseph Yeager

Published: *A Complete Historical, Chronological, And Geographical American Atlas, Being A Guide To The History Of North And South America, And The West Indies . . . To The Year 1822.* H. C. Carey & I. Lea (Philadelphia)

Hand-colored Map, 29 x 21 cm

David Rumsey Collection, P1373a-33

I n 1818, Illinois became the twenty-first state in the Union. The new state encompassed an area that was part of the Northwest Territory created by Congress in 1787; the states of Ohio, Indiana, Michigan, and Wisconsin were also organized from this Territory. Although its 56,345 square miles made Illinois the second-largest state in the Union by area, its 36,000 residents made it the smallest in population. This made the granting of statehood to Illinois problematic, because a federal statute required a territory to have a population of 60,000 before it could become a state.

Congressmen concerned that the territory did not have the necessary population insisted that a proviso be attached to the state's enabling bill; this rider stipulated that a census of the territory's population must be taken before it could form a state government. Nathaniel Pope, who was the Illinois Territory's delegate to Congress at the time, tried to have the census requirement removed from the state's enabling bill, but was unsuccessful. Illinois was forced to tally its residents, and it forwarded a census to Congress that was questionable at best. The census counted, for example, anyone on a territorial road as an Illinois resident—whether coming, going, or as was often the case, both. Counting simply continued until the 60,000 figure was reached.

As can clearly be seen on this early map of Illinois, the state's population was concentrated primarily in its southern and central regions, especially along the Mississippi River Valley and the Wabash and Ohio Rivers. The lands north and northwest of Illinois at this time were still territories, as this map indicates on those borders. When the Congressional committee considering Illinois' petition for statehood suggested that its northern border should agree with the Indiana state line, Pope argued—successfully this time—that the line 42° 30' should be used instead. This would push the border about sixty-two miles north of the provision made by the Northwest Ordinance, and much further north than Indiana's northern extremity. Pope eloquently convinced the committee that this would connect the new state with the northern interests of New York and New England through a Great Lakes port at Chicago (as the Erie Canal was soon to connect the Great Lakes to

New York). Pope also suggested that a canal connecting Lake Michigan with the Illinois River would do more than facilitate commerce: it would place Illinois into the political orbit of the northern states, thus "affording additional security to the perpetuity of the Union."

One unspoken issue here was slavery. The ordinance that had created the Northwest Territory outlawed slavery within its boundaries, and thus, Illinois had no choice but to enter the Union as a free state. Many settlers in southern Illinois, however, had migrated from the South and strongly sympathized with the pro-slavery cause. Moreover, southern Illinois was largely dependent on its trade relations with its neighbors to the south and west, all of whom had or would enter the Union as slave states. There was no question, then, where the allegiance of this part of the state would lie in the event the Union was threatened with dissolution. Thus, Pope's implicit line of reasoning was this: If Illinois were given a footing on the Great Lakes, it would have the opportunity to develop a thriving commerce with—and dependence on—the eastern states. This would provide a check on the interests of the southern part of the state, and help to ensure Illinois's commitment to Union. The soundness of Pope's argument came forth during the Civil War, as the northern portion of Illinois counterbalanced the secessionist tendencies of the state's southern

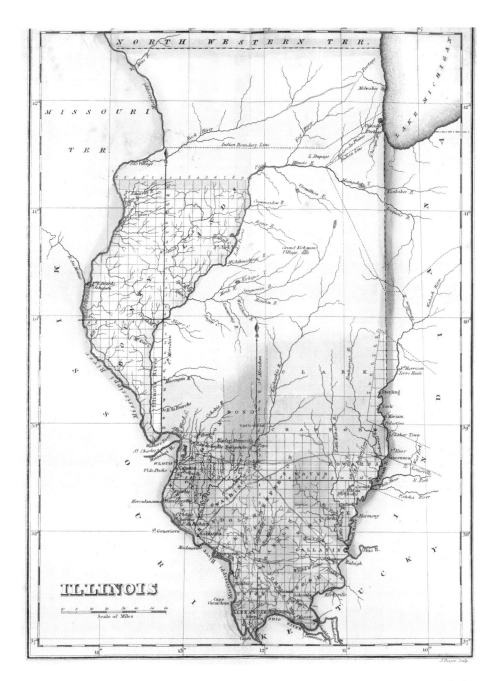

regions. Illinois proved to be an important part of the Union during the War Between the States.

The northern addition to Illinois has played an important role in the internal dynamics of state politics ever since. The growth of Chicago eventually placed more than half of the state's citizens in this area, which created a political split between the rural "downstate" interests and the urban center in the far northeastern reach of the state. Suburban growth around the city of Chicago, especially since the 1950s, has added a third factor to the dynamics of state politics. Thus today's political machinations can often be broken down to forces that reflect downstate, suburban, and Chicago interests.

FEDERAL TOWNSHIP PLAT

The Rector Plat

Title: Township 39 North of the baseline, Range 14 East of the 3rd principal Meridian,
Except that part of Section 16 which lies on the left or west side of the Chicago River
Date Issued: 1822
Cartographer: William Rector
Published: *Federal Township Plats* (Saint Louis)
Hand-colored, 55 x 66.75 cm
Illinois State Archives, RS 953.012

The Northwest Ordinance was a series of laws enacted by the United States Congress for the purpose of the settlement and political incorporation of the land in the Northwest Territory —that is, the frontier land west of Pennsylvania, north of the Ohio River, east of the Mississippi River, and south of the Great Lakes. Until about 1780, this land had been claimed by several states, including Virginia and New York. These states eventually ceded their territorial holdings to the federal government, and by the end of the War of Independence in 1783, specific procedures were needed to guide the settlement and division of the Northwest Territory.

The Land Ordinance of 1785 specified how this land was to be sold and owned; specifically, it created a rectangular system of surveying for the mapping and sale of this land. The statute decreed that the basic unit of land grant was to be the township, which was a square area measuring six miles on each side (where necessary, it allowed for fractional townships); it also established a coordinate system for locating townships relative to the intersection of a north-south meridian and an east-west base line. Each township comprised thirty-six sections, each section having an area of one square mile (640 acres). The law also required appointed surveyors to draw plats of the surveyed lands and empowered the federal government to sell the surveyed lands to the public.

In 1796, Congress created the office of U.S. Surveyor General, which was charged with the responsibility of surveying public lands. The surveying of the Northwest Territory began in Ohio and proceeded westward. It did not, however, spread across the territory in a continuous or contiguous fashion, for several reasons. First, the federal government did not have title to all the land within the territory, for much of the frontier was occupied by Native Americans. Although a series of treaties would cede most of the land to the United States, many of the areas reserved for aboriginal use were not surveyed until much later. Secondly, Congress had prioritized the surveying of this land: those areas for which there was a ready market were to be surveyed first. As a result, any portion of the territory where there was little demand for land was not immediately surveyed. Surveying also spread slowly in those parts of the country where there were extensive land claims made while the territory was under Spanish, French and British jurisdiction; these claims would have to be adjudicated before the land could be sold, and hence it was not directly surveyed. Thirdly, the progress of the survey was affected by numerous and interrelated changes that occurred in surveying practice. Some of these changes were necessitated by the type of land to be surveyed, some by changes in land laws, and some by the increasing sophistication of surveying equipment and surveying field methods.

The surveying of those lands that eventually would comprise the state of Illinois began in 1803, when the boundaries of the Vincennes Tract were charted by the Surveyor General. The Vincennes Tract was a parcel of land first ceded to the United States by the Treaty of Greenville, whereby Native Americans relinquished all claims to the land northwest of the Ohio River and east of a specified line. Although most of this land lies in Indiana, its western region was located in what would become the state of Illinois. After completing surveys of the Vincennes Tract, the Surveyor General's deputy surveyors started in southern Illinois in 1806. In 1816, Congress established the office of Surveyor General for Illinois and Missouri because surveying was progressing slowly in the Illinois military tract. The office's deputy surveyors, moving northward, intersected Illinois' northern boundary line in late 1831 and completed surveying the last of the state's townships in 1843. In 1855, the federal government issued the last contract for the resurvey of an Illinois township; and on the last day of October in 1863, the office of Surveyor General of Illinois and Missouri was closed. From 1868 to 1891, surveyors conducted occasional surveys of uncharted areas in Illinois such as islands and lakes.

The future site of the town of Chicago was surveyed by deputy

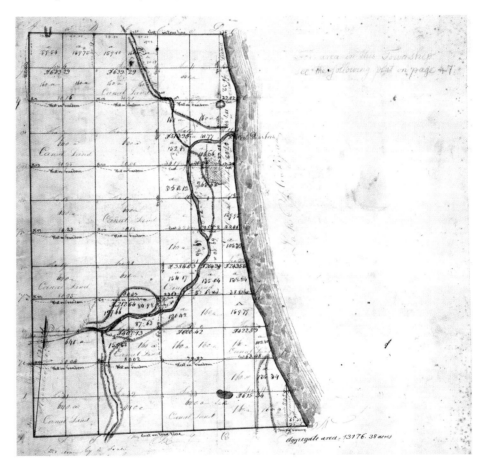

surveyor John Walls in June of 1821. The plat shown here was drawn by William Rector late in 1822, and is perhaps the only reasonably accurate depiction of local conditions in the Chicago area in this time period. Those sections owned by the Illinois and Michigan Canal Commission are designated "Canal Land," and Fort Dearborn is shown. To the left-hand side of the map (along the west fork of the South Branch of the Chicago River), "Portage House" is clearly marked. The dotted line proceeding to the west from the Portage House is labeled "Portage Road" and leads to the Des Plaines River valley (it is the only road marked in the area by the surveyor). The southern fork of the South Branch is identified as the "Head of Navigation," and is the point from which the Illinois and Michigan Canal would originate. The dark green lines on either side of the river are the limits of wooded groves, which made the land here valuable; a prairie swamp is noted in the right-hand corner of the plat.

THE THOMPSON PLAT

Thompson's Plat of 1830

Title: Thompson Plat

Date Issued: 1830

Cartographer: James Thompson

Published: Manuscript

Pen and Ink, 37 x 24 cm

Chicago Historical Society, ICHi-34284 (Copy certified by the "late commissioners" as "the identical map" used in the 1830 auction.)

In 1829, the Illinois General Assembly appointed a commission to dig a canal connecting Chicago with the Mississippi River by way of the Des Plaines and Illinois rivers; the commission was authorized to lay out towns, sell lots, and apply the proceeds to the construction of the canal. The canal commissioners employed James Thompson to lay out the town of Chicago.

James Thompson was a civil engineer and surveyor from downstate Randolph County, where he was also involved in local politics. Originally from South Carolina, Thompson had come to Kaskaskia in 1814 to teach school. He married, settled on a farm, and was elected a county commissioner and captain of the local militia. He also found work as a surveyor for a number of governmental agencies. One of the original canal commissioners was from Randolph County, and it was probably this connection that landed Thompson the job in Chicago. Upon completion of his task, tradition has it that Thompson was offered several of the town's lots as compensation for his services; Thompson refused, or so the story goes, and instead accepted a well-bred mare as payment. After his return to Randolph County, Thompson became a judge, served in the Black Hawk War, and also platted several other Illinois communities.

Thompson's plat of Chicago was to become the center of the future metropolis, and it set the pattern, location, and in many cases, the names of the city's streets and subdivisions. The territory that he surveyed was part of Section Nine of the 1821 United States land survey, which was one of the alternate sections of land that Congress had given to the canal commission. On today's maps, it extends from State Street west to Halsted Street and from Madison Street north to Chicago Avenue. More than half of this section lies north of the Chicago River, but Thompson chose to plat only the portion northward from Madison Street to Kinzie Street, and westward from State Street to Des Plaines Street.

Some of Thompson's street names refer to the locale—Canal, Water, and Market, and others honor famous national or local figures—Fulton, Carroll, Kinzie, Dearborn, Clark, LaSalle, Wells, Franklin, and Clinton. Randolph, Washington, Madison, and Jefferson Streets are not laid in order of presidential administration, which lends credence to the claim that they were

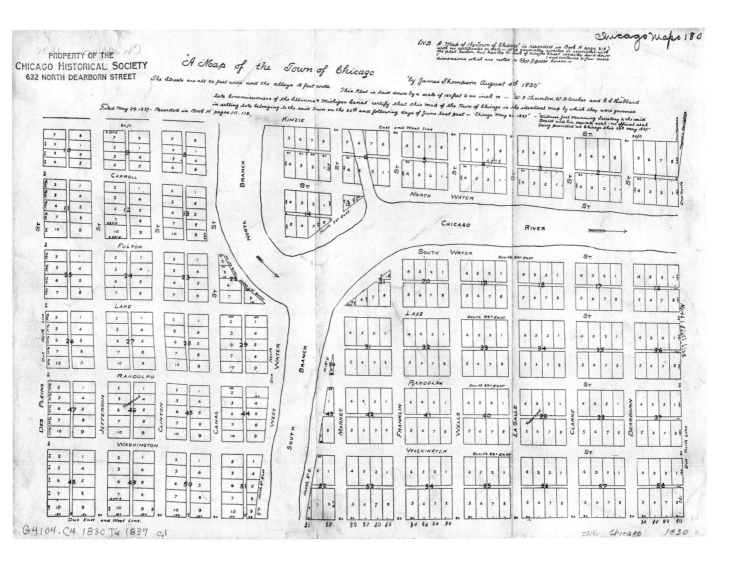

named after southern Illinois counties, and not presidents. Lake Street, which seemingly has no more connection to Lake Michigan than any other east-west street, probably was so named because it was the first street south of Fort Dearborn that could be extended to the lake.

It was originally thought that Thompson filed his survey and plat of the town of Chicago in Section 9, Township 39, Range 14 on August 4, 1830. Although the town was not incorporated until three years later, this was now Chicago's first legal geographic location. Thompson probably made at least two copies of the plat, one for the canal commissioners and one for public record. A month later, the public land was put up for sale: 126 lots were auctioned off at an average price of $35, and two eighty-acre parcels just west of the town plat went for $1.25 an acre and a similar plot for a few cents more. Many of the buyers were residents of the town who were out to ensure they had legal title to land on which they had built a structure. Others were simply interested in land speculation.

It is interesting to note that in the real estate frenzy of the day, Thompson's plat was not officially filed and recorded, and in fact, would not be until 1837—the same year that Chicago was incorporated as a city. By that time, land speculators had already produced several maps of the city. This, of course, does not detract from the importance of Thompson's plat, which may justly be considered the fundamental map of Chicago as an urban place.

ERADICATION OF THE NATIVE AMERICANS

The Edwin Rose Map

Title: Black Hawk War
Date Issued: 1832
Cartographer: Edwin Rose
Published: Manuscript
Pen and Ink, 24.4 x 20.1 cm
Newberry Library, Drawer Ruggles 408

In 1818, the year Illinois became a state, the northern quarter of the state was still occupied by Native Americans. Although there was no official census, their numbers have been estimated as follows: 1,600 Kickapoo along the Sangamon River Valley, 4,800 Potawatomi occupying northeastern Illinois, 3,200 Sauk and 1,200 Fox living near the mouth of the Rock River, and 2,400 Winnebago on a small portion of land between the Rock River and the eastern watershed of the Mississippi.

Chicago at this time was a racially mixed settlement of French Canadians, Anglo-Americans, Native Americans, and those of mixed ancestry. They lived just upriver of the newly rebuilt Fort Dearborn at Wolf Point, on the east bank of the south branch of the Chicago River (the "Forks" of the River where the north and south branches meet). A number of taverns and hotels were built in this area—places where, in the words of Donald Miller, "men and women of every color and class were welcome; and whisky, song, and dance were the great democratizers. Visitors from more civilized parts were shocked to see Indian braves spinning the wives of white fort officers around the dance floor . . . [and] Indian and white women drinking home-distilled liquor straight from the bottle." Chicago's earliest residents lived for today, enjoyed life on the frontier, and felt at home in the land of the Native American.

Great changes, however, would soon sweep over Chicago as the newly formed state of Illinois laid plans to link the Illinois River Valley by canal to the East, via the Great Lakes and the Erie Canal, which was opened in 1825. Chicago was to be the eastern terminus of the canal, which would be built using the proceeds from land sales along its route. Land sales were slow at first, but as the state's plan looked more certain, Eastern speculators would move in and begin to develop the area. There was, however, a problem: before the canal could be constructed or large numbers of settlers attracted to the area, the "Indian threat" would have to be removed. Unlike Chicago's earliest residents, the Eastern settlers migrating to Illinois did not want to live among the Native Americans, a people whom they typically viewed as an inferior and dangerous race.

By 1830, Illinois' non-Native American population had soared to over 157,000. As American settlers swept north and west across the state, more and more native groups abandoned their villages and farms for new lands west of the Mississippi. By the late 1820s, the Sauk and Fox villages near the mouth of Rock River constituted the last significant area of native settlement in Illinois. In 1828, the Indian agent for the Sauk and Fox tribes informed the tribal chiefs that they too should begin making preparations to abandon their villages, homes, and farms east of the Mississippi River in accordance with treaties they had earlier signed. Although the chiefs denied that they had ever ceded any of their lands, some of them, like Keokuk, argued that in the face of overwhelming numbers, they should accept the government's offer of land and retreat west of the Mississippi. Keokuk's principal rival, Black Hawk, felt that the Americans must have tricked the tribe's negotiators, for the tribe would never have willingly ceded their highly prized land along the Rock River.

In 1829, Keokuk crossed the Mississippi vowing never to return. Black Hawk, on the other hand, led a band of Sauk and Fox warriors and their families from their winter hunting grounds west of the Mississippi back across the river in the spring of 1830 and again in 1831. The Illinois governor viewed this last crossing as nothing less than an invasion of the state, and insisted that the federal government relocate these people, or he would call out the state militia to remove them "dead or alive over to the West side of the Mississippi." Confronted by an overwhelming show of force, a humiliated Black Hawk returned with his followers to the meager lands assigned to them west of the Mississippi.

In the spring of 1832, Black Hawk once again led a party of about 800 Sauk and Foxes, along with some 200 Kickapoos, east across the Mississippi. He hoped to return his people to their homes, or at least to lands on the Rock River, and to restore his honor as a warrior, which had suffered from the humiliation of capitulating to American forces nine months earlier. He also believed that he could force the Americans to accept the justice of Sauk and Fox claims and to admit the injustice of their own demands and actions.

The sight of the Black Hawk and his band set off panic among the new settlers, and led to a number of skirmishes, one of which ended badly for the state militiamen. Additional militia was called up—including Abraham Lincoln—and Black Hawk's party was pursued into Wisconsin. Eventually the militia and regular soldiers drove the exhausted and starving band to the Mississippi River, where most were slaughtered at the Battle of Bad Axe. Many of the victims were scalped by the white soldiers, and some of those killed included women swimming across the river with children on their backs. Those who made it across the river were tracked down and killed by Sioux warriors, the ancient enemy of the Sauk and Fox, who were working in support of the army. Black Hawk surrendered, was imprisoned for a time, and then sent on a tour of the new nation intended to impress upon him the number and strength of the American people. In his final days in captivity, he dictated an autobiography that was published as *Life of Ma-Ka-Tai-Me-She-Kia-Kiak, or Black Hawk*. He was eventually allowed to return to his land in Iowa, where he died in 1838.

The pen-and-ink map here has the added title on verso, "Map of Indian War of 1832, made by one who was there, Col. Edwin Rose." It depicts the region of northern Illinois and southern Wisconsin roughly bounded by Lake Winnebago, the Kankakee River, Peoria, and Prairie du Chien, and identifies rivers, towns, forts, and distances between points. The map details the routes taken by the U.S. Army troops in pursuit of Black Hawk; in particular, it shows Gen. Henry Atkinson's June 28 to July 9 route from

Dixon's Ferry northeast along the Rock River, and Lt. Col. Abraham Eustis's August 1 to September 1 route from Chicago to Rock Island. The map also identifies the marshes of the upper Rock River where Black Hawk and his band had holed up near Lake Koshkonong, and the path of their retreat northwest from the Wisconsin River.

The aftermath of the Black Hawk War signified that the "Indian threat" had been eradicated in Illinois, and that the state was now safe for settlement. Moreover, the soldiers and militiamen who had pursued Black Hawk returned home with stories of the natural beauty of the area depicted on this map, and descriptions of the sweeping prairies and sparkling lakes of northern Illinois and southern Wisconsin soon spread to the East in the form of books, pamphlets, and newspaper articles. The result was an avalanche of immigrants eager to take possession of the land, and thus began the development of what was to become the lifeblood of the future city of Chicago—its hinterland. The end of the Black Hawk War also signaled to the only remaining significant Native American land holders in the area, the Potawatomi, that their time too had come to leave Illinois.

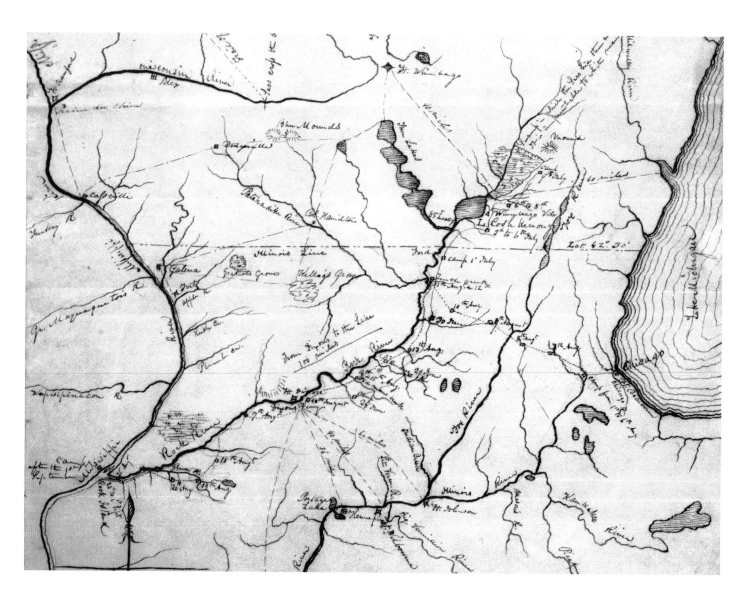

INCORPORATION AS A TOWN

The Conley and Seltzer Map

Title: A Map of Chicago: Incorporated as a Town August 5, 1833
Date Issued: 1933
Cartographer: Walter M. Conley and O. E. Seltzer
Published: *Chicago Sunday Tribune, Picture Section, August 13, 1933*
"Reproduced from a lithograph of the original," 33 x 47 cm
Author's Collection

On February 12, 1831, the Illinois state legislature authorized any community of over one hundred fifty inhabitants to incorporate as a town, with its limits not to exceed one square mile in extent. To incorporate, a majority of two-thirds of the community's eligible voters was required (eligible voters were white males over the age of twenty-one, who were either residents of the community for over six months, or were real estate holders in the community). If incorporation was approved, public notice was to be given, and after five days an election of town trustees was to be held. Incorporated towns could establish ordinances to remove and prevent nuisances, restrain and prohibit disorderly conduct, license

public shows, regulate markets, sink public wells, construct streets and sidewalks, and provide for fire protection. To finance their projects, towns could impose fines on ordinance violations, collect fees for the issuance of licenses, and levy and collect taxes on real estate not to exceed fifty cents per one hundred dollars of assessed value.

By 1833, the Potawatomi, once the principal land owners in Illinois, had been forced to sell almost all of their holdings. In August of that year, the Indian agent at Chicago sent word to the chiefs of the Potawatomi nations that the federal government wished to purchase the remaining five million acres of their land, which formed a semicircle around the village of Chicago. In anticipation of this

cessation, a group of villagers met at the Sauganash Hotel and voted to incorporate the village into a town. The exact day of this meeting is not known, but it is known that the first election of town trustees was held on August 10, 1833. Given the five-day mandate for this vote, this would mark the town's incorporation as August 5, 1833. At the time, Chicago barely had a population of 150 people, but the number of residents surged to over 250 by the end of the year. Many of the new settlers had come to town to witness the signing of the treaty with the Potawatomi, and decided that the town's future looked bright now that the "Indian menace" had been removed.

The first boundaries of the new town were Kinzie, Desplaines, Madison,

One Mile From Madison

½ Mile

Miss Eliza Chappel's School

THE FORKS
1. Mark Beaubien's Sauganash Hotel
2. The First Post Office 1833
3. Wolf Tavern
4. Sam Miller's Public House

The Wild Onion "Che-ca-gou"

SOUTH WATER STREET 1834

SOUTH BRANCH

SWAMP LAND

N W S E

TRAIL TO DANVILLE

Latitude 41° 53'
Longitude 87° 38'
Elevation 584 ft.

State Street in 1836

ROAD TO DETROIT

Mail over this week from

SITE OF DEARBORN MASSACRE at foot of 18th Street

Sand Hills

LAKE MICH

A
MAP
of
CHICAGO
Incorporated as a Town
August 5
1833

R.E. STELZER DES.
CAROLINE M. McILVAINE, HISTORICAL ADVISER

One Mile From Madison St.

½ Mile

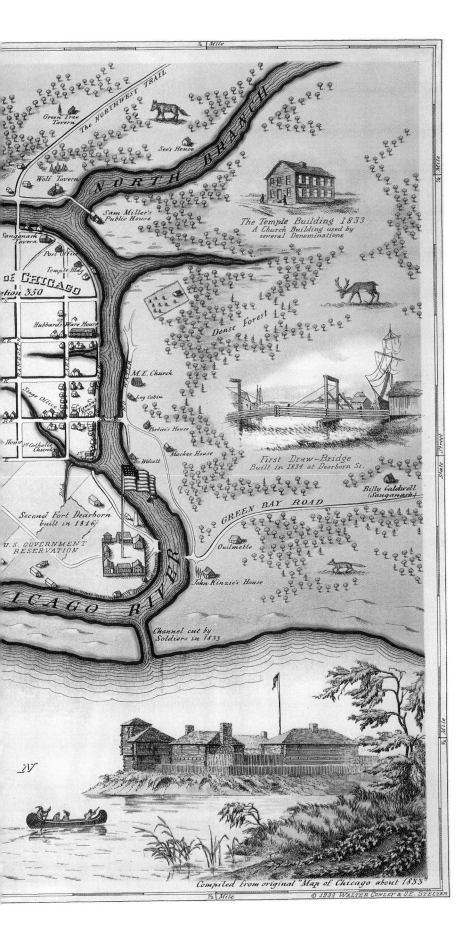

Compiled from original "Map of Chicago about 1833"

© 1933 WALTER CONLEY & O.E. STELZER

and State streets, which included an area of about three-eighths of a square mile. On November 6, 1833, the limits of the town were extended to an area of seven-eighths of a square mile. A special act of legislature was passed February 11, 1835, and under its provisions the area of the Town of Chicago was extended to about two and two-fifths square miles, with a population of 3,265.

This retrospective map presents many intriguing geographic, historical and demographic details about the town in its early days, including the locations of private houses, churches, taverns, cemeteries, and the second Fort Dearborn built in 1816. It was designed in collaboration with Caroline McIlvaine, who served as the Chicago Historical Society's librarian for the first quarter of the twentieth century. It notes that it was compiled from data provided by the "Original Map of Chicago about 1833" and records a resident population of 350.

The left side of the map pictures a wild onion plant, with the word *Checagou* below. From the language of the local Miami, it was actually derived from a word used to refer to the wild garlic plant that was abundant along the banks of the Chicago River. LaSalle was among the first to have found a similar term used by the Miami peoples to refer to the peninsula where the Chicago River emptied into Lake Michigan.

Prior to its incorporation as a town, the village of Chicago was centered on "The Forks," which was the name the early settlers gave to the area surrounded by the confluence of both branches of the Chicago River. Here we find the Sauganash Hotel, which was the first frame house built in Chicago, and was run by Mark Beaubien. The Wolf Tavern (a reference to Wolf Point, the angular prominence of the west bank of the Forks), and Sam Miller's Public House were also located here. Out on the Northwest Trail, which was later a plank road, was located the Green Tree Tavern, so named because of a solitary oak tree that stood nearby.

The village in its early days was a racially diverse settlement of Native Americans, half-breeds, French Canadians, and Anglo-Americans. A raucous lot, they lived isolated from civilization, traded in furs, and drank liberally in the taverns along the river. As more settlers arrived, additional houses were built along the south side of the main branch of the river to Fort Dearborn (South Water Street is depicted in the inset in the upper left corner). Elisa Chappel's school was started as a subscription school in 1833 and would later become Chicago's first public school. The Temple Building, built by Dr. John T. Temple, an ardent

Baptist, stood at Franklin and South Water Streets. The upper floor of this two-story building was used as school rooms, the lower floor rooms were used by the Baptists, Methodists and Presbyterians for worship services. Gurdon Hubbard began construction of a large, brick warehouse near the river, which skeptics nicknamed "Hubbard's Folly." Further down river, The Tremont House was built as a saloon and boarding house; in 1833 it was converted into one of Chicago's first fashionable hotels. The first stage line to run in Chicago opened in 1833 from Detroit. In 1836, the firm of Fink and Walker, which for years would enjoy a virtual monopoly on passenger transportation through the Midwest, began operations out of Chicago, with an office located at Lake and Dearborn Streets.

The first Catholic church in Chicago was built in 1833 on the southwest corner of State and Lake Streets. Saint Mary's Church was built by Augustine Taylor, who employed a new principle of construction that was to prove instrumental to the city's rapid growth. Traditional building methods used heavy, hand-hewn timbers and hand-carved mortise-and-tenon joints held in place by hand-cut dowels or handmade nails. This labor-intensive (and hence, expensive) process involved assembling an entire wall on the ground, which was then lifted into place by a large

crew of laborers. Taylor's method used much lighter pre-cut two-by-four studs that were held together by factory-made nails. This immensely reduced the cost of houses, which could be built quickly and efficiently by only two workers using basic carpentry techniques. Derisively called "balloon frame construction" (by carpenters who thought that a house so constructed would blow away in a strong wind), this type of construction is essentially that used to build houses today. Without these techniques, it is doubtful that Chicago could have transformed itself from a small frontier town into a teeming city as quickly as it did.

In November of 1836, a committee was formed to apply to the state legislature for a city charter, and to adopt a draft to accompany the application. A charter was prepared by this committee and submitted to the townspeople for approval at a meeting at the Saloon Building on Monday, January 23, 1837. After some minor alterations, the charter was approved and sent to the legislature. There, after certain amendments, it was enacted into law on March 4, 1837, and Chicago became a city with a population of 4,170. Interestingly, this charter divided the city into wards, yet it did not produce a printed map showing their boundaries. Rather, it was real estate interests that were to produce the first maps of Chicago.

THE REAL ESTATE BOOM

The Hathaway Map
The Wright Map
The Talcott Map
The Bradley Map

Title: Chicago With The School Section Wabansia and Kinzie's Addition.
Compiled from the Four Original Surveys as filed in the Cook County Clerk's Office
Date Issued: 1834
Cartographer: Joshua Hathaway, Jr.
Published: Peter A. Meisner (New York)
Lithograph, 72 x 50 cm
Chicago Historical Society, ICHi-05614

Title: Chicago
Date Issued: 1834
Cartographer: James Stephen Wright
Published: Peter A. Meisner (New York)
Lithograph, 47 x 38 cm
Chicago Historical Society, ICHi-34590

Title: Chicago with the several additions compiled from the recorded plats in the Clerk's office, Cook County,
Illinois. The lots in the original town…will be offered for sale…on the 20th of June 1836.
Date Issued: 1836
Cartographer: Edward Benton Talcott
Published: Peter A. Meisner (New York)
Lithograph, 57 x 93 cm
Chicago Historical Society, ICHi-37310

Title: Map of the City of Chicago Lithographed and For Sale at N. Currier's Office,
Corner of Nassau & Spruce Streets, New York
Date Issued: 1836–7
Cartographer: Asa F. Bradley
Published: N. Currier (New York)
Lithograph, 135.5 x 102 cm
Chicago Historical Society, ICHi-37866

By the mid-1830s, Chicago was in the midst of one of the most frenzied periods of land speculation in American history. The real estate boom was fueled by Eastern investors and property values soared. An 80-by-100-foot lot at the corner of South Water and Clark Streets that had a value of $100 in 1832 was sold for $3400 in 1834. The following year it sold for $15,000. The New York investor Charles Bronson purchased a tract for $20,000 in the fall of 1834; the following spring he sold the land for $100,000 to his friend Charles Butler. Butler subdivided the tract, offered it for sale within a month, and recouped the purchase price from the sale of just one-third of the lots.

As a parcel of land was subdivided and added to the original town, a new map of the entire community was needed. In the early 1830s, these took the form of various manuscript plats and plans, which were sent to Eastern investors to guide their investments. The first published map of Chicago appeared in 1834. Using the original surveys of the Town Plat and of three new additions, Joshua Hathaway, Jr. compiled *Chicago with the school section, Wabansia, and Kinzie's addition*. A notice in the June 18, 1834,

issue of the *Chicago Democrat* advertised for sale copies of a lithographic map of Chicago, most likely Hathaway's, since it describes the map using exactly the same wording as found in his legend. Little is known of the life of Hathaway, who arrived in Chicago with no money

and through a friend secured the job of compiling the map from George W. Snow, the regular surveyor. He later did survey work in Wisconsin, where he and Walter Newberry, Jr. invested in land in the Appleton area. The map itself was commissioned by John H.

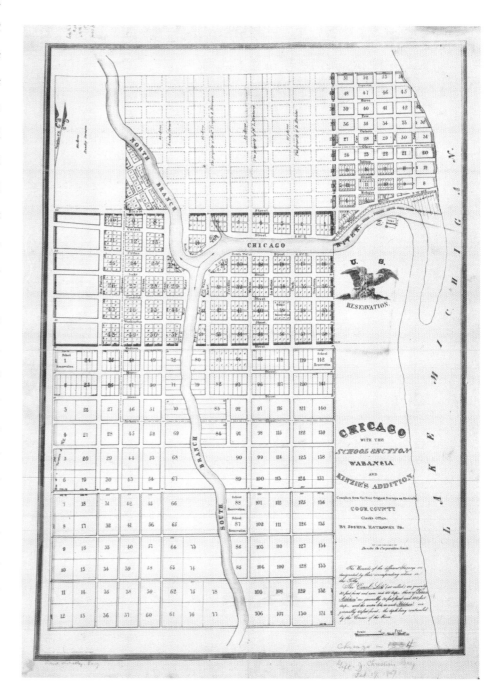

Kinzie to aid in the sale of his lots. Although the map is not dated and does not contain the lithographer's name, correspondence between Kinzie and his agent and partner in New York, Arthur Bronson, reveals that six hundred copies of the map were printed in 1834 by the lithographic firm of Peter A. Meisner. The map did not indicate it was a lithograph because Bronson was sure that very few people could tell that it was not struck from a copperplate. Six different impressions of the map were made on as many different types of paper. Although most of the maps were sold as individual sheets, some were sold on rollers, others in leather cases. On the original map the river and the shoreline are blue, and the legend is red, yellow and blue.

A similar, but smaller, real estate map of Chicago was also published by the firm of Peter A. Meisner in 1834. Drawn by John Stephen Wright, it is dated with the year of its publication, and shows many more blocks divided into lots than Hathaway's map. This is used as evidence that the Hathaway map was the earlier publication. Wright had sent an earlier manuscript version of the map to his uncle in New York, so that his uncle could follow real estate transactions being made on his behalf.

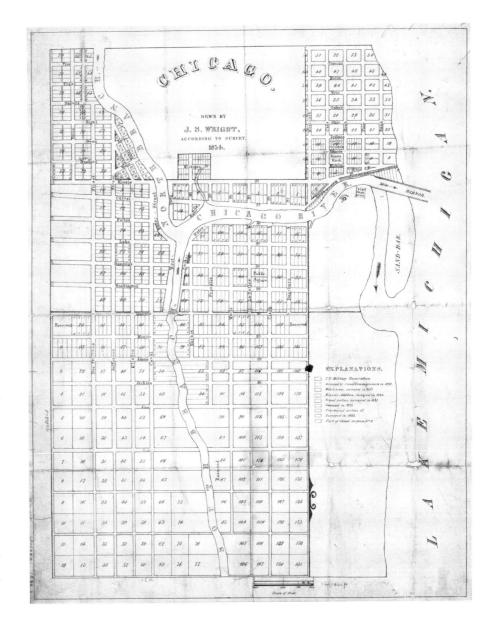

The map presented here is a fine tracing paper copy of this map. A map very similar to Wright's, but dated a year earlier, can be found in the archives of the Chicago Historical Society. It contains the note that it is a copy of the map "sent to Washington to secure an appropriation to improve the harbor, March 2, 1833." This same

year Wright had taken a census of the town of Chicago.

Wright first came to Chicago with his father in 1832 at the age of seventeen. He initially worked in his father's stores, but soon became a successful real estate dealer in the speculative fever of the day. By the time he was twenty-one, he had holdings worth over $200,000, a fortune

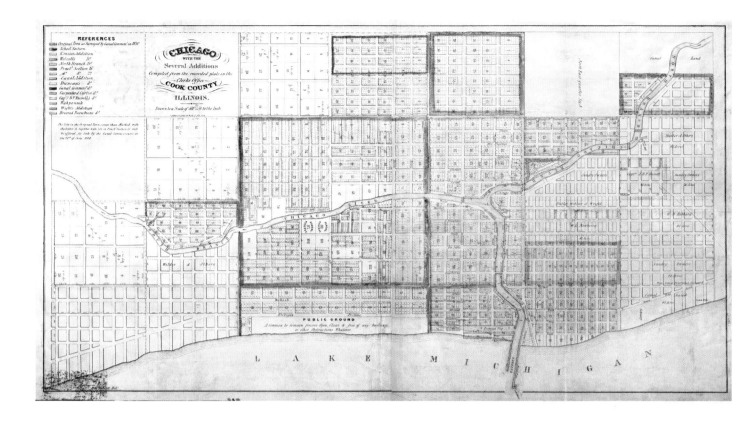

he would lose in the 1837 crash. He recovered by diversifying into the forwarding and commission business and into the sale of machinery. An ardent civic booster, Wright underwrote the construction of Chicago's first public school house in 1835, advocated a public park system connected by wide boulevards, and along with his father was a charter member of the First Presbyterian Church. He owned and edited the monthly newspaper, *Prairie Farmer*, and published several books, including *Chicago: Past, Present, Future*, in 1868.

The lithographic firm of Peter A. Meisner was to publish two other early real estate maps of Chicago. One, entitled *73 Building Lots in Chicago To be Sold at Auction by James Bleeker and Sons on Thursday, 22nd of October*, was published in 1835. The lots were located in the school section, and the plat featured an inset map showing where the lots were located. The second map, which is presented here, is a large and detailed map drafted by Edward Benton Talcott in 1836. Talcott had come to Chicago in 1835 to work on the Illinois and Michigan Canal, and would eventually oversee its construction. He also would find work as the city surveyor. Like John S. Wright, Talcott

remained in Chicago for the rest of his life, and is recognized as one who greatly shaped the future development of the city. His map was sponsored by the canal commissioners to stimulate interest in the city and to encourage the sale of lots in fractional Section 15. It presents more than twice the area of the 1834 maps, which required turning the plan horizontally to accommodate all the new subdivisions (note that the lake is at the base of the map with north set to its right-hand side).

The New York firm of Miller & Company also published a real estate map of Chicago in 1835. Entitled *Map of Lots at Chicago for sale by Franklin & Jenkins on Friday May 8, 1835 at 12 O'Clock at the Merchant's Exchange*, it is a large lithograph that presents two maps of Chicago: one is a general street map of the center of the city; the other is a detailed plat of a new subdivision west of the north branch of the Chicago River. The last map presented here is a very large map with decorative borders covering the area extending from Lake Michigan west to Damen Avenue and from De Koven Street on the south to Noble Street on the north. "In contrast to its decorative borders," notes Gerald Danzer, "the map is plain and uneventful. The diagonal roads are omitted, but a number of public squares were set at regular intervals across the city plan. The central part of the town is filled with numbered lots, but further from the river these details disappear in the plain blocks stamped with bold numbers. The map was apparently commissioned by Amos F. Bradley, a young mechanic, to compile a map that included all the subdivisions recorded up to that time. A great deal of fanciful material has been added to the map to fill up the undeveloped parts of the town."

Chicago's real estate boom came to a crashing halt with the Panic of 1837, which plunged the nation into a five-year-long depression. Real estate values plummeted, and land bought for $11,000 an acre in 1836 could not be sold for $100 four years later. As the real estate market evaporated, so did the need for maps. In fact, after the publication of the six maps detailed above, it would be more than a decade before another map of the entire city would be published. Even the chartering of the city of Chicago in 1837, which divided the city into wards, did not produce a political boundary map.

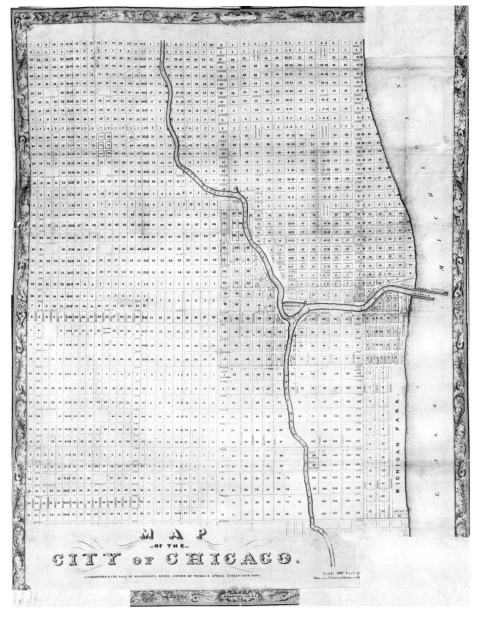

CITY REAL ESTATE AT A GLANCE

The Clougher Map
The Potter Map

Title: Map of Chicago and Vicinity
Date Issued: 1849
Cartographer: William Clougher
Published: Julius Hutawa (St. Louis)
Lithograph, 110 x 83 cm
Newberry Library, Map 6F oG4104 .c6 G46 1849 C6

Title: Map of Chicago
Date Issued: 1853
Cartographer: C. Potter
Published: Henry Hart (New York)
Lithograph, 213 x 133 cm
Chicago Historical Society, ICHi-29424

In 1850, Chicago was thirteen years old, its population was nearing 30,000, and the completion of the Illinois and Michigan canal and the coming of the railroads were about to create a new real estate boom. Although the built-up area of the city extended only a third of the way to the city limits, it would no longer be feasible to include all lots on a single map; rather, the city would begin to be documented by atlases of real estate and fire insurance maps on a lot-by-lot basis. In the late 1840s, however, there was still a demand for real estate maps of the entire city.

William H. Bushnell's large cadastral map "exhibiting recent additions, subdivisions, &c." was lithographed in New York by the firm of Saxony & Major, and was published in 1847. A similar *Map of Chicago and Vicinity*, compiled by Rees & Rucker, land agents, appeared in 1849. Shown here, this map was drawn by William Clougher and is unusual because it was lithographed by Julius Hutawa of Saint Louis, rather than by a New York firm.

While the Bushnell and the Clougher real estate maps were the last of their kind, the second map shown here was one of a kind—a hybrid between a real estate map and a street map. Considered the finest of the early maps of Chicago, it was drawn by C. Potter, surveyed and published by Henry Hart, and lithographed by Sarony and Company. Its huge size permitted a detailed representation of the entire city, showing every lot according to scale. As in the early real estate maps, it shows the ownership of the larger tracts. It was also a street map of the entire city and included hundreds of features like buildings, factories, railroads, and parks. It shows the voting wards of the city in different colors, and includes a beautiful vignette of the city courthouse.

Although this 1853 map was lithographed in New York, the other three maps of Chicago published that year were Chicago imprints. Soon Chicago was to surpass St. Louis in map publishing, and several decades later, more maps would be published in Chicago than in New York. Prominent names in Chicago's map publishing business included Rufus Blanchard, George F. Cram, Alfred T. Andreas, and the firm of Rand McNally and Company.

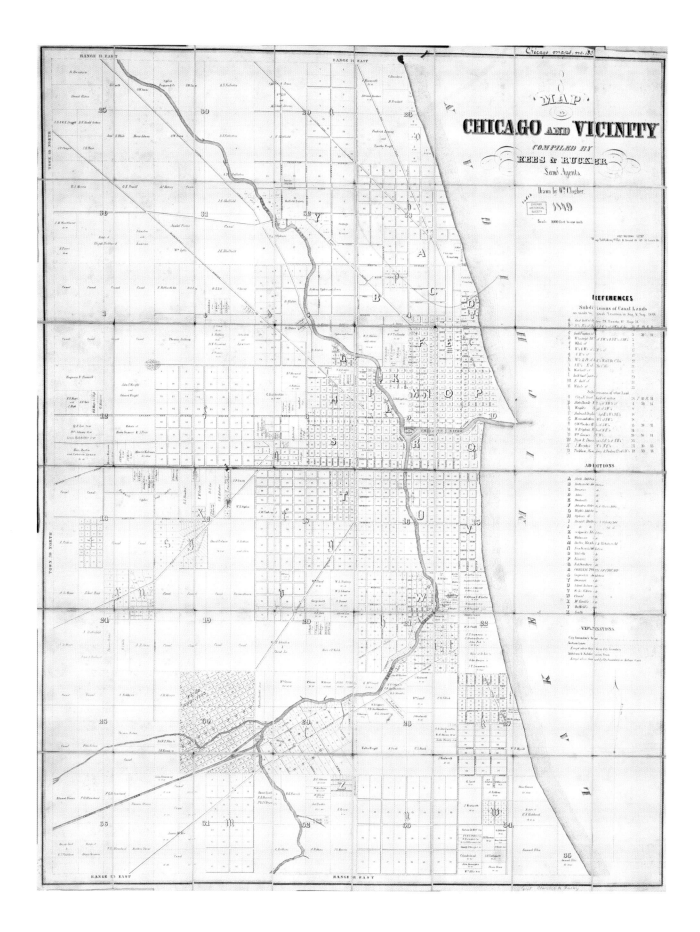

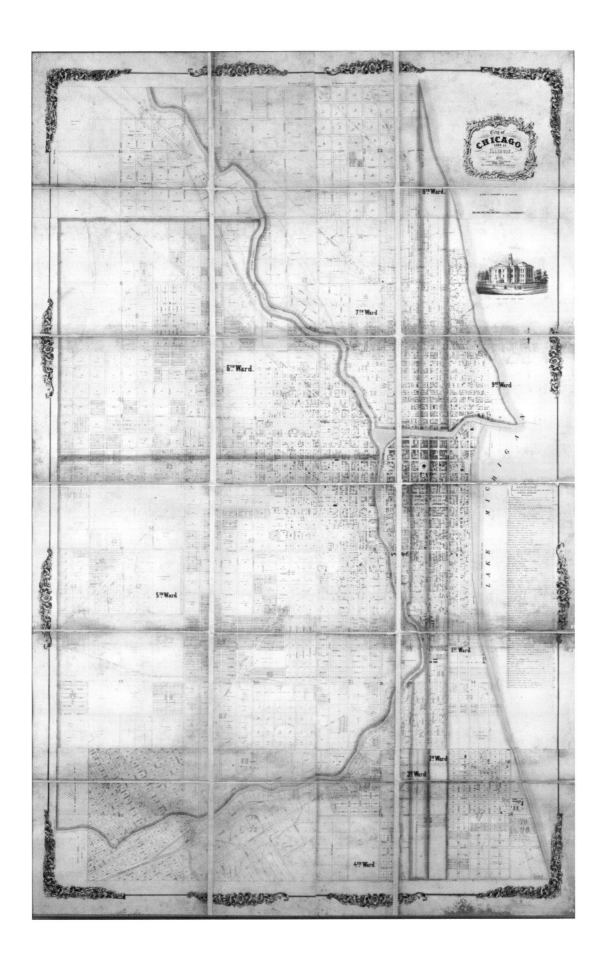

69

CITY DIRECTORY MAPS

The Burley Map

Title: Map of the city of Chicago
Date Issued: 1852
Cartographer: Augustus and Charles Burley
Published: *Udall & Hopkin's Chicago City Directory* (Chicago)
Folded Sheet, 33 x 25 cm
Newberry Library, Graff 4229

From 1839 to the late 1920s, various companies in Chicago published city directories; by 1844, the publication of a city directory had become an annual event. These directories typically included both residential and business listings and used information collected by company representatives who canvassed door-to-door throughout the city. A residential directory might list the names of everyone living at a city residence, their occupation, where they worked and their spouse's name. They often would indicate whether a person was an owner, renter, or boarder. If a person was listed as an owner, there might be a record of when the property was purchased.

As the city grew, these directories became more detailed, containing special sections pertaining to businesses, churches and organizations. They often included a "reverse" street directory that listed streets alphabetically with the names of people residing at each address. The need for a map to accompany these directories became obvious.

In 1849, O. P. Hatheway and J. H. Taylor published a directory with the note that "a beautiful steel engraved map" had been made for inclusion with the directory, but that the New York engraver had not sent it in time to include in the present edition. Whether this map was ever published is not known. In 1851, W. W.

Danenhower published a directory with a city street map, which was engraved by Doty & Bergen and printed by D. Morse in New York.

The map presented here accompanied the directory published in 1852 by Udall & Hopkins. Produced by Augustus and Charles Burley, it is probably the earliest contemporary map of the city that was printed in Chicago. Directory maps such as this one differed from the early real estate maps of the city. They were typically smaller in size and focused on streets, major buildings and landmarks. Street widths were not shown to scale, and lot lines and dimensions did not appear on these maps.

MAP OF THE CITY OF CHICAGO.

PUBLISHED BY A.H. & C. BURLEY.

1852

A ORIGINAL TOWN.
B SCHOOL SECTION.
C FORT DEARBORN ADDITION.
D FRAC. SEC. 15 Do.
E KINZIES Do. Do.
F WOLCOTTS Do.
G BUTLER WRIGHT & WEBSTERS
H SEDGWICKS Do.
I RUSSELL MATHER & ROBERTS Do.
J Do. Do. Do.
K WIGHTS Do.
L WABANSIA Do.

M CARPENTERS Do. Do.
N DUNCANS Do.
O CANAL Do.
P OGDENS Do.
R BUSHNELLS ADDITION
S JOHNSON ROBERTS & STORRS
T BROWNS Do.
U BUTTERFIELDS Do.
V ASTORS Do.
W NORTH Do.
X NEWBERRYS Do.
1 to 9 The Wards.

HOTELS.
1 TREMONT HOUSE
2 MATTESON
3 SHERMAN Do
4 CITY HOTEL
5 AMERICAN Ho.
6 HAMILTON Do
7 COMMERCIAL
8 UNITED STATES
9 NEW YORK
10 GARDEN CITY
11 BULLS HEAD
A COURT HOUSE
B MARKET
C Do
D Do

CHICAGO'S FIRST RAILROAD: THE GALENA AND CHICAGO UNION

The Colton Map

Title: Map Showing the Location of Galena and Chicago Union Railroad with its Branches and Connections in Illinois, Wisconsin, Iowa and Minnesota
Date Issued: 1862
Cartographer: G. Woolworth Colton
Published: G. Woolworth Colton
Lithograph, 36 x 64 cm
Library of Congress, Geography and Map Division, G4061.P3 1862 .G15 RR 414

In 1846, there was not a single mile of railroad track in Chicago. In ten years' time, the city would become the rail capital of the United States; and William Ogden, Chicago's first mayor and the builder of Chicago's first railroad, would become known as the "Railroad King of the West."

Ogden and a group of investors bought the rights to the Galena and Chicago Union Railroad in 1846, a railway that had been chartered in 1836 to connect Chicago with the lead mines at Galena. Ogden found that Eastern investors had little interest in his railroad and, to his surprise, that many Chicago merchants were opposed to the idea of a railroad. In fact, many local businessmen were afraid that a railroad would ruin the city. As things stood, farmers brought their crops to town in ox-drawn wagons, and often would stay a number of days to procure supplies and patronize the city's hotels, saloons, and other businesses. A railroad, they argued, would cause the city to lose this business, as farmers would no longer need to accompany their harvest. For this reason, the city was seen as better off with the modes of transportation already in place: shipping from the Great Lakes, the Illinois and Michigan Canal, and the network of plank roads leading to the city.

Unable to secure local or Eastern financing, Ogden set out to pitch the idea of a railroad to the farmers and merchants along its proposed route. He took on a partner from New England, Jonathan Young Scammon, and the two of them set out with horse and buggy to sell stock in their railroad. By 1848, Ogden had over $350,000 in stock subscriptions—not enough to build a railroad, but enough to start putting down track. Again Ogden faced opposition from local merchants, whose political clout prevented him from building a depot within the city's limits. Instead, the line began from the corner of Kinzie and Halsted Streets, which was then at the western edge of the city.

The steam engine "Pioneer" made its first run in the autumn of 1848 on the fledgling railroad's eight-mile-long line of track. On its return trip it carried a load of wheat it had picked up from a farmer traveling by ox wagon to the city, and a week later more than thirty loads of wheat were waiting at the Des Plaines River to be hauled into town. The city council quickly saw the error of its ways and allowed the railroad into the city.

Ogden immediately built an engine house on the north branch of the river, and later a depot on North Water Street, along with a drawbridge across the river. By 1850, the Galena and Chicago Union was already being recognized as a primary mode of transportation for Chicago. The *Chicago Tribune*'s "Annual Review of Commerce" for that year stated: "The three great sources and avenues of [Chicago's] commerce abroad are the Lakes, the Illinois & Michigan Canal, and the Galena and Chicago Union Railroad." By 1852, the Galena would carry over half the wheat that arrived in the city.

This map shows the location of the main line of the Galena and Chicago Union Railroad, with its branches and connections throughout the Midwestern United States. The railroad network is laid out on a map that includes drainage, cities and towns, and counties. The main line of the railroad network is emphasized, and the map has a table that charts the distance from Chicago to various Midwestern cities along the line. The lower margin is labeled "Entered according to Act of Congress in the Year 1862, in the Clerk's Office of the District Court of the United States for the Southern District of New York." The upper margin lists the longitude west from Greenwich.

Chicago's first railroad made money from the start, and Ogden's early success convinced Eastern investors that railroads in Illinois could be immensely profitable. The rail boom was on: by 1852, four more railroads served Chicago, two connecting with the East, one with the South, and another to the West; by 1856 that number had doubled, and on a daily basis Chicago saw fifty-eight passenger trains and thirty-eight freight trains. As the railroads grew, so did the city. In 1850, Chicago was a city of 30,000 people. In 1860, its population totaled 109,000. The entire state experienced tremendous growth over this decade, the end of which saw Illinois as the fourth most populous state in the Union. The center of this development was in and around Chicago, which almost overnight became a transportation and commercial center.

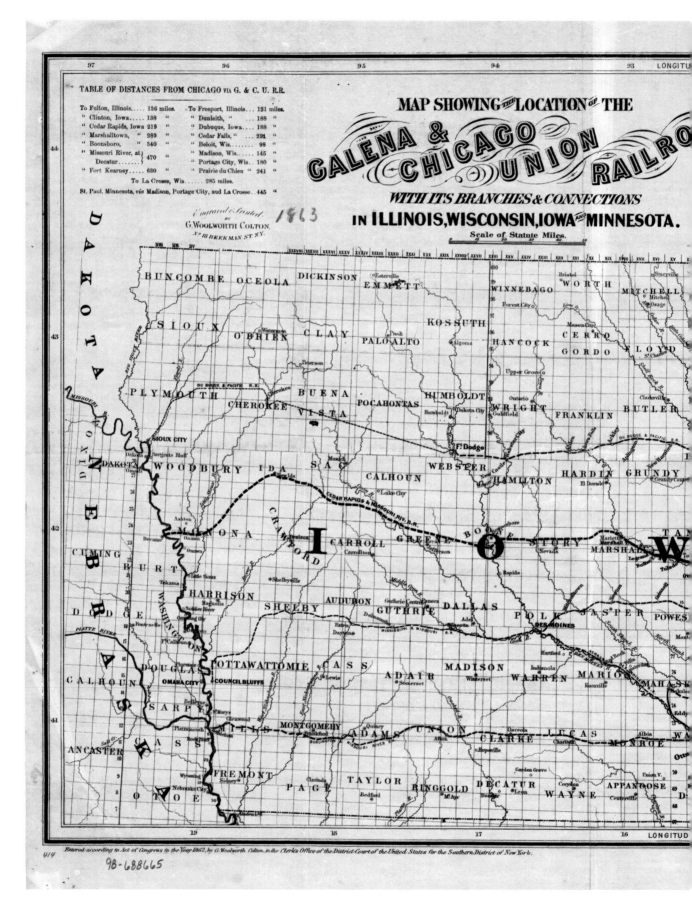

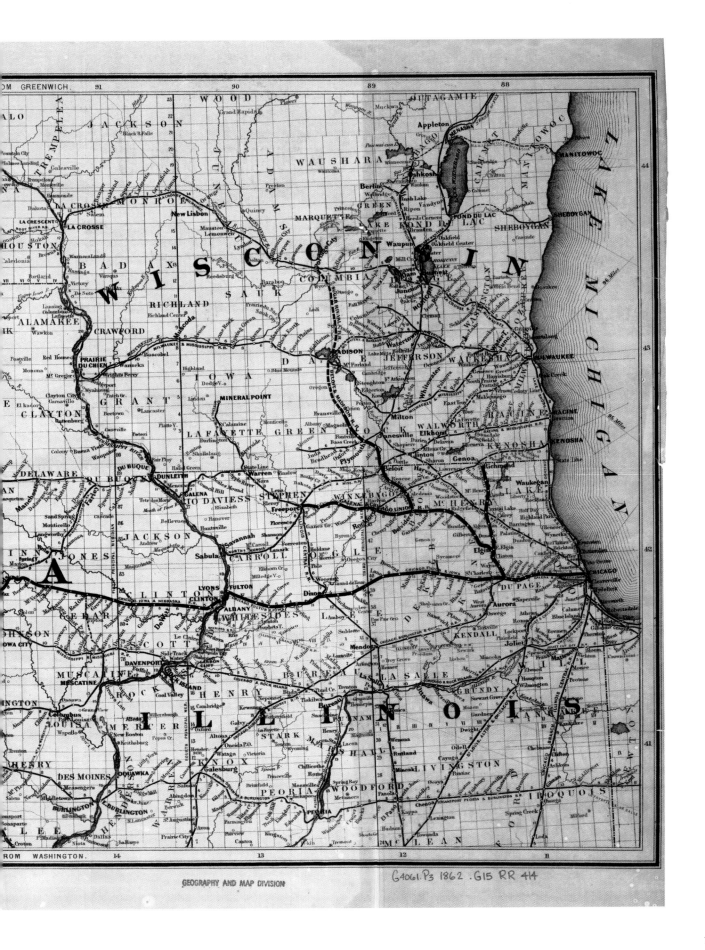

THE NATION'S RAILROAD CAPITAL

The D. B. Cooke Railway Guide Map

Title: D. B. Cooke's Great Western Railway Guide exhibiting all states with distances
Date Issued: 1855
Cartographer: D. B. Cooke & Co.
Published: D. B. Cooke & Co. (Chicago)
Lithograph, 73 x 101 cm
Library of Congress, Geography and Map Division, G4101.P3 1855 .D15 RR 203

In 1857, over three thousand miles of railroad track led to Chicago, making it the center of the largest railway network in the world. Over one hundred trains entered and left the city every day, and with them the products of farms and forests and, of course, people. The railroads transformed Chicago into the nation's largest transportation and commercial center almost overnight. One British visitor, who referred to Chicago as "the lightning city," wrote that, "The growth of this city is one of the most amazing things in the history of modern civilization."

Prior to the arrival of the railroads, steamboats handled most of the nation's commercial shipping needs, and the general direction of the nation's trade was from north to south. Thus, for example, Midwestern farm products would be gathered at the great river ports such as St. Louis, shipped south on the Mississippi River system to New Orleans, and from there by sea to the east coast. When the Erie Canal opened in 1825, the general direction of the nation's trade began to shift from north-south to east-west; and by about 1835, a large part of the traffic that had formerly been sent down the Ohio and Mississippi Rivers to New Orleans was now making its way across the Great Lakes and down the Erie Canal to New York City. The most important goods that were shipped via this route were lumber, meat and grain—the very same commodities that Chicago's railways would gather from its Midwestern hinterland and on which the city would make her early fortune.

Before the advent of the railroad, Chicago was unable to tap the potential of its hinterland. The Illinois and Michigan Canal, which underwrote the founding of Chicago, would serve as a conduit for goods coming from the country to Chicago's southwest. The only links to regions west and northwest of the city, however, were plank and toll roads, a relatively slow and inefficient means to transport goods to market. William Ogden, who had planned to revive a railroad that was designed to tap the lead mines of Galena, perceived this shortcoming; and in the same year the canal opened, he began operating a railroad to service these areas. He had funded the railroad by selling its stock to the farmers and merchants that lived along its proposed route, convincing them that this new mode of transport would be the most efficient means to bring their goods to market.

His railroad was an instant success, and showed Eastern capitalists that railroads could be built and run profitably in Chicago. "In succeeding years," writes Donald Miller, "Eastern investors, operating through Ogden and other agents in Chicago, built a spreading network of rail lines to the north, south, and west of the city, reaching into vast hardwood forests, deep minefields of bituminous coal, and to the largest region of continuously fertile land in the world." These railways allowed Chicago to fully exploit the riches of its hinterland, and Chicago soon became a prominent regional trade center.

Two of the most important commodities to come through Chicago were lumber and wheat. Ogden and other Chicago entrepreneurs had purchased entire forests in upper Wisconsin and Michigan, from which timber would be sent by lake boats to Chicago. The city's lumber mills would then process the wood, turning it into houses, schools, stores, and churches.

The latter would then be shipped via rail and canal to farmers and merchants on the treeless prairie. These same farmers used reapers made at Cyrus McCormick's Chicago factory to cut their wheat, which was shipped by rail to Chicago, and from there by boat to the rest of the world.

Chicago's location along the longest inland water route in the world practically insured it would become a major rail center. The Great Lakes and the Erie Canal linked Chicago to New York, and the Illinois and Michigan Canal connected Chicago to the Mississippi River and the Gulf of Mexico. By bringing rail lines to Chicago, the city would become a terminus of two great modes of transit, a prospect that Eastern investors were eager to promote.

St. Louis, of course, was also located on this same water route, was a major trade center, and by the time Ogden's railroad began its operations, was the nation's third-largest city. It too had an extensive hinterland from which it could gather those commodities sought by the East, including much of Southern Illinois and all of the upper Midwest drained by the Mississippi and Missouri Rivers. Chicago's chief urban rival remained loyal to river transport, however. When Chicago's railroads were set to cross the Mississippi River, St. Louis realized its

mistake, and tried to prevent their crossing by claiming that railroad bridges were hazards to boats trying to navigate the river. St. Louis was also reluctant to encourage outside investment, which would have been necessary for the rapid institution of a railroad building program. Chicago, on the other hand, eagerly sought Eastern investors, and in a very real sense, was a colony for Eastern capital—capital that indisputably made it the central mart of the region.

Chicago's geography was also instrumental in its emergence as the nation's largest rail hub. Railroads were destined to cross the continent, and in doing so, they played a fundamental role in creating a strong and unified nation: the railroads opened up the West and linked its development and destiny with the East. Lake Michigan, however, stood directly in the path of the shortest railroad route from the East to the far West and Northwest. Thus, railroads bound for these areas were forced to go around the lake's southern tip, and directly through Chicago, which became the great portal between East and West.

The first railroad from the East reached Chicago in 1852; by 1854, rail lines from Chicago stretched to the Mississippi. This map shows those railroads either "operational or in the process of construction" in the Great

Lakes area in 1855, and exemplifies a statement made at the time by the *Chicago Daily Democrat*: "With the use of a map, any person can see that all the [rail]roads and branches that we have noticed, aim at Chicago. From the east and west, north and south, it is the great center which they all seek." This map was published by David B. Cooke, a Chicago book dealer who acted as a local map publisher when the opportunity arose; he published a similar map of Illinois railroads the same year.

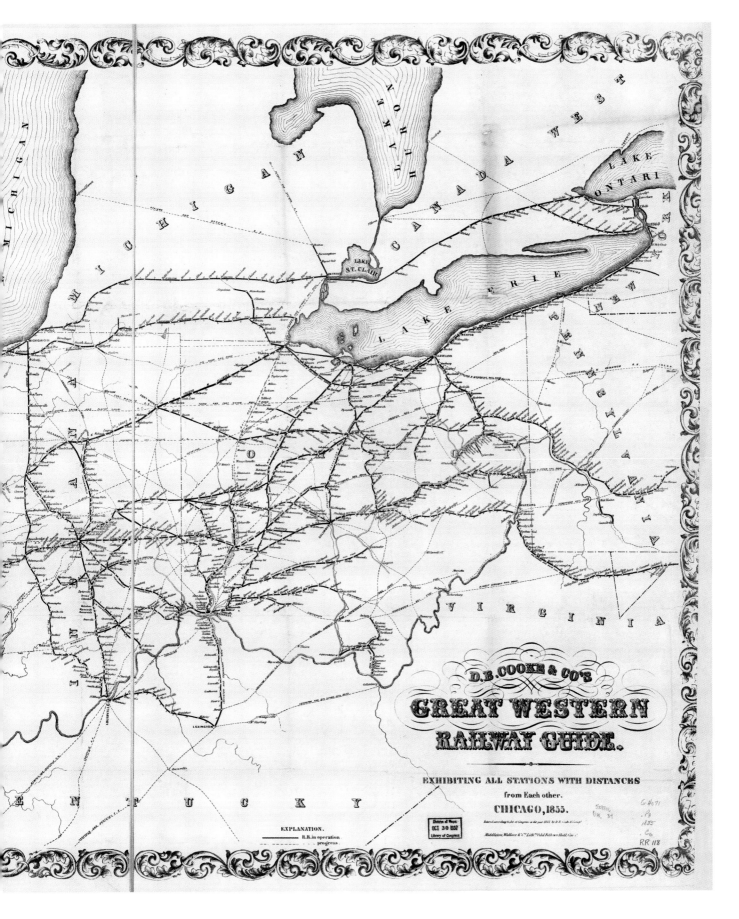

D.B. COOKE & CO'S

GREAT WESTERN
RAILWAY GUIDE.

EXHIBITING ALL STATIONS WITH DISTANCES

from Each other.

CHICAGO, 1855.

EXPLANATION.

——— R.R. in operation
‑ ‑ ‑ ‑ progress.

THE ILLINOIS CENTRAL RAILROAD

The Palmatary View

Title: Bird's-Eye View of Chicago
Date Issued: 1857
Cartographer: J. T. Palmatary (Engraved by Christian Inger)
Published: Braunhold & Sonne (Chicago)
Lithograph, 115 x 207 cm
Chicago Historical Society, ICHI-05656

Chicago's new railroads greatly altered the city's landscape. Wherever tracks were run—and they were run wherever the railroads desired—land use was immediately affected: depots and train yards dominated their surrounding neighborhoods, and commercial and industrial development quickly gravitated toward rail lines. Chicago literally grew up around its railroad tracks—it had to, as the railroads left only a single square mile in the center of the city free of their direct presence.

No railroad had a bigger impact on Chicago's physical environment than the Illinois Central. The "IC" was long a dream of Senator Stephen A. Douglas; he had campaigned in 1846 on a platform that called for the federal government to cede public lands to the state for the purpose creating a railroad that would run the length of the state and extend all the way south to the Gulf of Mexico. Douglas had a nationalistic vision in which the railroads served to bind different sections of the country together: future railways would tie the West to the East; the Illinois Central would link the North with the South, ending the South's growing desire for secession from the Union.

The IC was exceptional in two respects: it was a north-south railroad, and it was the first land-grant railroad. The railroad's land grant was approved by Congress in 1850, largely due to the efforts of three men: Douglas in the Senate, "Long John" Wentworth in the House of Representatives, and the publicist John Stephen Wright. At his own expense, Wright had 6,000 circulars printed and distributed, each bearing a petition to Congress to pass the "Douglas" plan; when the bill was about to come to the floor, Wright moved to Washington to personally lobby for it. The argument used to justify the grant was that the potential farmland of central Illinois would be inaccessible, and therefore without value, in the absence of such a railroad. As championed by Senator Henry Clay, the line of reasoning was that "by constructing this road through the prairie . . . you bring millions of acres of land immediately into the market which will otherwise remain . . . entirely unsalable."

Just as had been done with the Illinois and Michigan Canal, the railroad was to sell the lands granted to it, using the proceeds for construction. The Illinois Central Railroad Company was established by the Illinois State Legislature in 1851, and in 1856, the 705-mile railroad—the longest in the world—began regular service from Chicago to Cairo. The railway soon became known as "the St. Louis cutoff," as trade that previously had gone downriver to St. Louis now went to Chicago. In advertising and selling the two and one-half million acres of land along its route, the IC was a catalyst for growth in the central and southern regions of Illinois, attracting thousands of settlers and laying the foundations for agricultural, industrial, and urban development. This, in turn, provided the Illinois Central with its own economic lifeline, as these same settlers offered up their bounty for the railway to forward to Chicago.

The IC's entry into Chicago was to set off a battle that would not be resolved for nearly half a century. In 1836, the Illinois and Michigan Canal Commission, which was responsible for the original sale of lots in Chicago, had seen fit to set aside one parcel of land along the lakefront for public use. Indeed, their 1836 real estate map marked the lakefront with the words "Public Ground—A Common to Remain Forever Open, Clear, Free of Any Buildings, or Other Obstruction Whatever." This provision had distinguished Chicago from almost every other waterfront city in America, where the choice land along the water's edge was typically appropriated by manufacturing and transportation concerns. These industries would soon develop into a wall of unsightly buildings and grounds, foul the water with their waste and runoff, and cut a city off from what was once its most picturesque feature. By 1850, this was the fate of Chicago's riverfront; the lake, however, had thus far remained free of development.

The Illinois Central had originally wanted to enter the city to the west, where it would have direct access to Chicago's industrial district. It was unable to follow this route, however, because the land it would need had already been bought by the Chicago & Rock Island Railroad. After purchasing land from Senator Douglas in the Lake Calumet area directly south of the city, the railroad's directors requested access to Chicago's inner harbor on a line directly along the lakefront. After months of bitter haggling, a compromise was reached. The City Council would permit the railroad's trains to enter by way of a strip of land not on the lakeshore, but several hundred feet out into the lake. This would require the railroad's tracks to be laid on trestles, which the railroad would have to protect from the lake waters by building breakwaters and dikes.

For its northern terminus, the Illinois Central had purchased part of the old Fort Dearborn reservation as well as some land along the river. As seen in the lithograph here, trains approached on a trestle erected in the water from Twenty-Second Street to the Randolph Street Depot. The area between the seawall and the shore created a basin that city officials tried to get the railroad to fill in, so that the city could create a new park and promenade. When the railroad rejected this idea, Chicago's residents began to use the basin for swimming, sailing, and rowing. After the railroad received court permission to create a landfill extension of its terminal, dock and storage facilities, however, the basin became landlocked and "turned into a still pool filled with industrial debris, floating packing crates, and the bloated corpses of horses and cattle."

This striking 1858 view of the city clearly depicts the Illinois Central's tracks on the lakefront breakwater. Note the basin between the lakeshore and the breakwater. The tracks can be seen leading to the Illinois Central's terminal and branching out to warehouses at the mouth of the river. Individual buildings are clearly depicted along the city's grid, and the river is lined with warehouses for the storage of grain and lumber. The downtown area lies left (south) of the river, the North Side neighborhood of old settlers to the right. The patch of lakefront just north of the river was a disreputable area known as "the Sands," which became one of the major points of refuge from the Great Fire.

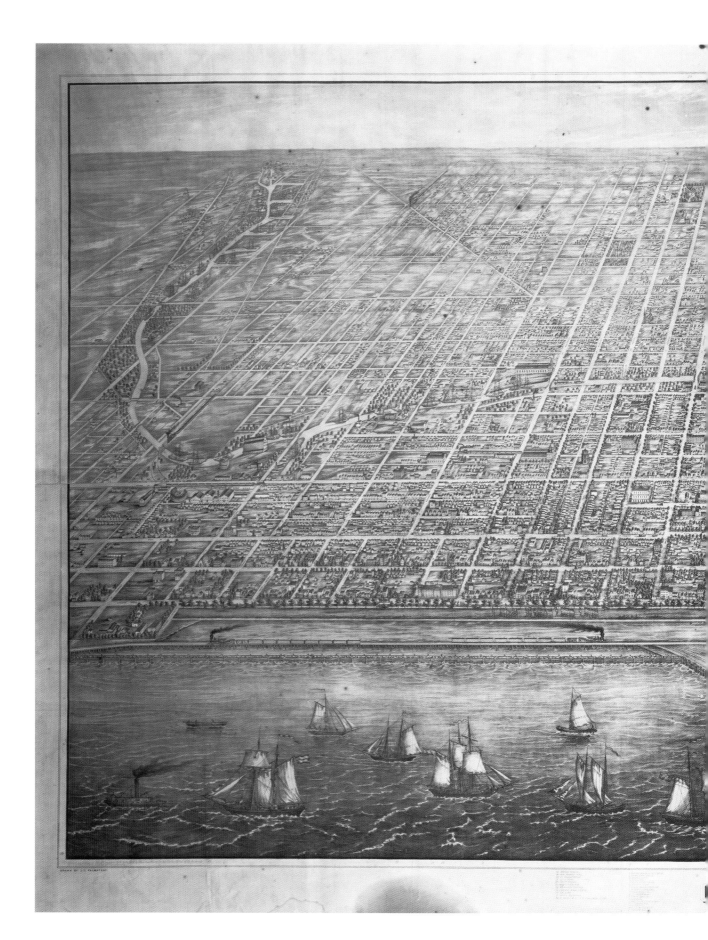

CHICAGO ILL.

HERLINE & HENSEL LITH S.E. COR. 7TH & CHESNUT STS PHIL.

COOK COUNTY

The Rees Map
The Flower Map

Title: Map of the counties of Cook and DuPage, the east part of Kane and Kendall, the north part of Will, State of Illinois.
Date Issued: 1851
Cartographer: J. H. Rees
Published: Ferdinand Mayer (New York)
Lithograph, 101 x 95 cm
Chicago Historical Society, ICHi-36660

Title: Map of Cook County Illinois with inset of map of Chicago
Date Issued: 1861
Cartographer: Walter L. Flower
Published: S. H. Burhans & J. Van Vechten (Chicago)
Lithograph, 172 x 157 cm
Chicago Historical Society, ICHi-27578

Cook County was organized in 1831 and originally encompassed the counties of DuPage, Will, Lake, McHenry and Iroquois, in addition to its present territorial limits. The county was named in honor of Daniel P. Cook, a pioneer lawyer who was the first Attorney General of the State of Illinois. Cook ran a newspaper while Illinois was still a territory, sat as a judge of the western circuit, and was instrumental in getting the Illinois Territory ratified as a state. He fought successfully to keep slavery out of Illinois, and served four terms in Congress as the sole Representative from Illinois during the years 1819 to 1827. While in Congress,

he secured a grant of government lands to aid in the construction of the Illinois and Michigan Canal. He lived a short life—dying at the age of thirty-three—and probably never set foot in what is now Cook County.

These two oversize maps depict rural Cook County in the early days of its development. The first map was drawn by J. H. Rees and also includes DuPage County (organized in 1839), eastern Kane and Kendall Counties (respectively organized in 1836 and 1841) and northern Will County (organized in 1836). The map shows county boundary lines as well as townships within these counties; the population of each township is given

as determined by the census of 1850. The Illinois and Michigan Canal is shown along with the Indian Boundary Lines; swamplands are noted, and the location of schoolhouses and post offices is marked. Rees also gives compass directions and the distance to various towns across the lake in Michigan. Existing Chicago railroads are depicted, as are three of the four plank roads that would lead to Chicago (shown are the Milwaukee and Chicago Plank Road, the Western Plank Road, and the Southwestern Plank Road).

Before European settlement, much of the Chicago area was crisscrossed with trails made by Native Americans, paths that held to

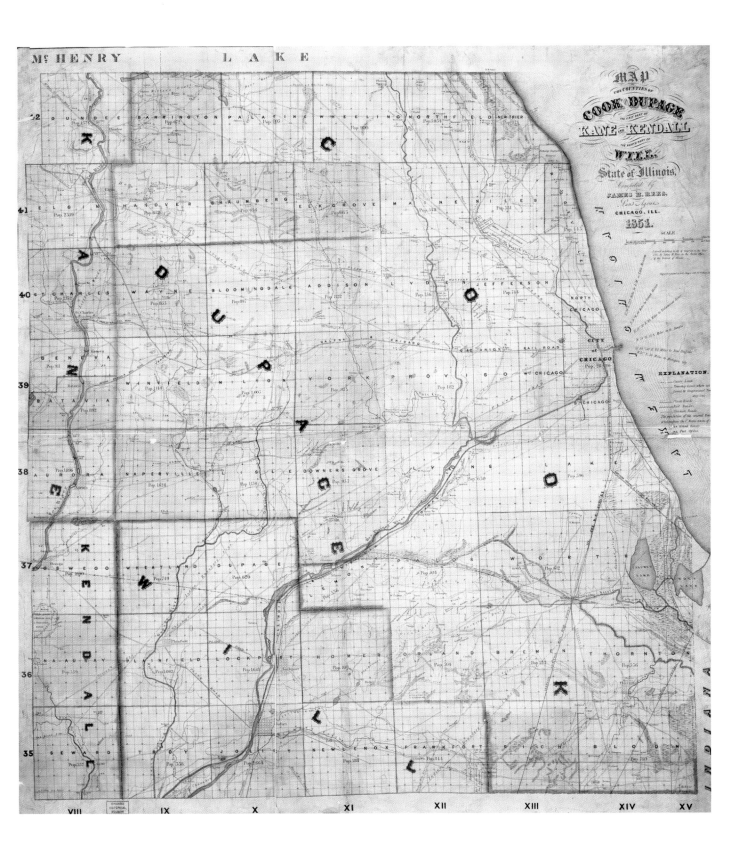

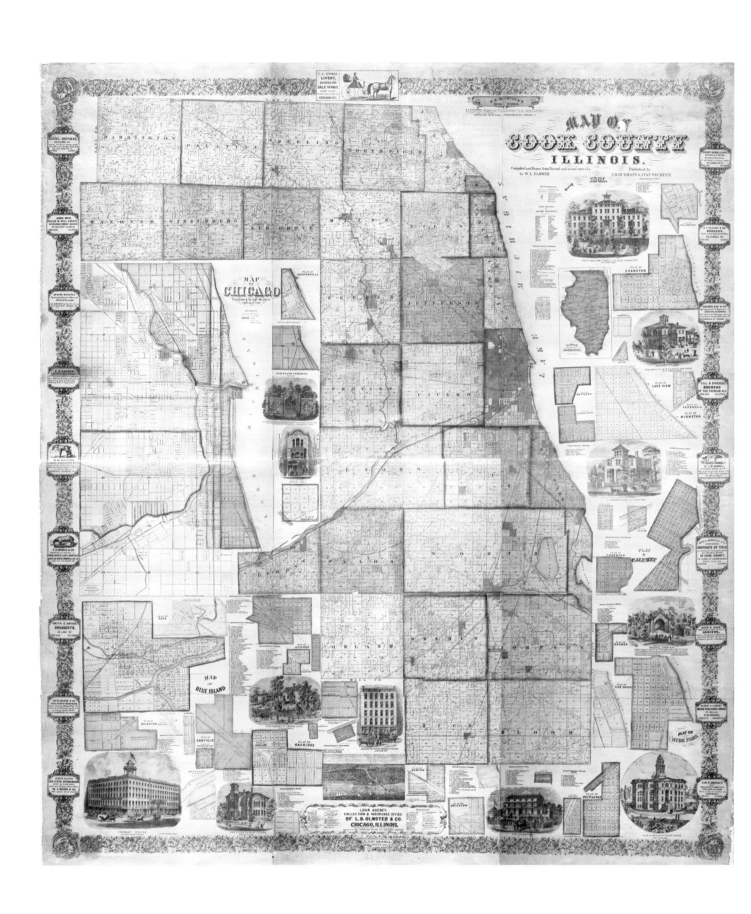

the high ground and were relatively dry. As settlers moved in, they tended to follow these trails, whether on foot or horseback. With the progress of settlement, however, there arose the demand to improve the area's roads — for it was one thing to follow a high, narrow trail on foot or horseback, and quite another to drive a wagon along it. The building of passable roads proved to be quite a challenge, however, for the prairie ground around Chicago was low and marshy. For a farmer whose wagon was laden heavy with supplies, a dirt road muddied by rain was impassable as the wagon's wheels would simply sink deep into the wet slough. Large stones were used as an attempt to provide a foundation on some roads, but they often either simply became absorbed in the muck or protruded high enough from the earth to break wagon wheels and axles. By 1850, the roads to Chicago were littered with broken down and abandoned vehicles.

Planking roads with wood—an idea imported from Russia via Canada—was an effort to overcome these problems. These roads were built by private companies, cost about $2,000 a mile, and involved laying three-inch planks crosswise on wooden stringers embedded in the ground. The roads were sixteen feet wide and the planks

were sometimes pine or hemlock, but oak and black walnut quickly proved their superiority for the purpose. Once opened, the company would charge a toll for using a plank road: toll gates were set up every five or six miles, and a four-horse vehicle would pay 37 $\frac{1}{2}$ cents to traverse a ten-mile stretch; a single team paid 25 cents and a single horse and rider half that amount. These roads were rough and noisy, although a marked improvement over previous roadways. The ground around Chicago soon extracted its own toll from the area's plank roads, however, as they quickly deteriorated in the marshy soil. Settlers were soon forced to the more permanent and expensive type of road-building that involved laying a substantial stone foundation which was then covered by gravel.

Walter Flower's enormously large map of Cook County is stated to have been "compiled and drawn from record and actual surveys." Because of its large size, Flower's map presents an historical snapshot of the Chicago area at the dawn of the Civil War that remains unparalleled in its richness of detail. Unmistakably a commercial venture, its border includes advertisements from various Chicago merchants. On its left side, there is an inset map of Chicago and another inset map of Blue Island.

The map also has an inset "diagram of the State of Illinois" that shows the state's counties and railroad lines. Plats of over thirty towns in Cook County are depicted, and business directories for many of these towns are also included on the map.

This striking map contains large scale pictures of various commercial concerns including the Tremont House Hotel, the Washington House, Bryan Hall, Graceland and Rosehill Cemeteries, J. J. Sand's Brewery in Milwaukee, and J. J. Sand's Columbian Brewery in Chicago. Also pictured are the Cook County Courthouse, Haase's Park near Harlem, Oak Ridge School in Cicero, the Farm residences of Thomas Cook and James W. Scoville, E. Haskin's House in Evanston, and Northwestern Female College in Evanston.

Owners of Cook County land parcels are listed on the map, and canals, wagon roads, school houses, churches, houses and streams are marked. Also referenced are railroads, city railways, bridges, section lines, and half section lines. The Indian Boundary Lines are shown on the map, and a platted Caldwell's Reserve is illustrated.

GUIDE MAP OF CHICAGO

The Blanchard Guide Map

Title: Guide Map of Chicago
Date Issued: 1868
Cartographer: Rufus Blanchard
Published: *Citizen's Guide For The City of Chicago. Companion to Blanchard's Map of Chicago.*
Rufus Blanchard (Chicago)
Lithograph, 53 x 41 cm
David Rumsey Collection, 4220.001

By 1871, in a span of less than forty years, Chicago had grown from a swampy frontier town to a metropolis of over 300,000. It had become the rail, livestock, grain, and lumber capital of the world; and its harbor received more ships than any other city in America. To both the nation and the world, Chicago had become a symbol of America's material might and of its reputation as the land of opportunity.

It was no wonder, then, that the city was a "must see" for anyone traveling west. "See two things in the United States, if nothing else," Richard Cobden advised a friend making his first trip to America, "—Niagara and Chicago." Visitors arrived in Chicago either by train or by lake boat, and stepped into a bustling, smoky, noisy, cosmopolitan city; its streets filled with "crowds of men, who looked like the representatives of every nation and tongue and people,—and every class of society, from the greenest rustic, or the most undisguised sharper, to the man of most serious respectability." So observed Caroline Kirkland, who wrote to her *Atlantic Monthly* readers that "to describe Chicago one would need all the superlatives set in a row. Grandest, flattest,—muddiest, dustiest,—hottest, coldest,—wettest, driest,—farthest north, south, east, and west from other places, consequently most central,—best harbor on Lake Michigan, worst harbor and smallest river any great commercial city ever lived on,—most elegant in architecture, meanest in hovel-propping,—most lavish, most grasping,—most public spirited in some things, blindest and darkest on some points of highest interest."

Tourists took both walking and riding tours of Chicago, bearing witness to its transformation from prairie town to city. But, as Ms. Kirkland noted, the city did not have much to offer in the way of culture: there was "no public park, no gallery of art, no establishment of music, no social institution whatever, except the church." She noticed "an appearance of extreme hurry" on the streets, but the scarcity of women made them seem, she wrote, "forlorn." This is not to say that Chicago was completely devoid of culture. Indeed, its city fathers were mostly educated, self-made men from New England and New York State; men who founded and supported a rich array of civic and cultural institutions once they made their fortunes. The historical, literary, musical, scientific, and civic associations established in Chicago during the 1840s and 1850s included the Chicago Historical Society, the Chicago Lyceum, the Academy of Sciences, the Chicago Musical Union, the Young Men's Association, the Orphan Asylum, and the Chicago Relief and Aid Society. Along with Chicago's common school system, these men also founded Chicago's first institutions of higher learning, among them the University of Chicago, Hahnemann Medical College, Rush Medical College, Female Seminary, and Northwestern University in the northern suburb of Evanston.

Chicago did have a theatrical tradition that began in the year the city was incorporated. Theatrical firms from the East staged plays in the Sauganash Hotel, and soon thereafter, in a playhouse, the Chicago Theater, located on Dearborn Street. In 1851, John B. Rice—the father of Chicago theater—built a brick theatre, and brought famous names to perform in Chicago. McVicker's Theatre opened in 1857, and Crosby's Opera House commenced business in 1865. Architecturally, the

city had grand, marble-faced hotels, such as the Palmer House, spectacular railroad terminals, and palatial houses that belonged to the city's titans of business and industry. The city's fashionable areas included Michigan and Wabash Avenues, and beginning in the 1860s, around Twenty-Second Street "along the Avenues"—Indiana, Prairie, Calumet, and South Park. The West Side along Washington Boulevard and Union Park also had a number of elegant houses. Other city sights included the million-dollar courthouse, which was set in the midst of a ten-acre square in the center of the city, the Chamber of Commerce Building, the Chicago Board of Trade, the city's new water tower, and a number of impressive stone churches.

It was not, however, Chicago's culture or architecture that drew most visitors to the city. Rather, they came to marvel at the city's display of can-do spirit and its free-wheeling expression of capitalism. It was, after all, the opportunity to make money that had fueled Chicago's rapid transformation into a center of economic activity. Indeed, the drive and determination of Chicagoans prompted one British visitor to characterize the city as "the very embodiment of the world-conquering spirit of the age." By the late nineteenth century, travelers were awed by Chicago's constant throbbing

of commercial activity: there were countless rows of lumber stacked along the South Branch of the Chicago River; grain elevators hovered over railroad tracks, trains, and ships, and became landmarks on Chicago's skyline; the Union Stock Yards, a square mile of penned livestock and packinghouses became the city's largest tourist attraction; Cyrus Hall McCormick's massive reaper works lay on the north side of the river; Potter Palmer and Marshall Field had turned downtown into one of the finest shopping centers in America; and Aaron Montgomery Ward made Chicago the nation's mail-order capital.

Chicago impressed visitors as a city where the interests of business took precedence over the individual. This was evident in the city's traffic patterns. First, there were the railroads. In other American metropolises, such as Manhattan, railroads were prohibited from entering the congested heart of city. Not so in Chicago, where the pursuit of money was unimpeded by government restraints, and the railroads steamed right into the center of town. Along with the trains came their tremendous bellows of noise and smoke, and an average of two people were killed or mangled every day at unprotected rail crossings. As one foreign visitor noted, "It's cheaper to kill people than to elevate the railroads, and human life in Chicago is nothing compared with money." Another problem was the city's river crossings. Due to the extensive river traffic—more than 270 lumber boats traversed the river every twelve hours—the bridges over the river would be swung open for long periods of time, causing extensive traffic jams on the city's streets. "As soon as the bridge closes, the impatient crowd rushes madly on," wrote journalist Noah Brooks, "giving a stranger the impression they are an active race, given to gymnastics and slightly crazed."

These "slightly crazed" pedestrians knew, of course, that the bridge was about to swing open again. In typical fashion, Chicago sought to alleviate this problem by a massive undertaking—it would build traffic tunnels under the river. Two tunnels were constructed, one under Washington Street that was completed in 1869, and another under La Salle Street that opened to the public in 1871. Such projects enhanced Chicago's "can-do" reputation, a trait to which visiting delegates to the 1860 Republican National Convention could attest.

Chicagoans were delighted to have their city of 100,000 chosen for the Republican Party's second presidential convention, which would prove to be the historic caucus at which Abraham Lincoln was nominated as the Republican candidate for president. There was one problem, however. The Republicans needed a meeting hall that could seat eight thousand, and they needed it in little more than six weeks. Chicago's business leaders, who paid for the construction of the hall, were up to the task. W. W. Boyington, the designer of Chicago's new water tower, was hired to create a two-story, wooden structure on the site of the former Sauganash Hotel at Lake and Market Streets. Nicknamed "The Wigwam," from a Native American word for "temporary shelter," the building was finished just in time for the convention and furnished with chairs borrowed from Chicagoans' homes. It had excellent acoustics; city groups used the building for other large meetings before it burned in the Great Fire of 1871.

Delegates to the convention and other visitors to Chicago needed a guide to orient themselves in the city, as did Chicago's steady stream of newly arriving residents. The earliest street guides began to appear in the 1850s and were typically made to be folded into a cover and tucked into one's pocket. Although Chicago was soon to become the center of the country's map industry, maps made in New York and Philadelphia dominated the local market until after the Civil War. This map was published by one of Chicago's first map publishers, Rufus Blanchard.

It was contained in the *Citizen's Guide for the City of Chicago*, which also included a twelve-page street guide and a city population table. The different colors on the map mark Chicago's wards, the system of political representation that was established when the city was incorporated in 1837 and would quickly become associated with patronage politics.

Street maps provided a fundamental gauge of the rate of Chicago's growth—this map, for example, required nearly four times as much space to show the city's entire street system as J. H. Colton's street guide, *The City of Chicago*, published just twelve years earlier.

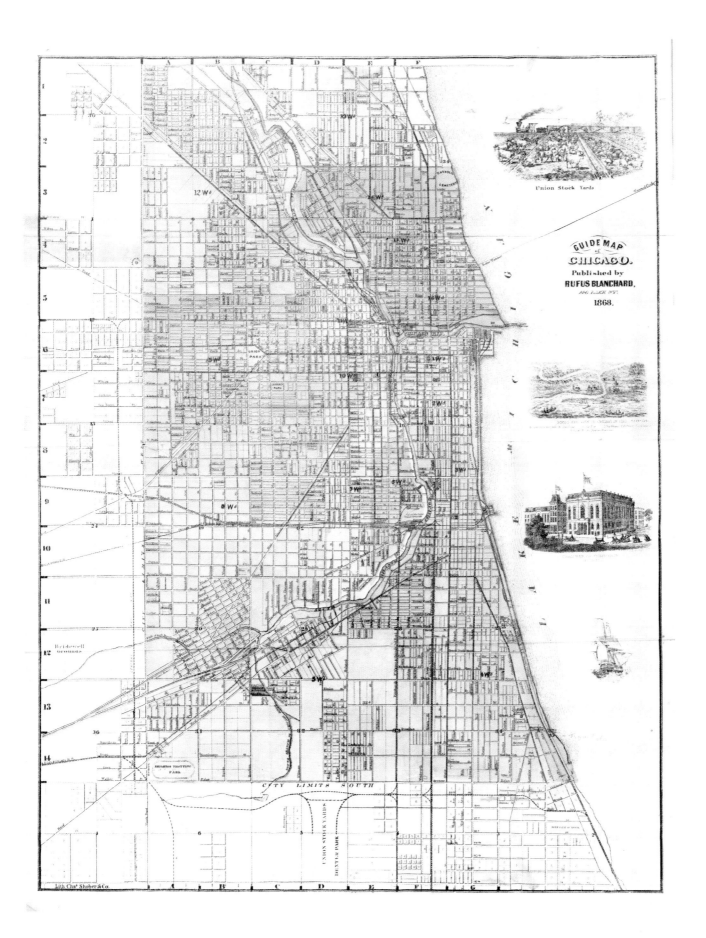

Union Stock Yards

GUIDE MAP
of
CHICAGO.
Published by
RUFUS BLANCHARD,
1868.

THE CHICAGO PORTAGE

The Steward Map

Title: Chicago Portage
Date Issued: 1904
Cartographer: John Fletcher Steward
Published: J. F. Steward (Chicago)
Blueprint, 43 x 60 cm
Newberry Library, Ayer 133.5 S84 1904

During the last Ice Age, four successive glaciers advanced and retreated over the Chicago area. These glacial movements greatly altered the landscape, grinding down elevations, filling valleys, and gouging out enormous basins, including the location of Lake Michigan. The last of these glaciers, the Wisconsin Glacier, receded about thirteen thousand years ago, and in its wake deposited concentric rings of glacial debris called moraines around the Chicago area. The largest belt of these rough, boulder-strewn ridges and mounds is the Valparaiso Moraine, which forms a crescent-shaped ridge around the southern rim of Lake Michigan. Named for the Indiana town which is situated upon it, the Valparaiso Moraine is as much as twenty-five miles wide with many high ridges, kettle-hole lakes, and marshes.

This moraine acted as a dam, holding the melting waters of the receding glacier between it and the glacier itself, forming a lake that covered the future location of Chicago. The water of Lake Chicago (as the lake at its greatest extent is called) reached an elevation of about sixty feet above the present level of Lake Michigan, and as this glacial lake receded over thousands of years to the present dimensions of Lake Michigan, its wave action and undertow worked to create the large flat plain that would become Chicago's most distinct natural feature. This lake plain is only slightly higher than Lake Michigan itself, and its tabletop flatness, as well as the layers of clay deposited by the glacier, made it extremely difficult to drain. The early town built on this plain would become a mud hole much of the year, and as

the town grew into a city, it would become afflicted by a succession of drainage-related health epidemics. The flat plain was ideal, however, for the laying out of streets, as well as rail and trolley tracks, and it placed no barriers in the way of Chicago's expansion to the north, south, and west.

The water of Lake Chicago receded in stages, first draining south to the Illinois and Mississippi Rivers through a gap in the moraines called the Chicago Outlet. This outlet became a Y-shaped passage whose arms consisted of two valleys, or sags, that cut through the Valparaiso Moraine near the southwest edge of the lake. The northern arm ran in a southwesterly direction along the present day Des Plaines River channel; the lake waters cut the southern fissure into the mile-wide Sag Valley, which runs in a more or less westerly direction through the moraines. After cutting the channel of the Des Plaines down to bedrock, the lake stabilized for a time, then dropped again after a new outlet opened to the north, shutting down the Chicago Outlet. However, the lake returned to the Chicago Outlet in later times, most recently during what is called the Nipissing Phase of Lake Michigan, a period that ended only four thousand years ago.

The two arms of the Chicago Outlet would play an important role in the development of Chicago, and are still visible today. The Calumet Sag Channel, a vital link in the nation's waterway system, runs through the Sag Valley. The northern gap through the moraines is sometimes referred to as the Chicago Portage, and is the site of the Illinois and Michigan Canal, the Chicago Sanitary and Ship Canal, and several major rail lines and highways. When Marquette and Joliet ascended the Mississippi to the Chicago River, they came through this glacial cut-through.

When the waters of Lake Chicago withdrew from the Chicago Plain, they uncovered a low, almost imperceptible morainic ridge—not ten feet high—that Joliet had the geographic sense to understand was part of a great continental divide. This drainage barrier separates two vast watersheds. On one side of this continental divide, the surplus rain and snow waters naturally drain toward

Lake Michigan. This surplus, combined with that from the watersheds of the other Great Lakes, eventually flows into the St. Lawrence River, which empties into the Atlantic Ocean. On the other side of this divide, water drains toward the Des Plaines and Kankakee Rivers and thence down the Illinois River to the Mississippi River, which empties into the Gulf of Mexico. Joliet deemed the narrow place in the continental divide at the "river of the portage" so strategically important that he sent a letter to his governor, and suggested that New France could command the continent by cutting a canal through the divide at this location.

Joliet's high regard for the area was based on the link it provided between the two great waterways on each side of the divide. In 1673, he and Marquette had traveled up the Mississippi to the Illinois River, and to the Des Plaines River. Canoeing up the Des Plaines they came to a place approximately midway between present day Summit and Riverside, Illinois. Here, at what is now known as the Chicago Portage, they came to a little creek that took them into a slough that came to be called "Mud Lake." Paddling to the eastern edge of this marsh, they came to a ridge that marked the continental divide. At this point they carried—or portaged—their canoes across one-and-one-half miles of open prairie to the West Fork of the

South Branch of the Chicago River, which led them east to Lake Michigan. Joliet immediately envisioned an immense waterway that stretched from the Atlantic Ocean to the Great Lakes via the St. Lawrence River, into the harbor at Chicago on Lake Michigan, up the Chicago River, through a canal across the continental divide, then down the Des Plaines and Illinois Rivers to the Mississippi and the Gulf of Mexico.

There were times when a portage was not even required to traverse the ridge between the great watersheds, particularly during wet seasons, when the waters of Mud Lake and the waters of the West Fork of the Chicago River connected and covered the continental divide at a depth of four to five feet. Conversely, during the driest periods, Mud Lake was waterless, and often both the Chicago and the Des Plaines Rivers would become merely a series of shallow pools.

Gurdon Hubbard was a venerated early settler of Chicago, and is often credited for being the person most responsible for locating the terminus of the Illinois and Michigan Canal at Chicago. He first came to the area in 1818, as a sixteen-year-old apprentice in the employ of the American Fur Company. Hubbard would spend the next ten years as fur trader in the Illinois frontier, and often crossed the Chicago Portage. In his autobiography, he wrote about his first portage across Mud Lake: "Four men…remained in the boat and pushed with poles, while six or eight others waded in the mud alongside…Those who waded through the mud frequently sank to their waist, and at times were forced to cling to the side of the boat, to prevent going over their heads; after reaching the end and camping for the night the task remained of ridding themselves from the blood suckers." It took three days to get the boats over the portage, and when the men reached the banks of the Des Plaines, they rested their "swollen and inflamed" limbs, and cursed "this miserable lake." It was an experience that would forever convince Hubbard of the need for a canal through this critical frontier portal.

Given the variation in the navigability of the rivers that led to the portage, La Salle had dismissed Joliet's "proposed ditch" as impractical. He did agree, however, with Joliet's assessment of the significance of the Chicago Portage. In a prophetic letter he wrote from a log hut on the portage in the winter of 1682–3, he predicted that through this "lowest point on the divide between the two great valleys of the St. Lawrence and the Mississippi … the boundless regions of the West must send their product to the East… This will be the gate of empire, this the seat of commerce." La Salle could not imagine, of course, that railroad tracks would run through the gate of the empire. On the other, Joliet's dream of

an immense inland waterway that traveled through the Chicago Portage would also become reality, albeit not until nearly three centuries later.

This 1904 blueprint map of the Chicago Portage notes that its "actual location… can be gathered by reference to John Andrew's map of 1782, Hull's map of 1812, the Govt. survey of 1822 and Lowe's map of 1852, fragments of which are given here." Inset maps reproduce details from an unidentified map of 1681, the Hutchins' map of 1778, the Andrews map, and the Hull map. Note that the Portage Road connects the Portage House on the west fork of the South Branch of the Chicago River and the Des Plaines River; the portage itself lies north of Mud Lake and covers a distance of approximately 10.5 miles.

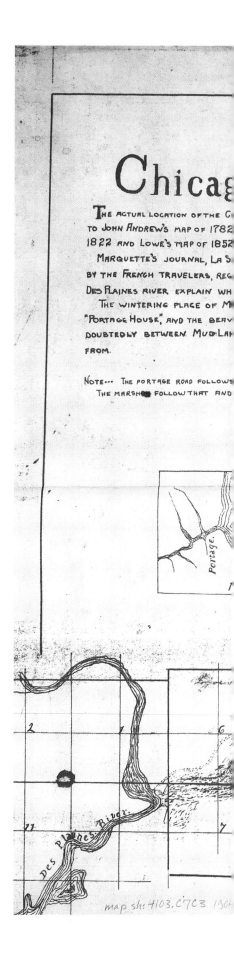

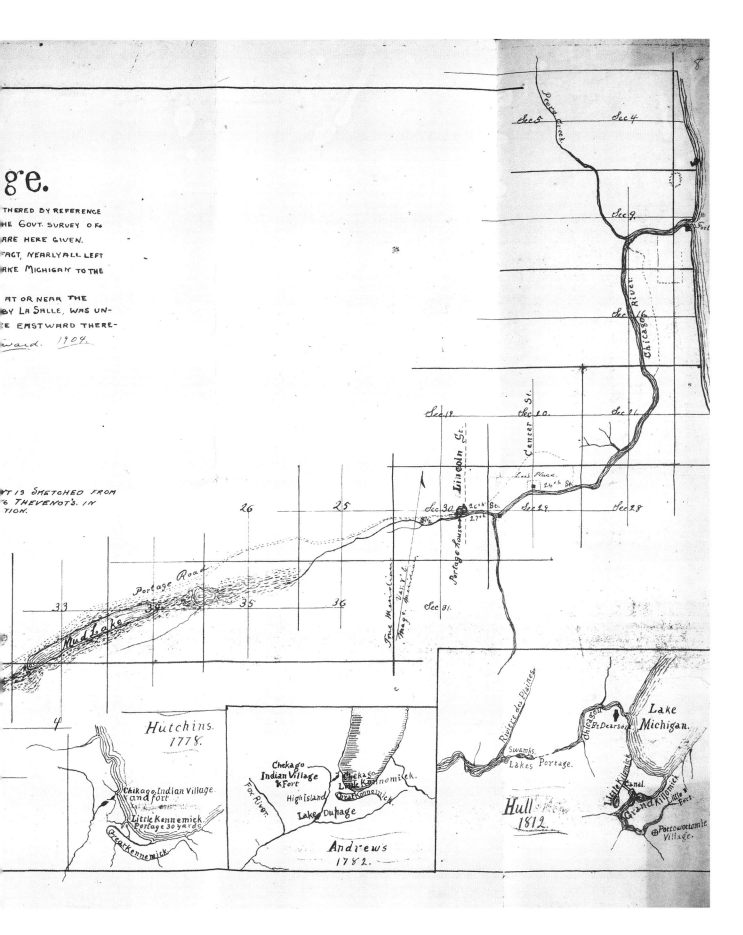

ge.

THERED BY REFERENCE
HE GOVT. SURVEY OF
ARE HERE GIVEN.
FACT, NEARLY ALL LEFT
RKE MICHIGAN TO THE

AT OR NEAR THE
BY LA SALLE, WAS UN-
E EASTWARD THERE-
ward. 1904.

T IS SKETCHED FROM
6 THEVENOT'S. IN
TION.

Peoria Creek

Sec 5   Sec 4

Sec 9   Fort

Sec 16   Chicago River

Sec 19   Sec 20.   Sec 21.

Lincoln St.   Center St.

Lees Place.
24th St.

26   25   Sec 30   20th St.   Sec 29   Sec 28
                                27th

33   34   Portage Road   35   36   Sec 31.
Mud Lake

4   Hutchins.
         1778.

Chikago, Indian Village
and fort
Little Kennemick
Portage 30 yards
Great Kennemick

Chekago
Indian Village
& Fort

Fox River

High Island
Lake Duhage

Chekago
Little Kennomick.
Great Kennomick.

Andrews
1782.

Riviere des Plaines

Swamps.
Lakes Portage.

Chicago
Ft. Dearborn

Lake
Michigan.

Hull
1812.

Little Killomick
Canal
Grand Killomick
Little
Fort
Pottowottomie
Village.

THE ILLINOIS AND MICHIGAN CANAL

The Sullivan Survey
The Long Map
The Irwin Map

Title: Official Survey of the boundaries of the Indian Lands ceded to the United States by the Treaty of St. Louis, August 1816
Date Issued: 1819
Cartographer: John C. Sullivan
Published: Manuscript
Ink, Watercolor, and Pencil on Tracing Paper, 37 x 107 cm
*Newberry Library, MS *map6F oG4102.N6B5 1819 .S8*

Title: Reconnaissance of a Journey to the Illinois Country
Date Issued: 1817
Cartographer: Stephen H. Long
Published: Manuscript
Ink, Watercolor, and Pencil, 101.6 x 66 cm (sheet #4 of 10)
National Archives, RG-77 Chief of Engineers Civil Works File Misc 15-Sheet #4

Title: Map and Profile of the Proposed Route for the Illinois and Michigan Canal
Date Issued: 1834
Cartographer: J.R. Irwin
Published: U.S. 23d Cong., 1st Sess., 1833-34, H. Doc. 546. Ser. 263, Index Map (Washington D.C.)
Folded Sheet, 55x 86 cm
Newberry Library, Smith map 6F oG4102.I4 1830 G8

The beginnings of the Illinois and Michigan Canal are to be found in a plan of national, as opposed to local, significance. Following the Louisiana Purchase in 1803, the idea of a national internal waterway connecting New York with New Orleans stirred the country's imagination. The route would connect New York to the Great Lakes via a canal from the Hudson River to Lake Erie, and the Great Lakes to the Mississippi River via a canal from Lake Michigan to the Illinois River. It was first mentioned in Congress in 1808, and four years later, embraced by the *Niles Register*: "By the Illinois River it is probable that *Buffalo*, in New York, may be united with *New-Orleans*, by inland navigation, through Lakes Erie, Huron,

and Michigan, and down the river to the Mississippi. What a route! How stupendous the idea! How dwindles the importance of the artificial canals of Europe compared to *this* water communication. If it should ever take place—and it is said the opening may be easily made—the Territory [of Illinois] will become the seat of an immense commerce, and a market for commodities of all regions."

The commercial need for such a route at the time was slight, but disasters on land during the War of 1812 (including the massacre at Fort Dearborn) amplified the military importance of a safe and passable highway from the Great Lakes to the Mississippi River. At the conclusion of the war, the opportunity

came to acquire the land through which to build a canal that would connect the two. In 1816, the federal government concluded the *Treaty of Saint Louis* with the Northwestern Native American tribes that had sided with the British during the war. This treaty included the cession to the United States of a strip of land ten miles north and ten miles south of the mouth of the Chicago River, and extending along the river in a general southwesterly direction to the Fox and Illinois Rivers.

The official survey of these "Indian boundary lines" was conducted by John C. Sullivan in 1819, and his map of this survey is the first map presented here. Prior to Sullivan's

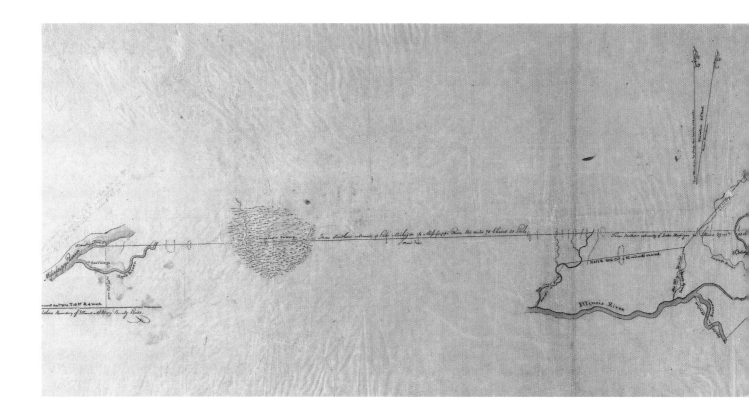

survey, Major Stephan H. Long of the U.S. Corps of Topographical Engineers had been ordered to make a preliminary investigation of a possible canal route for the Secretary of War. Long began surveying the area in September of 1816, and prepared a manuscript map, drawn at a very large scale, as part of his report. The portion of Long's map that includes Chicago is also shown here. In his report, Major Long remarks that "a canal uniting the waters of the Illinois with those of Lake Michigan may be considered of the first importance of any in this quarter of the country and, at the same time, the construction of it would be attended with very little expense, compared to the magnificence of the object." Shortly

thereafter, the Secretary of War urged Congress to construct a canal across the Chicago Portage.

In 1818, when Illinois was granted statehood, its northern boundary was advanced northward sixty-two miles from the "southerly bend" of Lake Michigan; this ensured that the canal would lie entirely within the state (it also placed Galena, with its valuable lead mines, within the state). This immediately had the effect of creating a local enthusiasm in the building of the canal, and while the federal government would have a continued interest, it was the state of Illinois that would become responsible for its actual construction.

The enthusiasm for the canal was

based on its potential economic benefits, but financing such a project was beyond the meager resources of the young state. In his inaugural speech, Shadrach Bond, the first governor of the State of Illinois, implored the federal government to help the state with the project by making a generous land grant. Congress responded in 1822 by granting the land on which to construct a canal, and in addition, a quantity of land "equal to one-half of five sections in width [about ninety feet], on each side of the canal, reserving each alternate section to the United States from one end of the canal to the other." This land was to be used to secure timber and other materials needed for

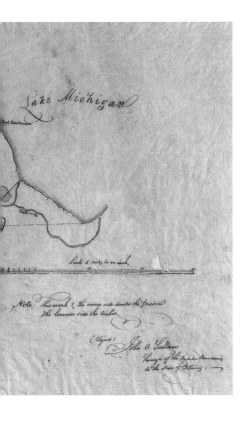

the construction of the canal. Although this grant would not be sufficient to underwrite construction costs, the state moved forward with its plans, and in 1823 created a canal commission of five members to determine the most feasible route for the proposed canal. The Commission hired an engineer, Colonel Justus Post, and a French mapmaker, René Paul, to survey the area between the Indian boundaries and recommend possible canal routes. In 1824, Post and Paul presented the Commission a map as part of their report. This map was the first detailed survey of the corridor of the canal, and in fact, of northeastern Illinois. It divides the area between the Indian Boundary Lines into square-mile sections, and shows five possible

canal routes. It was submitted to President Monroe to be the basis for the construction of the canal, in accordance with the federal Act of 1822. However, the map was misplaced and the canal was not begun before the Act of 1822 expired.

In 1825, the state legislature acknowledged both the value of the canal and the state's inability to finance its construction. Accordingly, help was sought in the private sector, and the legislature incorporated the Illinois and Michigan Canal Company, a jointly held stock company with an initial capitalization of $1 million. When the company failed, the state of Illinois again petitioned Congress for assistance, requesting a grant of public land, part of which would contain a canal and part of which could be sold by the state to finance construction of the proposed waterway. Congress responded in 1827. In addition to the area set aside for the waterway, the state was given alternate sections of land five miles on either side of the proposed route to be sold to finance construction.

After some delay, but obliged by the land grant, the state legislature established a three-person canal commission in 1829. Eager to promote land sales to raise money, the commission laid out the future cities of Chicago and Ottawa at either end

of the proposed route, and in 1830, the lots at Chicago were offered at auction to the public. Even with the land grant, however, the state lacked the means to finance the construction of the canal. In 1833, the legislature abolished the Canal Commission, and the Illinois and Michigan Canal project was abandoned. In its place, the legislature considered building a (less expensive) railroad.

The third map shown here was the result of a survey that aimed to show that—despite the pressure to build a railroad—a canal was indeed a practical project. The survey, begun in 1830, was conducted by the civil engineers W. B. Guion and E. Belin. Their field drawings are consolidated and reduced on the present map, which was drawn by Lt. J. R. Irwin of the U.S. Army and was printed as a government document. The map also presents a profile of the elevation of the land along the canal route, using the surface of Lake Michigan as its plane of reference. This profile makes it clear that most of the canal route lies below the level of Lake Michigan (and in fact, so does most of Illinois).

The abandonment of the canal project was short-lived, and by 1835 a new legislature and a new governor, Joseph Duncan, were committed to building the canal. A third canal commission was appointed and empowered to raise the funds necessary to complete construction of the proposed Illinois and Michigan Canal. In 1836, the Commission appointed William Gooding as Canal Engineer, and platted what were to become the towns of Bridgeport, La Salle, and Lockport.

On the Fourth of July, 1836, a ground-breaking by Commissioner Colonel William Archer at Canalport (later Bridgeport) marked the official start of the long awaited project.

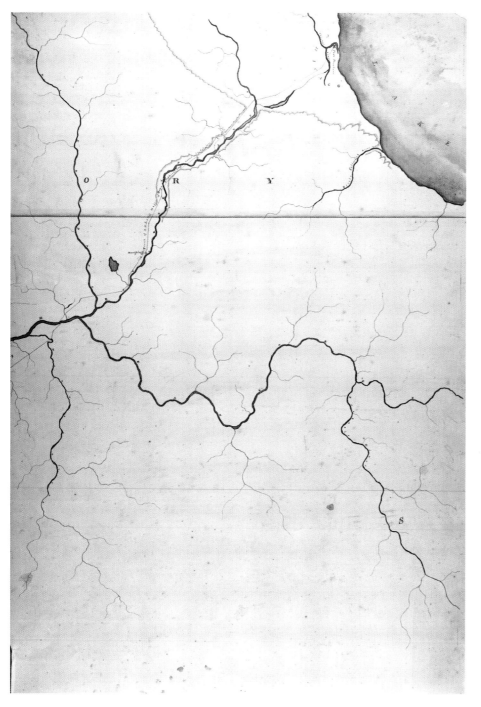

Although the excavation of the canal was fraught with engineering and logistical difficulties, the biggest hurdles were financial. In 1837, the state had launched a program of internal improvements and railroads that were to connect all parts of the state. Overly optimistic in its reach, the program brought the state to the verge of bankruptcy in 1840. Prior to this time, the state had been able to contract for loans to cover the costs of canal construction; now, with a depression sweeping the financial world, there was no capital available. The state dropped all of its internal improvement projects except the canal and began to pay contractors with state bonds and warrants promising payments at future dates. Things worsened, and in 1843 all construction on the canal ceased.

When the economy began to recover, capital became available to finish the canal; the state, however, would have to make certain concessions to its creditors. The legislature authorized the Governor to negotiate a $1.6 million loan, which would be sufficient to complete a shallower waterway than originally had been designed. In order to ensure successful subscription to the loan, the Governor pledged the canal, its property and all revenues generated by the canal to the canal bondholders in a deed of trust.

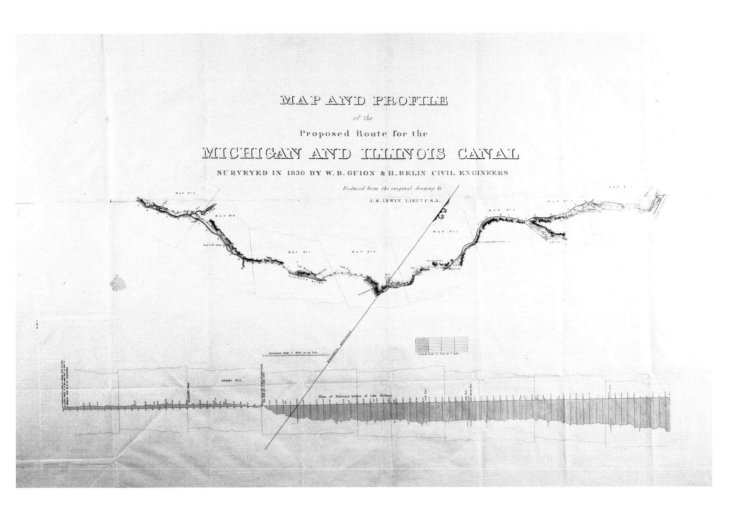

Once the principal and interest were paid to bondholders, the aforementioned assets would return to the state. During the period that the canal would be under a trust agreement, it was to be governed by a Board of Trustees composed of three members, two of whom would be chosen by bondholders and one appointed by the Governor. Under the Board's direction, construction of the ninety-six-mile-long canal was completed in 1848 at a total cost of $6,463,853. The trustees oversaw its operation until the debt was retired in 1871, at which time the canal reverted to state control.

The canal that Joliet had envisioned 142 years earlier was to have a profound effect on the development of Chicago and northern Illinois. Once the canal was put into operation, the produce of the Illinois River Valley, formerly shipped to St. Louis, began to flow into Chicago. Merchandise from the east, via the Erie Canal and the Great Lakes, and lumber from Michigan and Wisconsin, made its way down the canal to the river towns and from them to the settlements rapidly being extended northward and westward. Just six years after it opened, however, the Chicago and Rock Island

Railroad began operations along a route that paralleled the canal. The range of goods that were shipped via the canal diminished as the railroad's business grew, but bulk commodities continued to float the canal—especially lumber and grain, and a few other products such as sugar and molasses. Peak tonnage on the canal was not reached until the early 1880s, but thereafter gradually declined as freight continued to shift to the railroads.

THE CHICAGO HARBOR

The Howard and Harrison Map
The Allen Map
The Graham Map of 1854

Title: Map of the mouth of Chicago River Illinois with the plan of the proposed piers for improving the Harbor
Date Issued: 1830
Cartographer: William Howard and Frederick Harrison, Jr.
Published: Manuscript
Ink, Watercolor, and Pencil on Tracing Paper, 39 x 50 cm
*Newberry Library, Graff *1800*

Title: Improvement of the Harbour of Chicago
Date Issued: 1837
Cartographer: Capt. James Allen
Published: Capt. Thomas J. Cram's annual report, Engineer Department, U.S. Army
Annotated Blueprint, 66 x 82.5 cm
National Archives, RG 49 Old Map File Map #16

Title: Chart of Chicago Harbor Illinois, Shewing the MAIN ENTRANCE for Ships and the State of the BAR
Date Issued: 1854
Cartographer: J. D. Graham
Published: Edward Mendel, lithographer (Chicago)
Lithograph, 61 x 78.7 cm
Carl Kupfer Collection

The success of the Illinois and Michigan Canal would require the development of a reliable harbor on Lake Michigan at Chicago, the canal's eastern terminus. For the canal would not be of much use without a clear egress to Lake Michigan; nor would Chicago become a port of entry if it could not provide safe shelter to ships from the ravages of a stormy Lake Michigan. Once again, however, nature presented an obstacle. It was first reported by LaSalle, who not only had discerned the problems involved in building a canal, but noted that "there is still another difficulty which this ditch [the canal] one would make could not remedy...The Lake of Illinois always forms a sand bank at the entrance of the channel which leads to it. I doubt very much in spite of what anyone says whether this could be cleaned out or cleared away by the force of the current of the Chicago River when it was made to flow therein, since much greater currents in the same lake cannot do it."

What LaSalle had observed was that the mouth of the Chicago River did not naturally allow for a harbor; rather, it was blocked by a sandbar that acted to divert the final course of the river southward. The sandbar ran north and south, and was at times quite substantial, often with junipers and small willows growing on its north end that connected to the lakeshore. This sandbar presented several navigational hazards to any merchant ship attempting to enter the river. First, it made the harbor too shallow for a large ship to actually enter the river. Second, it would require a ship to make a sharp turn at the river's mouth, a difficult maneuver for large vessels. Third, it was impossible to accurately chart the sandbar, since its size and shape varied with the wind, lake levels, and storm activity. Accordingly, supply vessels that sailed to Chicago were forced to anchor outside of the sandbar and unload their cargo to small rowboats, or lighters, which would then have to be rowed more than a mile around the bar. Clearly, if Chicago's harbor was to become viable, the sandbar blocking its entrance would have to be removed.

During his survey of the proposed canal route in 1816, Major Stephen Long found that "The

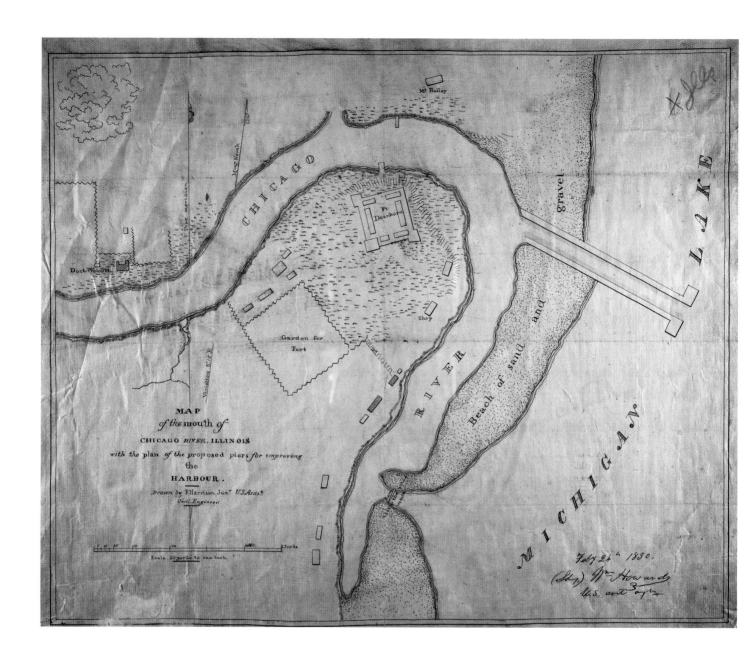

entrance into Lake Michigan…which is 80 yards wide, is obstructed by a sandbar about 70 yards broad." Long, who was sanguine about the effort required to build a canal, likewise thought that it would be straightforward matter to remove the sandbar: "Piers might be sunk on both sides of the entrance, and the sand removed between them." Moreover, since the river and its branches "are of sufficient depth of water to admit vessels of almost any burden" two or three miles inland, removing the sandbar would provide "a safe and commodious harbor for shipping." It would be almost two decades before work on such a plan would begin, but the problem of the sandbar would not be solved as easily as Long had envisioned. In fact, it would take years of experimentation and a great cost to make Chicago a safe port.

The first map shown here was prepared in 1830 by U.S. Assistant Civil Engineer Frederick Harrison, Jr. while he worked under William Howard, who in 1829 had been appointed by the U.S. Army's Engineering Department to supervise the surveying for the construction of the Chicago Harbor and the Illinois and Michigan Canal. This map, which depicts a pair of piers flanking a channel that extends southeasterly through a "beach of sand and gravel," was presented as part of a plan for improving the harbor. At the time of this drawing, soldiers garrisoned at Fort Dearborn, who were frustrated by having to skirt the sandbar in order to enter and exit the lake, had already cut a channel through the sandbar. The channel was wide enough to allow a yawl to bring supplies to the fort, and was one of a number of cuts through the sandbar made by the army between the years 1816 and 1828. None resulted in a lasting channel, however, as they more or less quickly would become clogged with sand.

In March of 1833, Congress appropriated $25,000 for a harbor improvement project, and work commenced in July of that year. Major George Bender, the commandant at Fort Dearborn, supervised the early harbor work, and was succeeded by Second Lt. James Allen in January of 1834. By July 12 of that year, the sandbar had been sufficiently breached (aided in part by a February storm that had created a channel through the bar) to allow the entry of the merchant ships: the entrance to the Chicago River was a channel 200 feet wide and three to seven feet deep, and was flanked by 700-foot-long northern pier and a southern

pier that was 200 feet long. On that day, the *Illinois*—a schooner of nearly 100 tons—sailed up the river to Wolf Point. The ship carried more than 200 visitors on board, and was greeted by an enthusiastic crowd along the banks of the river; when she docked at the wharf of Newberry & Dole, the *Illinois* was greeted with loud and repeated cheers.

Although the entrance of the *Illinois* delighted the citizens of Chicago, Lt. Allen realized the harbor was hardly adequate to accommodate the demand for increased ship traffic. Work on the harbor progressed slowly. By the fall of 1835, the north pier had been extended to a length of 1260 feet, and the south pier to 700 feet. These piers were built using limestone boulder-filled timber cribs, which provided the underwater foundation upon which the piers were built. A dredging machine was used to deepen the channel, and by 1837, the channel was a minimum of ten feet deep and only a small tongue of the original sandbar remained.

These harbor improvements were charted by the newly promoted Capt. Allen in the second map presented here. This blueprint map shows a well-defined channel to the river, protected by piers on both sides, depth soundings in and adjacent to the channel, and a series of sandbars that had begun to form north of the northern pier. Allen completed his tour of duty in Chicago in 1838, and

reported that "the harbor at present affords an easy entrance and secure shelter in the worst weather to the largest class of boats and vessels engaged in commerce of the lakes." He also cautioned, however, that the sand accumulating on the weather side of the north pier threatened to obstruct the harbor entrance, and that "the greatest solicitation is felt for its continued improvements and permanent security by all interested in the extensive navigation on this lake."

At this time, the federal government reorganized the bureaucracy of harbor building and maintenance, moving supervisory duties from the U.S. Army Engineering Department to the Corps of Topographical Engineers. Capt. T. J. Cram was subsequently made supervisor of work on all Lake Michigan harbors. In his 1839 report to the Chief of the Topographical Engineers, Cram noted that there were several inherent flaws in the design of Chicago Harbor; specifically, there were problems in the configuration of the piers that flanked the harbor's entrance. Cram observed that the northern pier was oriented in a direction that practically ensured wind and wave action would deposit sand in the harbor entrance. He thought that the width between the piers was too narrow, and also remarked that the southern pier was too long, since "vessels on missing the entrance during the action of the north winds, have been unable to round to and come in without striking the extremity of the pier." To remedy the situation, Cram endorsed a design recommended by his Chicago agent, James Leavenworth. Leavenworth had proposed a 405-foot extension of the northern pier in a sharp angle to the northeast. The idea was that this extension would slow the accumulation of sand at the harbor's entrance, and Cram deemed the project, which was completed in 1839, indispensable for "vessels to enter the channel, or to ride out the storm in times of the severest gales, in perfect safety."

In 1843, Capt. John McClellan became General Superintendent of Public Works for the west side of Lake Michigan. He reported that the 1839 extension to the northern pier had caused the shore north of it to "travel out along…[the pier] rapidly," and that if "operations [had] ceased for a few years longer, the shore would have reached and passed around the head of the pier and joined the bar at the entrance of the harbor." Since no funds had been appropriated for harbor work since 1838, little work had been done since the pier extension (although in 1841, concerned citizens of Chicago provided money for some dredging work to remove the ever accumulating sand at the harbor's entrance). To resolve both of these problems, McClellan proposed building another

pier north of the northern pier, a plan that was rejected as too costly. Instead, a crescent-shaped extension was added to the northern pier in order to bring it back in line with its original direction. This seemed to work as a breakwater, stopping the accumulation of sand out from the shoreline while also preserving the depth of the entrance to the harbor. In addition, McClellan built a fence north and parallel to the north pier in order to stop sand from blowing over the pier and filling the river; toward this end, he also planted grass along the shore.

In August of 1846, President James K. Polk vetoed the River and Harbor Appropriations Bill, which would have provided about $500,000 for the improvement of numerous harbors and rivers lying within the region of the Great Lakes. In his message to Congress, Polk argued that the bill unconstitutionally funded local improvements that although "in the language of the Bill were "called harbors…are not connected with foreign commerce, nor are they places of refuge or of shelter for our navy or commercial marine on the ocean or lake shores." He concluded that "It would seem the dictate of wisdom under such circumstances to husband our means and not waste them on comparatively unimportant objects." Needless to say, the citizens of Chicago—whose canal would open in two years—were

indignant. Indeed, the veto caused a widespread backlash of resentment in cities north and west of the Mason-Dixon Line (particularly those along the Great Lakes and in the Mississippi Valley), whose citizens saw the veto as being partial to southern interests.

In response to the veto, a River and Harbor Convention was held in Chicago in July of the following year. The meeting was to be a protest against the veto, and it attracted some 20,000 visitors from nineteen of the twenty-nine states in the Union. Among its more distinguished attendees were New York newspaper editors Horace Greeley and Thurston Weed, Senator Tom Corwin of Ohio, Erastus Corning, who would later become president of the New York Central Railroad, a half dozen governors, and numerous congressmen, including a little known congressman from downstate Illinois by the name of Abraham Lincoln. A resolution passed at the Convention admonished that the federal government had a duty "to improve navigable rivers and harbors for the benefit of all commerce, and that the Atlantic coast had been allotted an unfair portion of the money thus far expended in such improvements." Although the convention did not succeed in securing funds for harbor and river improvements, it did unite the northern and western states in their campaign for better facilities for water-

borne commerce. Moreover, the convention proved to be a spectacular success for its host city. Indeed, not only did Chicago favorably impress the throng of conventioneers (and in so doing, attracted eastern investors and their capital), it also awoke the city itself to its own self-importance in the developing nation.

In the fall of 1849, Lt. Joseph Dana Webster assumed the duties of general superintendent of western harbors on Lake Michigan. The last appropriation for work on Chicago's harbor had come in 1843, and Webster observed that sand was again creeping around the end of the northern pier and threatening to close the harbor. At the time, Webster recommended—as McClellan had—that a new pier be built 2000 feet north of the northern pier. By 1850, however, he had changed his mind and was convinced that the problem could be solved by the construction of a breakwater, or "jetty pier," at a distance northeast of the north pier. His thinking was that these two piers would concentrate the flow of water between them, thereby forcing the sand to drop at a harmless distance from the harbor entrance. No money was ever appropriated for this project.

In 1850, Chicago raised its own funds for harbor repairs and improvements, but by the spring of 1854, the harbor was virtually closed. After witnessing the destruction of four vessels and the loss of seven lives, as well as the damage wrought to two other vessels, Chicago's commercial interests were becoming frantic. The Chicago Board of Trade offered to pay all costs incurred in using a federal dredge to clear the harbor, but their offer seemingly fell on deaf ears. Accordingly, the Board of Trade, in cooperation with the city council, took matters into their own hands: they seized the federal dredge and began harbor clearing operations on their own. Shortly thereafter, Brevet Lt. Colonel James D. Graham arrived in Chicago to take over responsibility for harbor improvements. He retrieved the dredge and put it to work removing the sandbar that blocked the harbor.

It would not be the last time Graham was forced to deal with an indignant municipality "kidnapping" the dredge. The following summer Chicago's harbor entrance again became blocked by sand, but the dredge was in use in Kenosha. Rather than relinquish the dredge to Chicago, Kenosha city officials removed several of its vital parts, as well as other pieces of federally owned equipment from around the harbor. Graham was forced to confront city officials over their misconduct, and nine days later the dredge was returned (but only after the Kenosha City Council voted to give its "consent").

The last harbor map shown here was prepared by Graham in August 1854, shortly after he completed dredging the harbor entrance. When Graham had started his dredging operations in May, he found the water to be just over six feet deep. This prevented direct entrance to harbor, and he reported that "vessels coming in from the northward and bound for the harbor... were compelled to run [southward] as much as 1200 feet... and then double back on a northwesterly course in order to reach the harbor." As recorded on this map, Graham's dredging operations had removed enough sand to allow direct access to the harbor. The map also depicts the extensions made to the northern pier by Cram and McClellan. Graham retained the local lithographer and printer Edward Mendel, one of Chicago's first mapmakers, to produce this map. Mendel produced a limited number of additional maps for Graham (of the same title, dated 1857 and 1858), but most editions of Graham's maps were issued by Congress in House and Senate Serials.

In 1863, Graham reported that the harbor was in a "more or less delapidated [sic]" condition as no federal appropriations had been forthcoming since 1852. By the end of the Civil War, however, things would change. For Chicago had emerged as a major supply center for the Northern Army during the war, forcing the federal government to acknowledge its importance as a commercial center. From 1866 onward, appropriations for harbor improvements were steady and generous.

By 1871, the year of the Great Fire, Chicago was known as the "Queen of the Lakes," and more ships arrived in her port than in New York, San Francisco, Philadelphia, Baltimore, Charleston and Mobile combined. Chicago had not only surpassed Archangel and Odessa in Russia as the largest grain port in the world; it had also become the largest lumber market in the world. The Port of Chicago was now a mammoth exchange-engine, and on the lake ships heading east from Chicago with grain passed fleets carrying lumber heading toward Chicago from the north.

There remained, however, the problem of the sandbar. Constant dredging kept the channel clear, but Major Julius B. Wheeler, who was made Superintending Engineer of the harbor in 1866, would endorse a solution that broke with the original concept of improving the harbor by means of two piers. In 1867, a private firm, the Chicago Canal and Docking Company, approached Wheeler with a plan to provide docking elsewhere than on the Chicago River. Specifically, they proposed to build a boat basin just north of the northern pier with an entrance to the harbor; permission was granted, and the basin, called "Ogden Slip," was enclosed with cribwork by the Chicago Canal and Docking Company. Wheeler also recommended building a 455-acre enclosed harbor to south of the southern pier. This harbor would be created by constructing a 4000 foot long breakwater southward and at a right angle to the southern pier. He proposed that the far southern end be connected to the shore by a pier, and

that the harbor be dredged to twelve feet deep.

Given Chicago's stature as a port city, Congress was persuaded to appropriate $100,000 to commence construction of Wheeler's harbor in 1870. By then, Wheeler had been relieved of his duties by Maj. David C. Houston, who supervised the harbor's construction. Houston recommended against building the southern pier, as it was uncertain

whether wharves would ever be built along the lakefront. In 1874, Houston was replaced by Maj. George Gillespie, who oversaw the completion of the outer harbor breakwater, and reported that sand no longer accumulated at the harbor entrance. The problem of the sandbar had been solved, and as Gillespie testified, "mariners were showing increased confidence in the anchorage to be found" in Chicago's harbor.

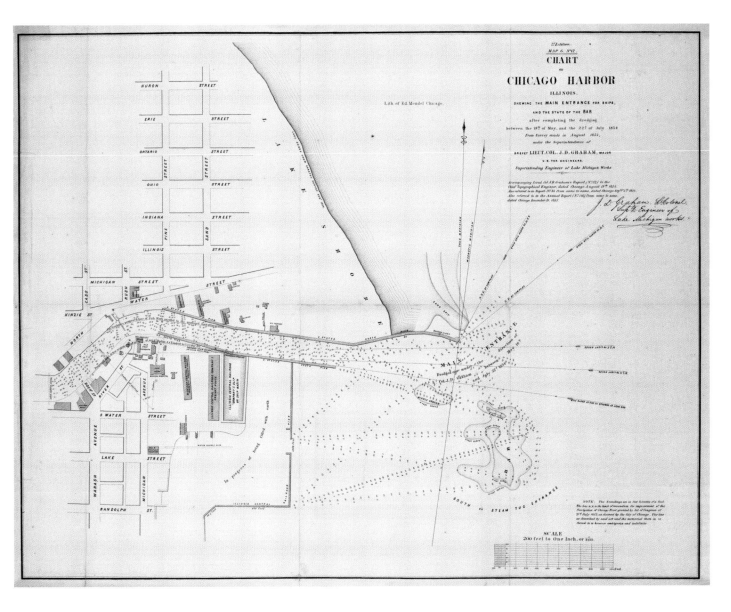

CHICAGO'S SEWER SYSTEM

The Board of Sewerage Plan of 1857

Title: Plan Shewing Sewers Laid under the Chicago Sewer Commissioners to the end of 1857
Date Drawn: 1858
Cartographer: Chicago Board of Sewerage Commissioners
Published: C. S. Chesbrough, *Chicago Sewerage Report of the results of examinations made in relation to sewerage in several European cities, in the winter of 1856–57* (Chicago)
Lithograph, 21 x 30 cm
Newberry Library, sc Fitzgerald map 1F oG4104.C6N46 1857 .C4

William B. Ogden arrived in Chicago in 1835 to supervise the sale of his brother-in-law's speculative land investment. There had been recent heavy rains, and when Ogden set out to inspect the property, he found himself knee-deep in mud and marsh. "There is no value in the land," he quickly wrote back to New York, "and won't be for a generation." Yet Ogden stayed on to fulfill his charge: he had the land drained, posted, and opened for settlement. When the lots were put up for auction, he was amazed at their selling prices—he sold a mere third of the property for $100,000.

This story has exemplifies two of the most important facets of the birth of Chicago: first, it began with one of the most frenzied chapters of land speculation in American history; and second, it was literally built in a swamp. More precisely, Chicago lies on a level lake plain with a base of hard-packed, poorly porous clay—land that drained so slowly its prairie grasses were often covered by one to three feet of water. Nevertheless, it is here that the land dealers and developers built a town, a town that would rapidly fill with settlers—and their waste.

Chicago's first sewer system consisted of little more than roadside ditches angled so as to flow toward the river. When rain fell on low-lying plain, these ditches often became clogged with garbage, leaving "standing pools of indescribable liquid." To make matters worse, livestock was typically penned in Chicago's alleys, and manure from barns was disposed in the town's streets. Water, garbage, and animal dung would accumulate under the town's wooden planked streets, which in hot weather created a stinking "miasma" that wafted into the shops of complaining merchants. And even when the sewer system worked, it simply washed sewage into the driftless river, which created cesspools "resembling in color and consistency a rich pea-soup." As the city grew, the river became a common sewer for tanneries, glue factories, distilleries, and packing plants. Chicago, one visitor remarked, should be called the "City of pestiferous odour."

Eventually, the contaminated river water would make its way to the lake, where it often fouled the city's new water system, which pumped lake water from an intake pipe just north of the mouth of the river. In 1854, Chicago was hit by a cholera epidemic that took almost six percent of its population of 66,000. It was the sixth straight year of epidemics, including dysentery and typhoid fever. Although the cause was not known, cholera was believed to be caused by polluted water and noxious fumes—"death fogs"—emanating from exposed sewage. In December, the city's frightened citizens organized a mass meeting and demanded action.

In response, the Illinois State Legislature established a permanent Board of Sewerage Commissioners for Chicago in February 1855. William Ogden was appointed to head the three-member commission, and he quickly brought in Ellis S. Chesbrough to design the first comprehensive system of underground sewers in the United States. Chesbrough, a self-educated canal and railroad engineer, had earlier designed Boston's water distribution system. Since he had no experience in building sewers, he began by visiting a number of European cities in order to study their sewage systems, and finally decided to build a system that combined both household waste and storm water in a single line of pipe that would empty into the Chicago River. Chesbrough lamented using the river as a disposal basin, but it was far preferable to using Chicago's freshwater reservoir, Lake Michigan. He was immediately confronted, however, with a problem: since the city lay only several feet above the river, a sewer system could not be laid underground.

By the spring of 1856, Chesbrough convinced the Commissioners that the level of Chicago's streets was far too low to adequately drain his sewer system. Accordingly, he made a radical proposal: if the street level grade was raised six to ten feet, sewers could be laid directly on top of the existing streets, covered with dirt, and then paved to create guttered streets. As the sewer lines moved away from the river, they would be elevated at an angle so as to allow them to flow into the river by gravity. The higher street level would not only accommodate the sewer pipes, it would also allow for the laying of underground gas and water mains. Chesbrough's plan would, of course, also require the city's buildings to be elevated as well.

Chesbrough's proposal survived a court battle, and the city began the construction of its new sewer system and the process of raising the city up out of the muck. The river was dredged to accommodate the increased sewage load, and the dredged soil was used to cover the system's pipes. The plan was for buildings, horse car tracks, lampposts, and even shade trees to be lifted to the new street level. Owners of buildings were expected to pay for elevating them, and while most did, some refused, leaving their stores and houses in "holes" in relation to the elevated buildings on the rest of the block. As a result, Chicago was for years built on several levels, and it became a city of "ups and downs" as its boarded walkways descended and ascended to and from the old street level.

George M. Pullman, who had solved similar problems along the Erie Canal, engineered much of the lifting of early Chicago buildings. Buildings were jacked up and a foundation built under them without interrupting the occupancy of the building. The raising of Chicago out of the mud would continue for two decades, but by the end of 1857, the city had a working sewer system. This map shows the main lines of the system, along with the sub-main lines, pipes, manholes, and catch basins that had been laid by the end of that year.

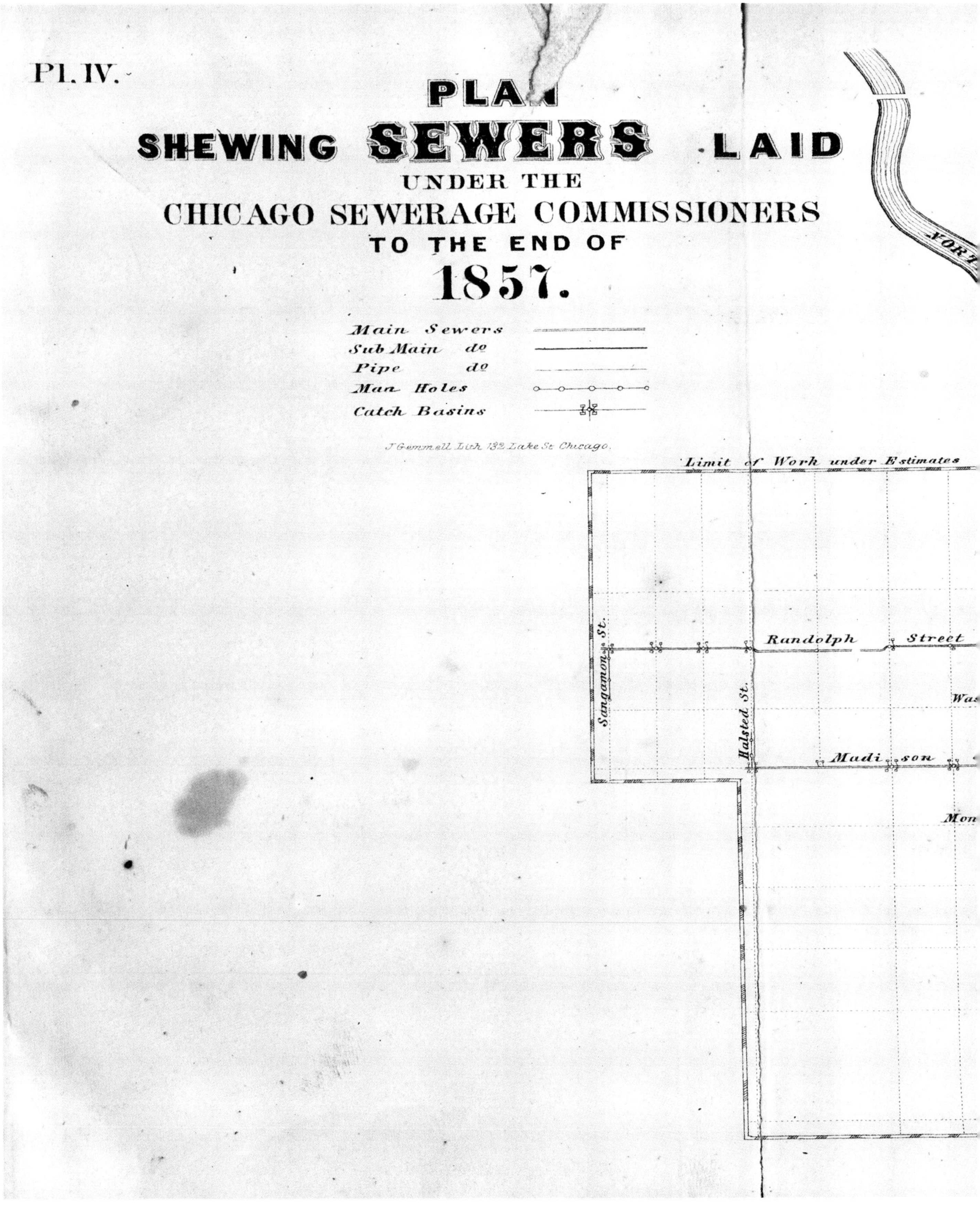

Pl. IV.

PLAN
SHEWING SEWERS LAID
UNDER THE
CHICAGO SEWERAGE COMMISSIONERS
TO THE END OF
1857.

Main Sewers
Sub Main   do
Pipe   do
Man Holes
Catch Basins

J. Gemmell Lith. 132 Lake St Chicago.

Limit of Work under Estimates

Sangamon St.

Randolph   Street

Halsted St.

Was

Madi son

Mon

Ohio St.

Rush Street

Clark Street

Kinzie St.

Wells St.

La Salle St.

North Water Street

St.

Dearborn St.

Wolcott St.

Street

River St.

CHICAGO   RIVER

South Water Street

Lake Street

Market street

Franklin St.

Wells St.

St.

Clark St.

St.

St.

State St.

Wabash Av.

Michigan Avenue

Randolph Street

Franklin

Wells

Lasalle

Washington Clark

Dearb.

Street

State

Wabash

Michigan

BRANCH

Madison St.

Monroe Street

Scale 1200 Ft. to 1 Inch

Limit of Work
Under Estimates

113

CHICAGO'S WATER SUPPLY

The Original Municipal Water System
The Tunnel and Water System of Chicago

Title: Map of Chicago's Original Municipal Water Supply System
Date Issued: 1933
Cartographer: Chicago Bureau of Engineering
Published: *A Century of Progress in Water Works* (Chicago)
Printed Sheet, 15.2 x 10.2 cm
Illinois State Library, 628.1 C532

Title: Map from *The Tunnels and Water System of Chicago: Under the Lake and Under the River*
Date Issued: 1874
Cartographer: Wallis
Published: J. M. Wing & Co. (Chicago)
Printed Sheet, 23 x 92 cm
Newberry Library, G8962.895

When Chicago was originally chartered in 1833, its three hundred fifty residents had little concern for the availability of drinking water—the Chicago River, Lake Michigan, and shallow wells provided abundant sources of water. When in little over a year Chicago added several thousand to its population, the village trustees arranged for the construction of a public well at Hubbard Street and Wabash Avenue. Residents would either carry water home in buckets from this well, or purchase it from peddlers who sold water carried on mule-drawn carts for ten cents a barrel. As Chicago's development pushed further from the lake to the west and south, however, it soon became impractical to rely on transporting water with buckets and water carts. Moreover, the town's wells and the river were being fouled by the rapidly growing volume of residential and industrial waste. So, the town looked to Lake Michigan for its water.

In 1836, the Illinois legislature granted a seventy-year charter to the Chicago Hydraulic Company to supply lake water to the town. Completed in 1842, the company's water system consisted of a crib in Lake Michigan located 150 feet from shore, an iron pipe from the crib to a pump well on shore, a steam pump that forced water from the well to an elevated reservoir at Lake Street and Michigan Avenue, and a distribution system comprised of two miles of hollowed-out cedar logs. The system, which cost approximately $24,000 to construct, was often plagued by fish clogging its pipes, filthy water after storms, and ice during the winter. Chicago's rapid growth soon overwhelmed this privately owned system.

In 1852, the first municipally owned waterworks in the United States was incorporated to supply Chicago's demand for water. The Chicago City Hydraulic Company purchased the rights of its privately held predecessor, and immediately began to develop a new supply system. The new waterworks, which was overseen by a

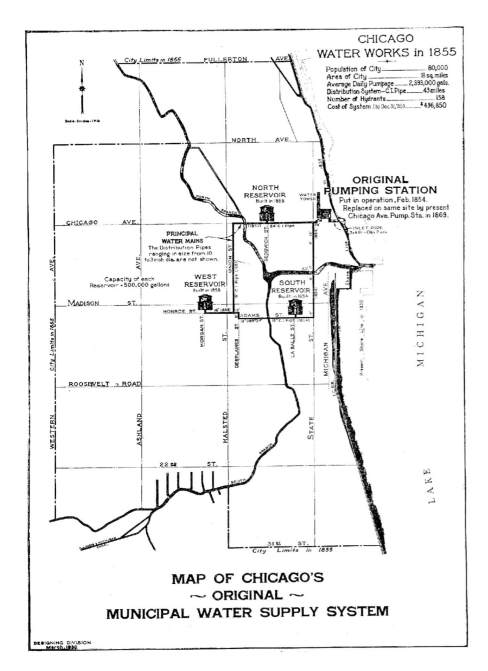

CHICAGO WATER WORKS in 1855

Population of City	80,000
Area of City	18 sq. miles
Average Daily Pumpage	2,393,000 gals.
Distribution System~C.I.Pipe	43 miles
Number of Hydrants	158
Cost of System (to Dec 31, '55)	$496,850

ORIGINAL
PUMPING STATION
Put in operation, Feb. 1854.
Replaced on same site by present
Chicago Ave. Pump. Sta. in 1869.

PRINCIPAL
WATER MAINS
The Distribution Pipes
ranging in size from 10
to 3 inch dia. are not shown.

NORTH
RESERVOIR
Built in 1856

Capacity of each
Reservoir - 500,000 gallons

WEST
RESERVOIR
Built in 1858

SOUTH
RESERVOIR
Built in 1854

MAP OF CHICAGO'S
~ ORIGINAL ~
MUNICIPAL WATER SUPPLY SYSTEM

DESIGNING DIVISION
March, 1939

three-person Board of Water Commissioners, was completed in 1854, and the system is shown on the first map here: it consisted of a suction well in Lake Michigan originally located six hundred feet from shore; a timber intake pipe, three feet by four feet in section and laid in a trench in the lake bed; a pumping station incorporating a steam engine and stand pipe, located at Michigan Avenue and Chicago Avenue; and a distribution system consisting of a wrought-iron reservoir and nine miles of iron pipe. The pumping station had a capacity of eight million gallons per day, but like the earlier system, its capacity was quickly exhausted by the burgeoning city. Additional storage tanks were added to the system in 1856, and a second pumping station, with a twelve-million-gallons-per-day capacity, was constructed in 1857. Concerns over the system's capacity, however, quickly became eclipsed by concerns for water quality.

Chicago continued to grow and become more industrialized, and the Chicago River served as the repository for both its residential and commercial waste. The river water would eventually make its way to the lake—especially during spring floods—contaminating the water supply. It had been hoped that purer water could be obtained by extending the water intake further out into the lake, and an effort was made to maintain a crib at a position six hundred feet from shore. Rough water and inadequate technology made the project unsuccessful, and the intake had to be placed closer to the shore. In 1854 a cholera epidemic prompted the city, in early 1855, to appoint a Board of Sewerage Commissioners to address concerns for sewage handling and the quality of the water supply. Ellis S. Chesbrough was hired as Chief Engineer for the Board, and was immediately dispatched to Europe to gain first-hand knowledge of the water and sewer systems of a number of its great cities. Upon his return, he designed and constructed a new sewage system for

115

Chicago, one that efficiently drained the city's waste directly into the Chicago River.

As a result, the condition of the river—and of the city's drinking water—grew worse yet. Pollution was not the only problem for water system. Small fish were attracted by warm water of its shoreline collecting basin and were frequently sucked into the system's pipes, which in turn poured them into the sinks, bathtubs, cups, and cooking pots of Chicagoans. When the fish got into the city's hot water reservoir, they "came out cooked, and one's bathtub was apt to be filled with what squeamish citizens called chowder." Immediate action was required, and in 1861, the Board of Sewerage Commissioners and the Board of Water Commissioners were merged to form the Bureau of Public Works. Ellis Chesbrough was named to head this new public organization.

In 1863, Chesbrough proposed that Chicago's water supply problems could be solved by drawing its fresh water some two miles offshore—well away from mouth of the polluted Chicago River. This would require the construction of a five-foot brick tunnel under the lake, which would make it the longest tunnel ever constructed at the time. The proposal was criticized

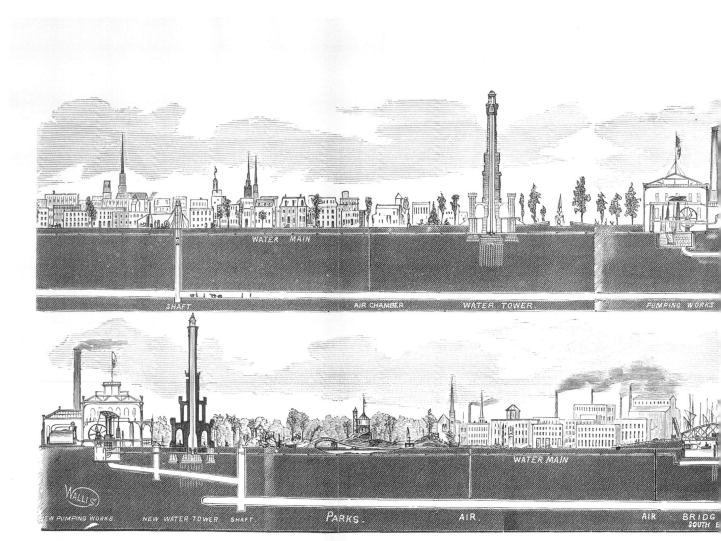

SECTIONAL VIEW OF THE WATER SYSTEM OF CHICAGO, SHOWING THE CRIB IN LAKE MICHIGAN, THE ORIGIN

as being technically impractical, and so a number of field tests were conducted to evaluate its feasibility. Soil borings in the lake bed, beginning twenty feet from shore and continuing to two-and-one-quarter miles from shore, indicated the lake bottom was sand-covered clay of variable firmness. At two and one-quarter miles from shore the lake was found to be thirty feet deep, and the lake water at this depth was clear and approximately fifty degrees Fahrenheit. These findings convinced critics that Chesbrough's plan for the Chicago water supply system was sound.

Construction on the new water system began in 1864, and the water intake system was dedicated in March of 1867. As a feat of engineering, it was described as the "eighth wonder of the world." By 1869, a new pumping station and water tower, designed by William W. Boyington in a castellated Gothic Revival style, were built on the site of the old structures at Michigan and Chicago Avenues. In 1872, a second tunnel was added to the system. The tower and pumping station were among the few buildings to survive the Chicago Fire, and both stand today as a memorial to an outstanding feat of engineering and as a Chicago landmark.

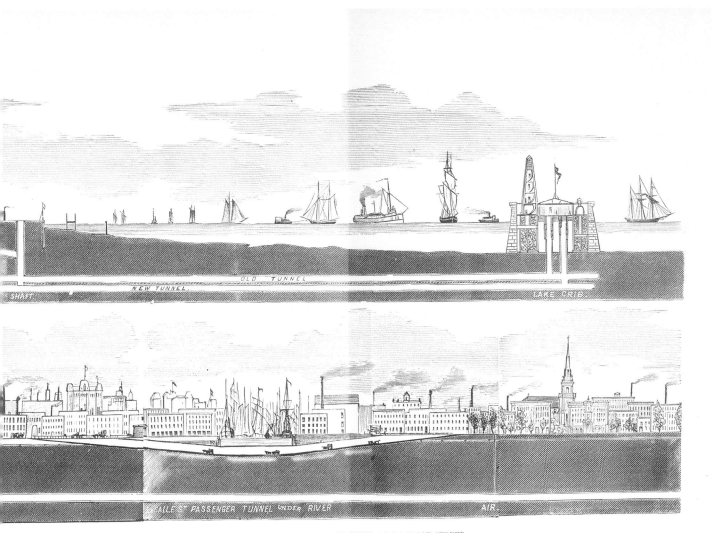

POND LAKE TUNNEL, THE TUNNEL UNDER THE CITY AND THE TUNNEL UNDER THE RIVER AT LA SALLE STREET.

REVERSING THE FLOW OF THE CHICAGO RIVER

The Sanitary District Map of the Chicago Drainage Canal

Title: A Map prepared by the Sanitary District
Date Depicted: 1895
Date Issued: 1895
Cartographer: D. MacDonald, W. Kramer and Edgar Williams
Published: Sanitary District (Chicago)
Blueprint, 4 sheets, 188 x 141 cm
Newberry Library, Case G 10896.166

Ellis B. Chesbrough's water supply system was both an engineering marvel and the pride of Chicagoans, and its new water tower became—and still remains—a special symbol of Chicago's civic energy and resourcefulness. The tunnel system that brought the city its water never performed as successfully as Chesbrough had hoped it would, however. The western winds, rainstorms, and spring floods that he thought would periodically cleanse the Chicago River of its waste also served to periodically drive the sewage out past the intake crib and into the city's water system.

In the meantime, Chicago continued to grow at an unprecedented rate, and as the city grew, tanneries, glue factories and other new industries discharged effluent directly into the river. Bubbly Creek, the old South Fork of the Chicago River, became a notorious open sewer as the newly constructed Union Stock Yards dumped its slaughterhouse offal into the stream (the waterway's new designation derived from the bubbles caused by decaying matter that filled the river bottom). The city's health officials began to advocate antidumping laws, but the capitalists who controlled Chicago warned that such measures would drive commerce from the city. The *Chicago Tribune* agreed that the river must remain the city's main sewer line, and later recommended that the City Health Department be disbanded and its duties turned over to the police.

Once again the city turned to Chesbrough for a solution to its problem. Ellis B. Chesbrough advocated a radical measure that he had broached when he first came to town: reverse the flow of the Chicago River. By making the river run backward, the city could send its waste through the Illinois and Michigan Canal to the Illinois River and eventually the Mississippi River. Those waters, he argued, would dilute and "deodorize" the city's waste. Chesbrough was well aware that a number of European cities employed sewage farms for their waste, and that many European engineers deemed the recycling of waste into fertilizer as the best method of sanitary disposal. He did not believe, however, that Chicago's taxpayers would agree to foot the bill for the building of the pumps that would be necessary to move sewage to irrigation farms; nor did he believe that Chicago's land developers would stand idly by if valuable acreage at the edge of the frantically growing city was set aside for this purpose.

With state permission and funds from a $3 million bond issue, Chesbrough dredged the Illinois and Michigan Canal to a depth that the river would flow back into it. In the summer of 1871, the "deep cut" was complete, and with the help of powerful pumps at Bridgeport, the Chicago River began to flow southwest down the canal. An enthusiastic observer commented that the "black river" would soon be "clean enough for fish to swim in." Chicago business leaders hailed Chesbrough's "permanent solution" by giving him a testimonial and $11,000 for devising a plan to purify the river without "interfering with large and rapidly increasing manufacturing interests" or the "unparalleled growth" of the city.

The "permanent solution" lasted about a year. By then Chesbrough had conceded that the city would not be able to discharge its sewage "into the river for all time to come without producing injurious results." One problem was the "deep cut" canal was still eight feet above the

bottom of the Chicago River, so that the lowest and most polluted waters of the river did not drain into the canal, even when pushed by the huge pumps at Bridgeport. To make matters worse, William Odgen and John Wentworth had taken advantage of the deepened canal to drain Mud Lake in order to sell off the old swampland as real estate. To do so, they dug a ditch that connected the West Fork of the South Branch of the Chicago River to the Des Plaines River. The following spring, heavy rains flooded the ditch, which caused almost all of the Des Plaines River to divert into the South Branch of the Chicago River, which in turn backwashed into the lake. Silt from Ogden-Wentworth Ditch soon settled at the bottom of the canal, and negated the entire effort of the dredging and deepening operation of the previous year. The current of the reversed river began to slow and eventually stopped; in one year's time the river was back to its old stagnant, fetid self.

In 1873, cholera struck the city again, and smallpox and dysentery epidemics would continue in the city throughout the next decade. In the summer of 1879, Chicago experienced thirty straight days of rain, and the ordinarily shallow Des Plaines River turned into a raging torrent of water.

Its flood waters poured over the Chicago Portage and into the Chicago River, causing the carrier of nearly all of Chicago's sewage to back up into the lake beyond the intake pipes for the water system. Chicagoans who were forced to boil their drinking water, soon became indignant, and began to demand that the city's sewage and water supply problems be resolved.

In 1885, a near disaster would force the city into action: six inches of rain fell in less than a day, flooding much of the city. Urban legend has it that the flood caused widespread outbreaks of cholera, typhoid, and other waterborne diseases that claimed the lives of twelve percent of Chicago's population (in fact, the rate of death from waterborne disease for the entire year was not far from normal). What the flood of 1885 did cause was an enormous anxiety among Chicago's residents, who understood all too well how lucky they had been. In response, Illinois' elected officials developed a grand plan that would combine sewage drainage with a steamship canal that would finally give Chicago its grand waterway to the Mississippi and New Orleans. In 1889, the state legislature created the Sanitary District of Chicago, one of the first regional authorities in the nation. It was charged with the building and operation of a new canal, along with its

ancillary projects; in 1892, ground was broken for the Chicago Drainage Canal, which would later be renamed the Sanitary and Ship Canal.

As depicted on the map here, the Sanitary and Ship Canal runs parallel to the old Illinois and Michigan Canal, cutting through the south fork of the Chicago Outlet between the Great Lakes and Mississippi Basin at Summit. It extends in a southwesterly direction twenty-eight miles from Chicago to Lockport, linking the south branch of the Chicago River to the Des Plaines River. The new canal does not have a traditional system of locks, but rather is a continuous waterway, which prompted its engineers to dub it "the Ditch." Many Chicago boosters touted it as a man-made river that "counteracted" nature itself, making the Chicago River flow southward, as it had done eons ago when the site of Chicago lay at the bottom of Lake Chicago.

With the help of a widened and deepened Chicago River, the canal would draw a far greater volume of water from Lake Michigan than the shallow Illinois and Michigan Canal (the new canal was designed to carry a normal flow of ten thousand cubic feet of water per second). The Sanitary District claimed that this strong-running stream would "sanitize" Chicago's sewage by a process of oxidation and dilution by the time it

reached Joliet. The canal was dug to a depth of twenty-five feet, and is 160 feet wide at its narrowest point and 306 feet wide at its widest. It is larger than the Suez Canal in Egypt and at the time represented the largest earth-moving project in the world. In fact, new methods of earth-moving and new types of earth-moving machines were invented in the eight-year process of building the Sanitary and Ship Canal. These new technologies became known as the "Chicago School of Earth-Moving," and would later be employed in the construction of the Panama Canal.

In December 1899, with work nearing completion, the State of Missouri sought an injunction against the opening of the Sanitary Ship Canal, claiming that it would imperil the St. Louis water supply. Fearful that their massive project was in danger, the Sanitary District acted quickly and secretly, without informing either the mayor or the governor. At dawn on January 2, 1900, the nine Chicago Sanitary District Commissioners, along with two newspaper reporters, gathered to watch the demolition of the temporary dam which separated the Chicago River from the new channel. The flow of the Chicago River had been permanently reversed, the first river in the world to flow away from its mouth.

St. Louis still took Chicago to

court, but the case was eventually dismissed when a report by scientists concluded that the canal's dilution process worked: the Chicago River's wastewater was clean by the time it reached Joliet. It would not be until the 1930s that the canal became part of a transportation channel to the Mississippi, however. To complete this task, locks and dams had to be built along the Illinois River to make it navigable for deep-water vessels.

The new canal, along with the St. Lawrence Seaway, which opened in 1959, would make Chicago the nation's fifth-largest port, and would finally complete the inland water highway from the St. Lawrence River to the Gulf of Mexico that had been dreamed of since the days of Marquette and Joliet. In 1955, the American Society of Civil Engineers named the Chicago Sanitary and Ship Canal one of the seven wonders of American engineering.

CHICAGO'S DEEP TUNNEL PROJECT

The TARP Map

Title: Map of Tunnel and Reservoir Plan
Date Issued: 2002
Cartographer: Metropolitan Water Reclamation District of Greater Chicago
Published: Separately
© *MWRDGC2002-7*

Chicago has worked for over a century to preserve the purity of its freshwater reservoir, Lake Michigan. Today, Chicago's eight million people draw over 2.4 billion gallons of fresh water from the lake every day. None of this water is meant to return to Lake Michigan; instead, Chicago sends its wastewater through a network of tunnels, canals, and rivers that draw water away from the lake and eventually into the Mississippi River. That, at least, is the way Chicago's sewer system was designed to work.

As Chicago continued to grow in the twentieth century, so did its sewer system. By 1930, Chicago had over 3,200 miles of sewers under its streets, making it the most extensive sewer system in the world. During the Great Depression, the Works Progress Administration took over the construction of new sewers in Chicago, and over six years added an additional 192 miles of new sewers. Following World War II, the city and its environs continued to grow, and vast new areas within the city and beyond were built up and paved over. This new era of urban sprawl overwhelmed Chicago's combined sewer system.

Chicago's combined sewers were designed to accept both storm water and sanitary waste, which means that when it rains, storm runoff drains into a combined sewer where it mixes with the sewerage flow from homes and industry. By the 1950s, Chicago's sewer system could capture and treat two billion gallons of wastewater per day; a single rainstorm, however, could produce five billion gallons of runoff. Basements and streets would become flooded, and the Sanitary District had no alternative but to allow the excess mixture of raw sewage and storm water to spill directly into the Chicago River as "combined sewer overflow." When the excess deluge became large enough to raise the level of the river above that of Lake Michigan, the locks were opened and the untreated water released into the lake. By the early 1970s the problem had grown so severe that raw sewage was being dumped into the river an average of every four days, and Chicago's beaches had to be closed to the public about twenty-five percent of the season.

Once again Chicago was faced with the problem of defending Lake Michigan from its wastewater.

To address the problem, another bold and massive project was launched: a flood control system called the Tunnel and Reservoir Plan (TARP). Under this plan, 109 miles of huge underground tunnels would be burrowed under the city to collect combined sewer overflow and convey it to large storage reservoirs. After a rainstorm had subsided, the overflow could then be conveyed from these reservoirs to treatment plants for cleaning before going to a waterway.

Construction of the tunnel and reservoir system, known as the "Deep Tunnel," began in 1975. As can be seen on this map, the system consists of four tunnel systems: the O'Hare System, the Mainstream System, the Des Plaines System, and the Calumet System. These tunnels cover a total area of 375 square miles, and serve the city of Chicago and fifty-one neighboring communities. The Mainstream Tunnel is 35 feet in diameter and was bored in limestone rock 240 to 350 feet below ground. It holds one billion gallons of water and was put into operation in 1985. The system's three reservoirs are the O'Hare Reservoir (completed in 1998), Thornton Reservoir and McCook Area Reservoir. Excavation for all the tunnels was completed in 2004, and the entire tunnel system is scheduled to be operational in 2006. When all the reservoirs are complete in 2014, the

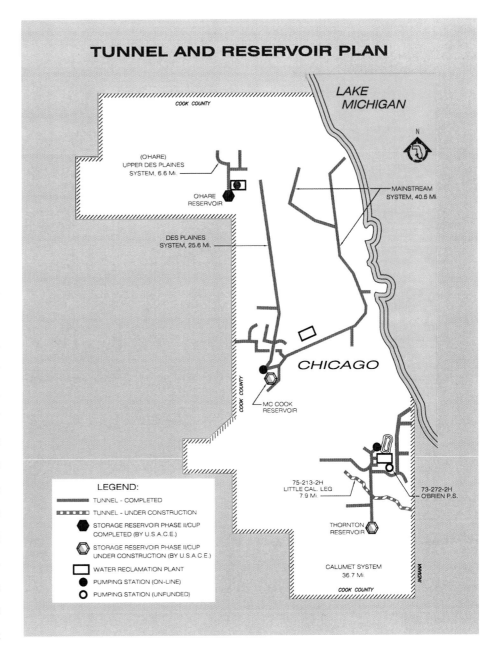

Deep Tunnel system will have a capacity of eighteen billion gallons.

The Mainstream Tunnel is one of the world's largest rock tunnel bores, and was constructed by huge tunnel boring machines. (Since tunnel contractors would be working beneath homes, businesses, and streets, excavation by extensive blasting was ruled out; the tunnel-boring machines cause less rock disturbance, noise and vibration). Tunnels this size had never been bored before, and the machines used in this operation were the largest such machines ever built. This technology has led to other major projects, including the "Chunnel" bored under the English Channel.

THE GREAT FIRE

Richard's Map of the Great Conflagration

Title: Richard's illustrated and statistical map of the great conflagration in Chicago
Date Issued: 1871
Cartographer: R. P. Studley Company / J. Keppler
Published: R. P. Studley Company (St. Louis)
Lithograph, 29 x 69 cm
Newberry Library, map6F oG4104.C6 1871 .R6

In October of 1871, Chicago suffered one of the worst urban disasters in history as a large portion of the city was destroyed by fire. At the time, Chicago was the fastest-growing city in the world. In just under four decades, it had grown from a town of three-eighths of a square mile to a city of eighteen square miles, and its population had grown from barely 150 to 340,000. Where once was a muddy swamp now stood the rail, grain, lumber, and livestock capital of the world.

The likelihood of the Great Fire was not unforeseen. In 1868, the fire department had warned the mayor and the city council of "the grave defects in which our city [is] being built." Almost every building outside of the central business district was constructed of wood, and even the marble buildings downtown had wooden cornices, long wooden signs on their fronts, and mansard top stories made of wood. Almost every roof in the city was made of wood, and covered with felt, tar, or shingles. The city had miles of raised wooden sidewalks, and even the streets of the business district were lined with planks of pine. The fire department also warned that a great number of the city's strikingly beautiful new stores, hotels, and multi-story buildings were poorly constructed by "swindling" contractors. As reported by the *Chicago Tribune*, they were "firetraps pleasing to the eye," but all "shams and shingles."

By the fall of 1871, this city of pine was literally a tinderbox. Just an inch of rain had fallen since the Fourth of July, and in its October 8 edition, the *Tribune* warned that the drought had "left everything in so flammable a condition that a spark might set a fire which would sweep from end to end of the city." In only a few short hours, this prophecy would be fulfilled. The fire started around nine o'clock that Sunday night in the O'Leary family barn, which was located at DeKoven and Jefferson Streets. Mrs. Catherine O'Leary was a thirty-eight-year-old woman who ran a dairy business, and within the first few hours of the fire, a rumor started that she had brought a lantern to the barn, and that a cow had kicked it over, starting the hay on the floor of the barn on fire. An official inquiry established that Mrs. O'Leary, her husband, and their three children were asleep in bed when the fire started, and that in fact, a neighbor had to awake them and alert them to the fire in the barn. The legend, however, lives on.

Chicago's fire department at the time of the Great Fire numbered only 185 men, and the day before, the entire force had battled for seventeen hours to contain a fire that consumed a four-block area just south of the business district. The night of the Great Fire they were exhausted, and to make matters worse, they were sent to the wrong neighborhood when the fire alarm first went out; when they finally arrived at the O'Leary residence, they found the fire raging out of control.

A southwest wind from the prairie had freshened that night, and the fire quickly spread to a block of shanties on the West Side. Flaming timbers were blown toward the South Branch of the river, where planing mills and furniture factories were located. These were soon engulfed in flames, and the fire spread to neighboring grain elevators. By eleven-thirty flaming material blew over the South Branch of the river at Van Buren Street, setting a horse stable on fire. Another flaming brand crossed the river and ignited the South Side Gasworks on Adams Street. From these two spots a new and larger fire started, and even the greasy river itself was ignited. After the gasworks went, three

blocks of pine rookeries called Conley's Patch were burning, and the fire raced toward the heart of the city. First the "fireproof" mercantile buildings along LaSalle Street were consumed; by one o'clock the Chamber of Commerce was gone, and less than two hours later the Court House fell, its great bell clanging until the end. The Brigg's Hotel, Marshall Field's new marble store, Joseph Medill's *Tribune* building, and the Palmer House all were destroyed.

After leveling the near West Side and the business district, the fire sent a piece of burning wood across the main branch of the river that landed in a railroad car containing kerosene. From this point, the fire spread in a diagonal line from west to east, across the North Side to the pumping house of the Waterworks. Within minutes the pumping house was devoured by flames, and the city was without water. The city was now at the mercy of the fire, which swept in all directions from the Waterworks. Many residents sought refuge on the open ground northwest of the city or in Lincoln Park and the abandoned cemetery at its south end. Thousands had been pushed to the edge of the lake, and were trapped throughout the night on the Sands, an area north of the river along the lake, near William Ogden's lumberyard. The next morning the lumberyard burst into flames, and the fire then consumed

Ogden's railroad depot, McCormack's Reaper Works, and, south of the river, the Illinois Central terminals.

The fire was stopped at the south end of the city late Monday afternoon after reaching a firebreak that had been created by blowing up buildings. The fire ended on the north side Monday night; it had spread to the city limits, where it found nothing else to burn. Late Monday, a rain began to fall. The fire had run its course, and the rain ensured it would not flare up again.

The Great Fire destroyed more than 73 miles of streets and 17,000 buildings. More than 100,000 people— nearly one third of the city's population—were homeless; 120 bodies were recovered; many others were drowned or vaporized (the coroner estimated the total number of deaths to be around 300). An official inquiry determined that shoddy construction, lax building inspection, and a poorly equipped fire department were to blame for the fire.

Richard's map, the map presented here, is larger and more colorful than the many similar maps that appeared with accounts of the fire. It includes a bird's-eye view of Chicago, which, like nearly all such views of Chicago, takes a vantage point looking to the west from Lake Michigan above the Chicago River. The city is shown engulfed in orange flames, and

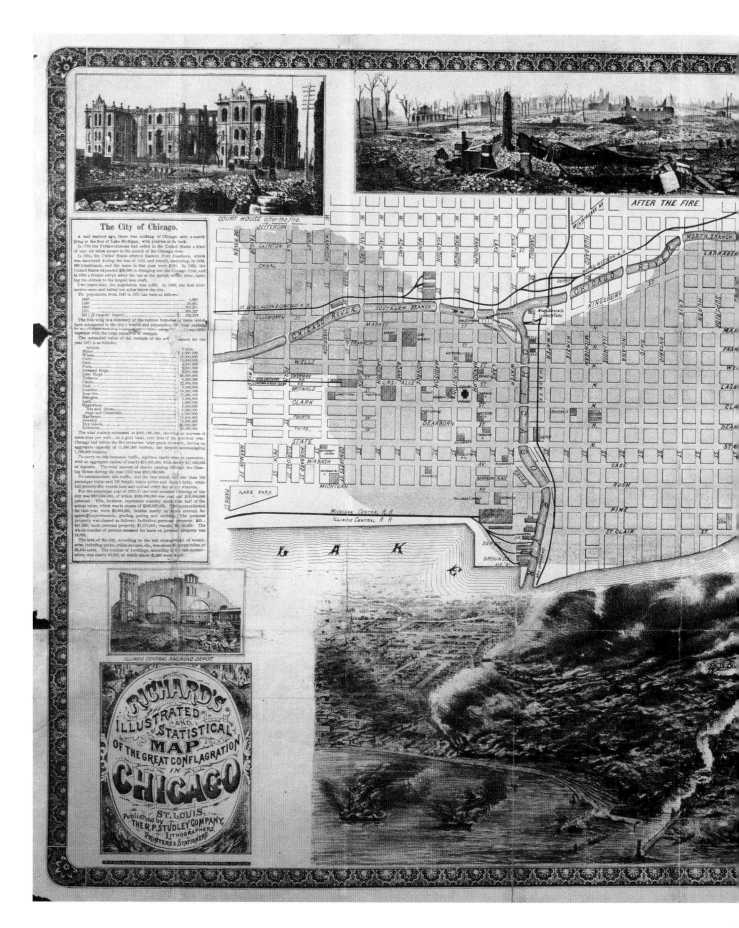

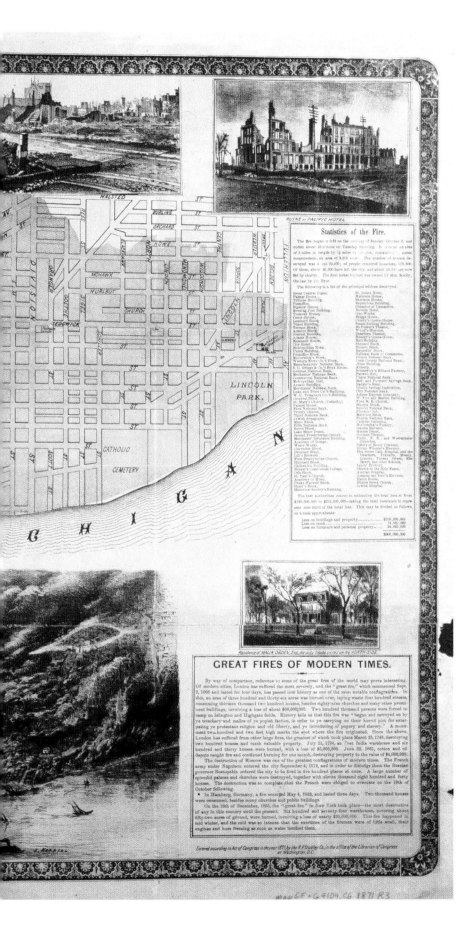

covered by clouds of gray smoke. The O'Leary cottage is located at the upper left-hand point, and one can clearly see how the fire moved north and east from there. It also shows that the fire jumped both the south and main branches of the Chicago River, and that the North Division suffered the most extensive damage.

The power, and no doubt the popularity, of the panoramic map both lie in its almost pictorial representation of its subject matter. The bird's-eye view here, along with its accompanying text frame, is clearly intended to show that even in its destruction by fire Chicago was larger and grander than other cities suffering similar devastation. Local newspapers were quick to report that the Great Fire could only be compared to the London Fire of 1666, or perhaps to Napoleon's burning of Moscow in 1812. And yet these earlier fires still paled in comparison to the Chicago fire, which destroyed more than twice the total area of both of them combined. The rebuilding of Chicago would require not only a collective effort from its citizens, but also resources and capital from those living elsewhere in the country. By detailing the enormity of the Great Fire, this map was meant to help realize both.

THE NEW CITY

The *New Chicago* Map

Title: Map of Chicago's business district in 1872 showing the extent of reconstruction following the fire of 1871
Date Issued: 1872
Cartographer: E. Burnham & Son
Published: *New Chicago: a full review of the work of reconstruction for the year, embracing a mention of every structure built or being built in the city* (Chicago)
Wood Engraving, 24 x 33 cm
Newberry Library, map2F G4104.C6 1872 .B3

One of Chicago's earliest and biggest promoters was William Bross, a part owner of the *Chicago Tribune*. Two days after the fire, he was on his way to New York to buy new equipment for the newspaper. As one of the first eyewitnesses to reach the East, reporters were eager to hear his stories of the fire. While there he also addressed local business leaders. He was quick to tell them that the Chicago fire had opened new opportunities for investment in the city: "Go to Chicago now!" he exhorted New York's capitalists, "You will never again have such a chance to make money!" Bross predicted that within five years the city would be completely rebuilt, and that it "would have a population of one million by 1900." Bross's friend and fellow Chicago booster John Stephen Wright likewise declared that "Five years will give Chicago more men, more money, more business, than she would have had without this fire."

The Great Rebuilding of the city began almost immediately after the fire, and no city has recovered from a large-scale disaster as quickly as Chicago did. Within days pioneer businesses sprang up in the ash-filled rubble of the city and proprietors of burned-out downtown firms were setting up shop in provisional structures. Marshall Field, to cite but one example, set up retail operations in a brick barn on the South Side, all the while contemplating plans for a new store back on State Street. Within a week of the fire, almost 5,500 temporary structures had been erected throughout the city, and over 200 permanent buildings were under construction. By the first anniversary of the fire, the entire downtown area was nearly completely rebuilt. The next year was to see an even more vigorous period of rebuilding, when the city dumped thousands of tons of debris into the basin between the Illinois Central trestle and South Michigan Avenue. This land would become a park, and on the far north end of its grounds was built the enormous glass and iron Inter-State Exposition Hall, designed by W. W. Boyington.

In effectively leveling the city's landscape, the Chicago fire hastened social and economic trends that were in motion before the disaster. One such trend was the residential movement away from the central business district. In the summer before the fire, over twenty-five thousand people from all walks of life lived in the immediate vicinity of the central business district, which included a mix of commercial, industrial and cultural buildings. In the rebuilt city, business establishments replaced downtown housing, pushing dwellings to the perimeter of the city; a decade after the fire, almost no one lived in the heart of the city. Another trend was the agglomeration of allied business concerns within localized regions of the city. Potter Palmer had begun this development by centralizing retail shops along State Street. After the fire, other types of enterprise were to follow suit. To pick a pertinent example, the various industries involved in making, publishing, and distributing maps came together after the fire in the new Lakeside Building at the corner of Clark and Adams. This increased the efficiency of the mapmaking industry, and contributed to the rising dominance of Chicago's mapmakers.

State Street still remained the center of downtown retail activity and industries continued to hug the river and the rail lines. The biggest change after the fire was the size and height of downtown. In fact, the rebuilding of downtown after the fire took place in two phases. The first phase ended with the depression of 1873, and resulted in a downtown that looked much the same as it did in 1871 except that it was larger and a few stories higher. In the 1880,

however, a new wave of construction began, and in a little over a decade, the entire downtown was again completely rebuilt. This time downtown Chicago was more than twice the area of the central business district before the fire, and it was converted into the world's first vertical city, as skyscrapers replaced the buildings that had been built just a decade before. The architects who designed and built these tall buildings made innovative use of fireproofing methods and materials, and as a result the new buildings of Chicago's central business district were the safest in the world from fire.

This map appeared the year after the Great Fire in *New Chicago: a full review of the work of reconstruction*, which

was published by the *Chicago Times*. The fine print just below the map reads, "In the above diagram only permanent structures are included. None of the shanties which disfigure the lake front, or any portion of the South Division's burnt district, are given. Wherever a building of brick, stone or iron has been completed, or even commenced, the area which it covers is shown in black, the white portion representing that portion of the south side's burnt section upon which no rebuilding has yet begun. As the great interest in the work of reconstruction centers in the South division, or great business heart of Chicago, the diagram presents only that portion of the city."

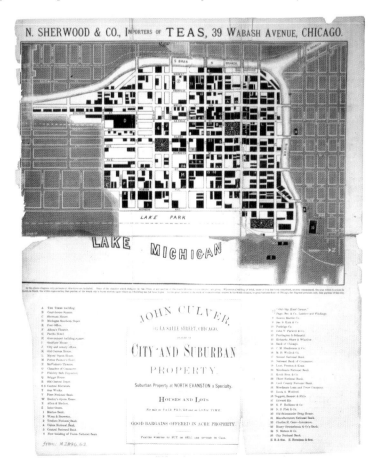

THE STREETCAR CITY

The Chicago Surface Lines Map

Title: System of Chicago Surface Lines
Date Issued: 1928
Cartographer: Chicago Surface Lines
Published: Chicago Surface Lines (Chicago)
Folded Sheet, 53.3 x 28.6 cm
Author's Collection

Mass transit in Chicago began with Franklin Parmalee's horse-drawn omnibuses in 1853. These slow and unsteady "urban stagecoaches" were replaced by horse-drawn railroad cars in 1858, when Parmalee and other investors chartered the Chicago City Railway Company.

Horse cars were a tremendous improvement in mass transportation, as the cars rode on rails, affording not only a smoother ride, but also allowing the horses to pull larger vehicles. The problem with horses, however, was pollution. Chicago's horse car system employed over seventy-five thousand horses, and their iron-shod feet produced a deafening clatter on the city's streets. Their manure turned the city's gutters into rank-smelling brown streams when it was raining, and, in dry weather, pulverized manure blew into the faces of downtown shoppers.

The cable car proved a faster, cleaner, and quieter alternative. The first line installed in Chicago was along State Street from Madison Street to Twenty-First Street. In January of 1882, a cheering throng of over three hundred thousand watched the inaugural run of the Chicago City Railway's State Street line. By 1894, the city was home to the largest cable car system in the world, with eighty-six miles of track, eleven steam power plants, and over fifteen hundred cars. The cables looped around in the downtown area before making return runs to the residential areas. The term the "Loop" thus became synonymous with downtown Chicago even before the completion of the elevated railway system that now encircles the business district and which remains today a defining city landmark.

Although the flat streets and urban topography of Chicago proved to be ideal for cable cars, another technology was soon to replace them—the far less expensive and more efficient electric trolley. After 1892, nearly all new streetcar construction in Chicago was electrified; by 1906, all of Chicago's surface cars were electric trolleys.

The transformation of Chicago into a Streetcar City was primarily due to efforts of one man, Charles Tyson Yerkes. This was the Gilded Age, a time, to paraphrase Mark Twain, when the chief end of man was to get rich, dishonestly if he could, honestly if he must. It was also a time when urban transit systems were owned and operated not, as today, by municipalities, but by powerful and power-hungry capitalists. Yerkes, a banker from Philadelphia, fit Twain's description to a tee. He had served time in jail for stock fraud, was subsequently pardoned, and arrived in Chicago to "make his fortune" in 1881. He immediately began to search for profit-making ventures, and it was not long before the city's street railways caught his eye.

Chicago's streetcar system in the early 1880s was woefully inadequate. It was a slow, horse-powered system with not enough lines to serve a city whose growing population now numbered over a half-million people. Before he would leave town, Yerkes would modernize and greatly expand the city's archaic system. He began in 1886, by acquiring (with two Philadelphia partners) a controlling interest in the North Chicago City Railway, a company with a low stock price and room for expansion and modernization. Next he obtained control of the Chicago West Division Railway. He immediately replaced the horse cars used by both of these companies with cable cars. Yerkes then leased and renovated two tunnels owned by the city to run his cars under

the Chicago River; this eliminated the frequent delays caused by the constant opening of swing bridges to accommodate river traffic. He completed an integrated cable system by 1893, and by 1901, he had installed electricity for 240 miles of his system and added an additional five hundred miles of track connecting the city and its suburbs. (During this time, Yerkes had also constructed the north-side elevated tracks, and the elevated Union Loop, which encircles downtown Chicago.)

A master manipulator of stocks, bonds, and entire companies, Yerkes created a web of companies by which he owned, operated and built various parts of his transit system. He would employ whatever measures were necessary to further his business interests. To extend his lines, Yerkes needed franchises for the use of public land, and like many other businessmen of the period, he routinely resorted to bribery to control both municipal and state politicians. When bribery was not successful, he sometimes engaged "professional vamps" to seduce, and then blackmail, lawmakers. Once his franchises were in hand, Yerkes would build tracks out to empty land on the edge of the city that he had secretly bought in advance. He would then make a fortune by selling the land to housing contractors. Yerkes routinely watered down the value of the securities of the companies he owned, and he overcapitalized his

holdings by at least $62 million; he kept the favor of his stockholders, however, by returning dividends of between twelve and forty-two percent.

Yerkes' opulent lifestyle, which included a Chicago mansion on Michigan Avenue and a renaissance palace on New York's Fifth Avenue, his half-dozen mistresses, and his brazen political thievery made him reviled in the eyes of the city's newspaper editors, the mayor, and the public. In 1897, the "Goliath of Graft" attempted to gain complete control of the city's transit system, and part of his plan was to have the city council extend his land franchises for fifty years. This required the approval of the state legislature, which did so without exacting any payment. The public was outraged, and in the 1899 election, the "boodle" legislators who had voted for Yerkes were defeated and the law was repealed. Yerkes' days in Chicago were over, and in 1901 he sold his interests in the financially overburdened streetcar and elevated systems; part to his Philadelphia associates Peter Widener and William Elkins, and part to Marshall Field. Yerkes moved to New York and then went abroad to build the London Underground. Chicago was glad to get rid of him, but he left behind one of the finest urban transportation systems in the world.

In 1906, electric streetcars literally covered the city, and nearly all of its residents were within walking distance of a line. The route pattern was rectangular, with service along nearly every section-line street, some half-section streets, and most of the major diagonal arteries. In 1907, five companies were granted franchises for the entire one-thousand-mile system; seven years later the entire system was put under management of the Chicago Surface Lines, creating the largest streetcar system in the world. Its volume of traffic reached 634 million fares in 1913; in 1929 that figure soared to nearly 890 million. It has been said that the streetcar city was the most livable urban form ever invented. By 1959, Chicago's streetcars were a thing of the past.

This twentieth-century map shows the streetcar system near its peak. Published by the Chicago Surface Lines, it was accompanied by a "sightseeing and route guide" entitled *Seeing Greater Chicago by the Chicago Surface Lines*. The first half of this pamphlet presented "What to See in Chicago," giving a number of points of interest in the city and directions on how to get to them via streetcar. The latter half of the booklet detailed the various streetcar routes. As one can gather—and see from this map—streetcars could literally "take you everywhere" in the city of Chicago.

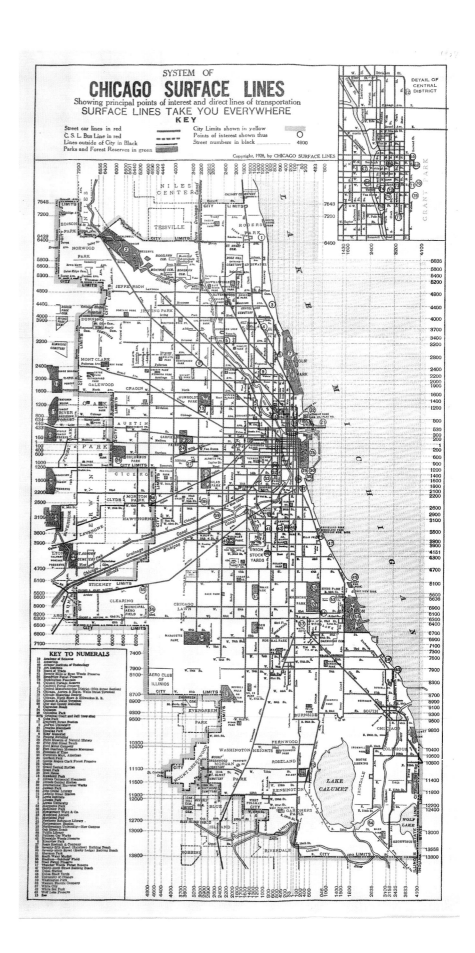

CITY PARKS AND BOULEVARDS

The Wüllweber Map

Title: Map of Chicago showing the Water Works System, Parks & Boulevards, Publics Buildings, & Railroads
Date Issued: 1886
Cartographer: O. L. Wüllweber
Published: City Map Department (Chicago)
Lithograph, 67.3 x 39.2 cm
Chicago Historical Society, ICHi-37869

Chicago's growth in the first few decades of its existence was so rapid and widespread that little or no provision was made for public parks or plazas. The irony in this fact is that in 1837, the newly incorporated city adopted "Urbs in Horto," or "city set in a garden," as its motto. This motto was intended to portray Chicago as a beautiful gateway to the fertile lands of the west. But in 1839, the only park in the city was Dearborn Park, a square located on the grounds of Fort Dearborn (currently the site of the Chicago Cultural Center). Michigan Avenue served as a promenade, but only for the wealthy residents whose mansions faced Lake Michigan from the west side of the street. Three years later, Washington Square was built, followed by Lincoln, Jefferson, Union, Ellis, and Vernon Parks. These seven parks, totaling 290 acres, served a city with a population of 229,000.

By 1847, incoming Mayor James Curtiss decried the lack of open space in the city, exclaiming in his inaugural speech that "one of the most prominent evils which exists in our city, is the want of public grounds. Scarcely a city in the Union, perhaps in the world, is so poorly provided for, in this respect. Grounds which but a few years since were thought too far out for any such purpose, now exceed in value any sum which we should perhaps be willing to pay. Something ought and I think can be done to remedy this evil." Two years later, the real estate developer and Chicago promoter John S. Wright answered the mayor, writing that "I foresee a time, not very distant, when Chicago will need for its fast-increasing population a park, or parks, in each division. Of these parks I have a vision. They are all improved and connected with a wide avenue, extending to and along the Lake Shore on the north and south, and so surround the city with a magnificent chain of superb parks and parkways that have not their equals in the world."

Wright's vision of a chain of parks and boulevards around the city was opposed by many of the city's real estate developers, who thought it a waste of open space. On the other hand, advocates of a park system touted its health and recreational benefits. Park trees would clean and refresh the city's "contaminated" air, and the pastoral setting of parks would attract the everyday worker, replacing the temptations of the saloon and gambling den. In 1866, the *Chicago Times* published a plan based on John S. Wright's concept. It proposed a continuous encirclement of the city with a 2,240 acre park, 14 miles long by one-quarter mile wide, and boulevards lining each side of the park strip. Although the plan was never implemented, it did provide the foundation for Chicago's park and boulevard system, authorized by state legislation three years later.

Ultimately, Chicago's park system was built—like nearly all of nineteenth-century Chicago—for the financial gain it would bring. Paul Cornell, himself a real estate operator, sold the city's developers on the idea of a park system by convincing them that it would increase the value of the land around it. Cornell's model was New York City's Central Park, which— besides attracting large crowds—had tremendously raised the value of its surrounding real estate. It should be noted that Cornell's interests were more than just material. In fact, he

and his fellow park promoter J. Young Scammon (William Ogden's associate) were deeply interested in the city's betterment; their hope, originally planted by Ogden, was that a system of city parks and cultural institutions would help control Chicago's runaway capitalism.

In 1869, the State of Illinois passed the "Parks Law" that established three park districts for Chicago, one each for the north, south, and west sections of the city. These districts were created as independent municipal corporations, and a parks fund was created for each of the corporations on the basis of the assessed valuation of the taxable real estate within each area. This legislation not only outlined the powers and duties of the park districts, but also detailed the location of the parks and connecting boulevards shown (in green) on this map. This system of parks and boulevards was located outside the city limits, and was intended to encourage the orderly expansion of the young city.

Park development immediately became the order of the day, and Cornell and other park promoters got themselves appointed to park district boards. Over the next three decades, over $46 million was spent on parklands, some of it, of course, finding its way to board members and

their associates who owned land where the new parks were located. Besides the desire to get rich, however, the board members wanted Chicago to have a first-class park system, and set out to hire the finest landscape designers available, including Frederick Law Olmsted, Calvert Vaux, William Le Baron Jenney, and Swain Nelson.

By 1893, Wright's vision of a park system was nearly complete. Chicago had recovered from the Great Fire, and was set to host to the World's Columbian Exposition commemorating the four-hundredth anniversary of Columbus's voyage to America. Visitors to the fair were so impressed with the beauty of Chicago's parks and boulevards, that they dubbed it the "Emerald Necklace" of Chicago. Similar boulevard systems were later developed in Boston, Kansas City, and Washington, D.C.

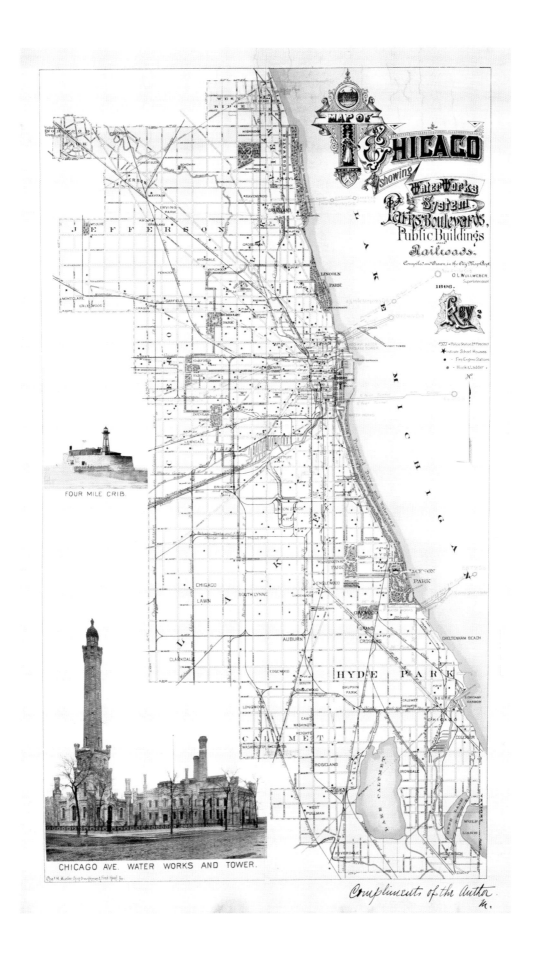

FOUR MILE CRIB.

CHICAGO AVE. WATER WORKS AND TOWER.

Compliments of the Author.

ANNEXATION

The Manstein Map

Title: Map showing territorial growth of the city of Chicago: to accompany the annual report of the Map Department, R. A. Manstein, superintendent, 1891
Date Issued: 1891
Cartographer: Charles M. Müller & Roderick A. Manstein
Published: Globe Lithographing & Printing Co. (Chicago)
Lithograph, 48 x 28 cm
Newberry Library, sc map 2F oG4104.C6G4 1891 .M8

On June 29, 1889, Chicago more than doubled in size as voters in a surrounding 125 miles elected to join the city. Annexed into the city were part of the Town of Cicero, the Town of Jefferson, the Town of Lake, the City of Lake View, and the Village of Hyde Park. There had been a long and bitter campaign against the merger, as its opponents argued that incorporation into the city would bring vice, crime, taxes, and other negative aspects of metropolitan life into their suburban existence. Winning the day, however, were the opportunities to gain the city's police and fire protection, as well as to be served by its water and sewage systems.

The following year, parts of the Village of Gano, South Englewood, and the Villages of Washington Heights and West Roseland were annexed into the city. In 1893, the Villages of Fernwood, Rogers Park and West Ridge all joined the city. Chicago now encompassed an area of 185 square miles, and its population was over one million people; the only American city with more people was New York. Other populated areas around Chicago, such as Evanston to the north, and Oak Park and Maywood to the west, remained independent of the city. These suburbs effectively formed a barrier to any further expansion of Chicago in their direction.

Annexation was the inevitable consequence of Chicago's amazing growth, as the city found its old boundaries could no longer contain its burgeoning commerce and growing population. Its growth followed the now familiar process of urban displacement: as commercial facilities expanded in the center of the city, old neighborhoods of housing gave way and residential construction was forced to the edge of the city and into the suburbs beyond.

This map was published shortly after the city's greatest period of expansion, and gives a chronological and geographical representation of the various areas annexed by Chicago. It begins with the area of the original town (shown in white), then shows the size of the city when it incorporated in 1837 (the area shaded in green). The extensions of 1847 and 1853 are shown in blue; those of 1863 and 1869 in yellow. The 1889 annexation of the towns of Hyde Park, Lake, Jefferson and Lakeview are depicted in pink; 1890 annexations are shown in brown and hazel.

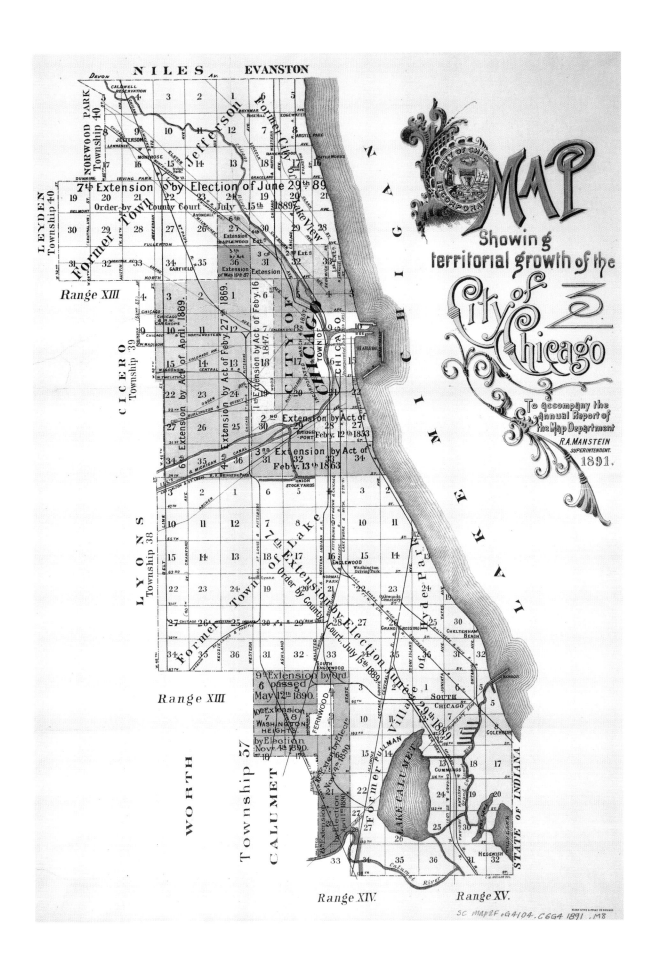

FIRE INSURANCE MAPS

The Robinson Map

Title: Outline and Index Map from Robinson's atlas of the city of Chicago, Illinois, Volume 1
Date Issued: 1886
Cartographer: Elisha Robinson, Roger H. Pidgeon, James P. Brown, George E. Ryan, L. F. Graether, W. S. McDonald, W. S. Miller
Published: Elisha Robinson (New York)
Lithograph, 28 x 35 cm
Newberry Library, Baskes A6 0011

Chicago's Great Fire may have been the largest conflagration the world had ever seen, but it was by no means usual—indeed, fires were a common occurrence in the late nineteenth-century urban environment. Chicago had already seen a number of large fires, and like many other cities, Chicago was plagued by primitive fire-fighting equipment, inadequate water supplies, and a city made of highly combustible materials. The threat of fire was greatly exacerbated in Chicago by the use of balloon-frame construction in its rapid transformation from a small frontier town into a teeming city. In fact, in the fastest-growing city in the world, almost any kind of construction was permitted as long as it made money for the builders and landlords. The attitude of the typical commercial building owner was that it was far cheaper to insure against fire loss—and the city was full of insurance companies—than to employ sound construction methods.

Fire insurance maps originated in fire-prone London toward the end of the eighteenth century, and were used to assist large fire insurance companies and underwriters in determining the risk involved in insuring individual properties. Underwriters there needed accurate, current, and detailed information about the buildings they were insuring, and this information was recorded on maps of the city. London underwriters also wrote most of the fire insurance for buildings in American cities both before and immediately after the Revolutionary War, and a number of American cities were surveyed in order to access fire risks. After the War of 1812, when many business ties with the British were severed, American companies began to provide domestic fire insurance.

During the first half of the nineteenth century, most American fire insurance companies were small and based in a single city. Consequently, the underwriters could themselves examine properties they were about to insure, and there was little need for special fire insurance maps. However, as insurance companies became larger and expanded their coverage to numerous cities, a mapping industry developed to support this need. These maps not only provided construction details for individual buildings, they also offered a more general assessment of the distribution of risk across neighborhoods.

George T. Hope is generally credited with having advanced the idea of specialized and detailed fire insurance maps in the United States. Hope was the secretary of the Jefferson Insurance Company in New York City, and in 1849 or 1850, he began to compile a large-scale map of a portion of New York City for use in calculating fire risks on business and residential structures. He hired William Perris, an engineer trained in England, to make the surveys and to draft a map of the city from the lower tip of Manhattan Island to Twenty-Second Street. To ensure that the proposed map would include all essential information, Hope formed a committee of fire insurance officials, with himself as chairman, to direct the project. The committee agreed that the map should identify the construction materials in all buildings by a system of colors, formulated a set of appropriate cartographic symbols, and set a format and scale for the map. The standards adopted by the Hope committee were used, with few modifications, on most fire insurance maps for a century or more.

Although there were many fire insurance atlas publishers in the United States in the late nineteenth century, by the early twentieth century the field was dominated by one company, the Sanborn Map Company of New York. Fire insurance maps thus are commonly referred to simply as Sanborn maps. From the 1870s until the 1950s, the Sanborn Map Company produced some 700,000 map sheets that covered over 12,000 American cities and towns. These maps were sold on a subscription basis, and had to be constantly revised to reflect changes in the urban landscape. Since it was very costly to produce new map sheets, these changes were often issued on correction slips that were to be pasted over existing sheets. For this reason, although a fire insurance atlas may bear the date that it was originally published, the information it contains is effectively the date of its last revision. Until after World War II, most Sanborn maps were drawn at a scale one inch to fifty feet on 21-by-25-inch sheets of paper. They detailed the location, height, number of stories, and material composition of all buildings within a city or town, noted the strength of fire departments, location of water and gas mains, and labeled most public buildings by name. Buildings were color-coded according to their composition: pink symbolized brick, blue for stone, yellow for frame construction, and so on. The work of coloring maps fell to individual artists, who painted on lithographs (sometimes also hand-drawn) as printing often proved uneconomical for small orders.

Sanborn maps were sold primarily to national or regional underwriting associations, and in the 1930s Sanborn maps commonly cost between $12 and $200.

Fire insurance maps are no longer widely used by the fire insurance industry, for myriad reasons. The slow decline of insurance cartography began as early as the mid-1920s, when some companies began replacing maps with the "line card" method of recording risk; present-day companies, of course, use computers to store their liability and risk records. One reason for this decline was the constant growth of the nation's cities, which made keeping maps up to date a cumbersome and expensive process. So too have improved fire codes, better fire protection methods, and modern building construction techniques rendered the detailed local information provided by fire insurance maps superfluous, as insurance companies are more likely to rely on inspection services provided by their own or an independent fire insurance rating organization. Today, fire insurance maps are used for a wide variety of

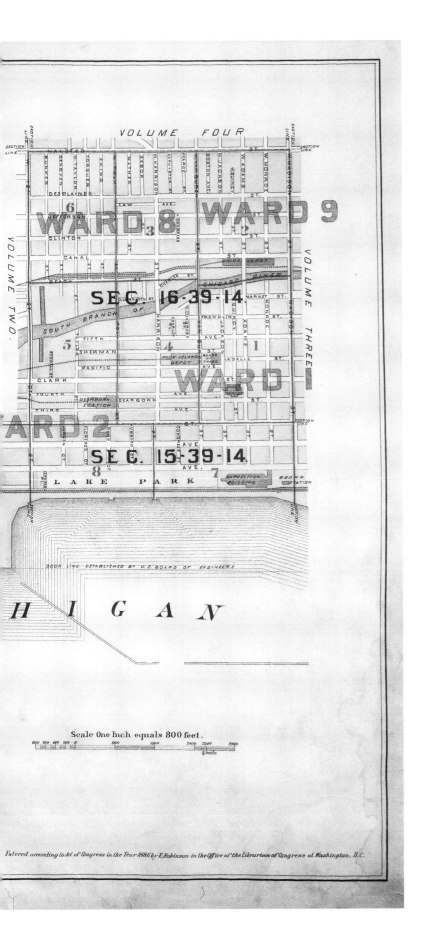

research purposes including genealogy, urban history and geography, historical preservation, and environmental studies.

The fire map presented here is not from the Sanborn series; rather, it is drawn from *Robinson's Atlas of the City of Chicago*, which was first published in 1886. This map is the Outline and Index Map for Volume 1 of the (5 volume) atlas. This volume covers the lakefront from Madison Street on the north to Pershing Road on the south.

PULLMAN'S TOWN

The Western Manufacturer View

Title: Manufacturing Town of Pullman and Car Works
Date Issued: 1881
Cartographer: Western Manufacturer
Published: Supplement to *Western Manufacturer 9*
Folded Sheet, 26.8 x 74 cm
Chicago Historical Society, ICHi-38519

Shortly after the Civil War, George Mortimer Pullman, the former Chicago building raiser, organized the Pullman Palace Car Company. Pullman almost single-handedly revolutionized train travel, which prior to the introduction of his railroad cars confined passengers in coaches that were little more than rickety wooden boxes with seats or benches, poor heating and ventilation, and inadequate springs that made for a rough ride. The luxurious interior of the Pullman Palace Car included carpeted floors, upholstered seats, electrically lit chandeliers, table lamps with silk shades, and advanced heating and air conditioning systems. Pullman's railroad cars were also revolutionary for their service. Courteous employees, efficient baggage handling, prepared gourmet meals, dining cars, and cleanliness made these cars a popular choice for those passengers willing to pay a slight surcharge. In the words of one woman rider, they transformed the "dreaded journey" between New York and Chicago into "a mere holiday excursion."

Chicago at the time was riding the crest of an enormous population boom, and the city attracted both foreign immigrants (in 1870, over one-half of the city's population was foreign-born) and native migrants in search of work and good wages. While many of the city's new residents found opportunity, they also found squalor; indeed, the typical working-class neighborhood was an overcrowded, unsanitary, and unappealing part of town. It was also a time of labor unrest, not just in Chicago, but across the country and internationally. Issues about wages and hours, the safety of working conditions, and the replacement of laid-off workers with lower-wage irregulars during times of economic downturn led to confrontations between labor and management and between labor activists and police and other armed authorities.

In late July of 1877, the Great Strike, as it came to be called, shut down the entire railroad system in the United States, moving westward from Boston and New York, to Baltimore and Pittsburgh, and in a few days reaching Chicago, the nation's railroad hub. Workers from a variety of industries, many of them immigrants and socialists, rioted in Chicago's streets, burning railroad property and shutting down the stockyards, lumberyards, rolling mills, and just about every other industrial enterprise. The city responded by calling out the police along with armed volunteers, the National Guard, and the U.S. Infantry. Violent confrontations took place on Halsted Street, at Sixteenth Street, on Archer Avenue, Goose Island, at the Burlington Yards, and many other locations. After three days, the rioters were finally corralled by the mass of armed militia. Nationwide, a hundred workers had been killed; thirty had been killed in Chicago, where another several hundred had been wounded.

Immediately after the strike, the Citizen's Association, a law-and-order group of business leaders led by Marshall Field, donated money to the Chicago Police Department for the purpose of procuring an arsenal that included four twelve-pound Napoleon cannons, a Gatling gun, and other light artillery pieces. At the Association's urging, the city also began building armories to house National Guard units. Chicago would be well-armed to face any future labor uprising. George Pullman was a member of the Citizen's Association, but his reaction to the Great Strike was to seek a radical new solution to the "labor problem"—by engineering social reform.

In the 1870s, Pullman was manufacturing his railroad cars in Detroit, but by the end of the decade he was in search of a Chicago area site on which to construct a larger, modernized plant. Why not, he thought, set this new factory in the center of a town built especially for his workers? Pullman's idea was to improve the relationship between capital and labor by creating a safe, clean, culturally enriching environment for his workers; his workers, in turn, would undoubtedly respond with loyalty, honesty, and commitment to hard work. Here was his chance to engage in enlightened capitalism: his company town would be a place where "all that would promote the health, comfort, and convenience of a large working population would be conserved, and … many of the evils to which they are ordinarily exposed made impossible." Such evils for Pullman included not just saloons, brothels, and gambling houses, but also political bosses, labor agitators, and even meddling priests or ministers. Free of such temptations, his town's environment was sure to improve the moral character of its residents, and would make for an efficient and contented workforce.

In 1880, after purchasing four thousand acres of land just west of Lake Calumet, Pullman began construction of his model town, which he named for himself. He hired the architect Solon Beman and the landscape designer Nathan Barrett to collaborate on the design and building of the town. At its center was the virtually self-sufficient Pullman Palace Car Company factory complex, which was dominated by a large clock tower. Although some critics panned their uniformity, the town's brick houses and apartment buildings were well constructed with many state-of-the-art conveniences, including indoor plumbing, gas, and regular trash removal. Residents could enjoy man-made Lake Vista, as well as the town's meticulously maintained parks and promenades. The large Arcade building, which foreshadowed the modern shopping center, contained a restaurant, a bank, a library, a post office, a theater, and numerous other privately owned shops. Market Hall contained sixteen stalls that were leased by the Pullman Land Association to private businesses for the provision of fresh meats, produce and other market goods. Hotel Florence, which was named for Pullman's daughter, stands not far from the Arcade building, and housed many visitors touring the model city.

Pullman insisted that his town be financially solvent, and, in fact, that it return a six-percent profit (he required an eight-percent return from his manufacturing enterprise). Toward this end, the town and factory complex were designed to be as efficient as possible. All waste and excess materials were to be recycled. Thus, for instance, scrap wood from the factory fueled the town's Corliss engine, which powered the machinery in Pullman. The engine's condensation filled Lake Vista, and workers used the ice from the lake on Pullman cars. The Corliss engine also pumped sewage from the town to a nearby Pullman-owned farm, where it was used as fertilizer for produce that would be sold back in the town.

In 1896, the town of Pullman was presented an award for the "World's Most Perfect Town"; it had a population of approximately 12,000, of which about half were Pullman employees and the remainder, their family members. It was, to be sure, "Pullman's Town"—for George Pullman maintained almost absolute control over all aspects of life in the town. The town's only newspaper was edited by the company publicist, the only elections in town—for the school board—were often rigged by the company, and a company-appointed pastor at the town's only church reminded his congregation that their employer was "just below the angels" (Pullman assumed that his residents would be satisfied with one church and with that form of worship he himself had chosen). Pullman chose which stores could set up shop in his town, he chose which books could be offered by the library, and even which plays and musical entertainment could be presented in the theater. Town residents were not allowed to own their own homes, and their leases all had a

MANUFACTURING TOWN OF PULL

Supplement to the "WESTERN MANUFACTURER," Nov. 30th, 1881; COYNE & Co., Publishers, and SOLICITORS OF PATENTS, Chicago.

clause that allowed Pullman to evict them with ten days' notice. Alcohol was not permitted to be sold in town, except at the tavern at the Hotel Florence, which only served out-of-towners. To ensure the townsfolk complied with his policies, company spies or "spotters" stood watch for any resident who behaved to the contrary.

Residents unhappy with Pullman's close paternal control over their lives voted to annex their town to the city of Chicago in 1889, but the annexation did little to alter Pullman's tight-fisted governance of the town.

Then the depression of 1893–4 set in. To ensure that neither he nor his investors suffered financial loss, Pullman drastically reduced the factory's productivity, and cut his worker's wages by one-third. He did not, however, make any corresponding reduction in the rent he charged his employees for their living quarters, in the town's store prices, or in the utility charges he charged town residents. Quite predictably, his workforce rebelled, and the result was the famous Pullman Strike of 1894. The strike began in May and turned violent in July when federal

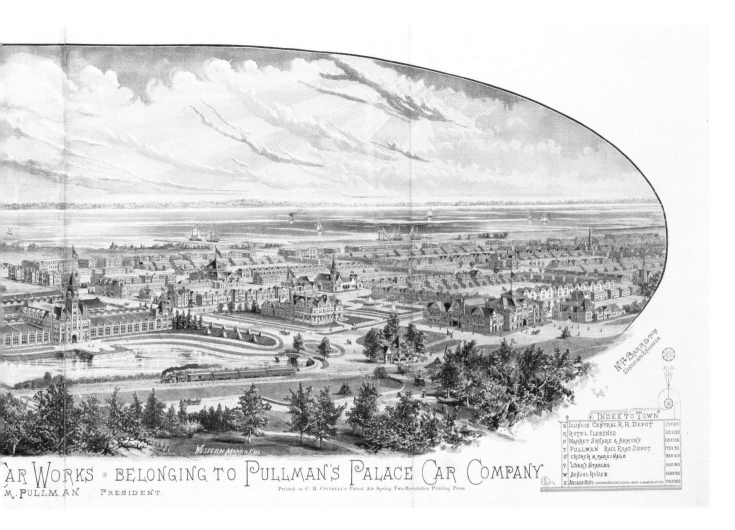

AR WORKS · BELONGING TO PULLMAN'S PALACE CAR COMPANY.

M. PULLMAN PRESIDENT.

Printed on C. B. Cottrell's Patent Air Spring Two-Revolution Printing Press.

INDEX TO TOWN		
Q	ILLINOIS CENTRAL R.R. DEPOT	25 X 45
R	HOTEL FLORENCE	105 X 150
S	MARKET SQUARE & ARMORY	110 X 100
T	PULLMAN RAIL ROAD DEPOT	175 X 130
U	CHURCH & PARSONAGE	95 X 100
V	LIVERY STABLES	112 X 160
W	SCHOOL HOUSE	150 X 190
X	ARCADE BLDG (CONTAINING STORES, THEATER, LIBRARY & MUNICIPAL OFFICES)	170 X 250

troops quashed the strikers; shortly thereafter the strike collapsed.

The strike ended George Pullman's attempt to solve the "labor problem." Indeed, his heavy-handed paternalism, which as early as 1885 a journalist referred to as "a well-wishing feudalism," actually undercut the very values he wished to instill in his workers, namely, stability, order, and loyalty to the company. For his land-use and intrusive surveillance policies ensured that few of his workers actually felt "at home" in the town of Pullman; as soon they could

afford to, many left the town and bought homes in nearby communities. Pullman could not understand the failings of his approach, and he died a bitter man in 1897.

In 1898, the Illinois Supreme Court ordered the Pullman Company to sell the nonindustrial land in the neighborhood to its inhabitants, determining that the Pullman Palace Car Company was not authorized to provide non-manufacturing services such as property rental. The Pullman Company continued to manufacture railroad cars at its plant in the

neighborhood until 1957. In 1960, developers sought to demolish the town and build an industrial park in its place. The neighborhood's residents formed the Pullman Civic Organization and worked to defeat this plan. Its residents also worked to gain landmark for the neighborhood, and Pullman became a State Landmark in 1969, a National Landmark District in 1971, and a City of Chicago Landmark in 1972. Today hundreds of Pullman houses continue to undergo privately funded renovation and restoration.

THE WORLD'S COLUMBIAN EXPOSITION OF 1893

The Randy McNally View

Title: Bird's-Eye View of World's Columbian Exposition, Chicago, U.S.A., 1893: showing grounds and views of the buildings—looking northwest
Date Issued: 1893
Cartographer: Rand McNally & Co.
Published: Rand McNally & Co. (Chicago)
Lithograph, 68 x 100 cm
Chicago Historical Society,ICHi-25161

In 1893, Chicago hosted the World's Columbian Exposition, a celebration—one year late—of the four-hundredth anniversary of Columbus's discovery of the New World. Hailed as "the greatest event in the history of the country since the Civil War," the Fair ran from May through October, and was the largest tourist attraction America had ever seen. Authorized by an act of Congress, it was truly the first World's Fair, with over fifty nations participating in "an international exhibition of arts, industries, manufactures, and the products of the soil, mine, and sea."

The main site of the Fair was located in Jackson Park, and was bounded by Stony Island Avenue on the west, Sixty-Seventh Street on the south, Lake Michigan on the east, and

Fifty-Sixth Street on the north. Smaller buildings and concessions were strung along a small strip of land between Fifty-Ninth and Sixtieth Streets that connected Jackson Park to Washington Park. This eighty acre strip became known as the Midway Plaisance. Jackson Park covered 533 acres, and had two miles of frontage on Lake Michigan. Nearby Washington Park covered 371 acres, and the amount of space the Fair actually covered was 633 acres.

The design and construction of the fairgrounds was overseen by Daniel H. Burnham, whose architectural firm had built some of the nation's first skyscrapers, including the Montauk Building and Masonic Temple in Chicago and the Flatiron Building in New York. Frederick Law Olmsted, the

venerable landscape architect who had designed New York's Central Park, laid out the Fair's setting. A Board of Architects was convened by Burnham to conceive the general design of the Fair's buildings and the Court of Honor, and was constituted primarily of Eastern architects who had received their training at the Academie des Beaux-Arts in Paris. Burnham also commissioned the architects who would carry out the design and construction of some two hundred additional buildings. Some of the most renowned artists of the day contributed statuary, among them Augustus Saint-Gaudens and Daniel Chester French, along with a newcomer, Lorado Taft.

Burnham, Olmstead, and the Board arrived at a most unusual and spectacular Fair plan. Olmstead worked with the swampy landscape of Jackson Park, creating a system of waterways and lagoons that were fed by Lake Michigan. These bodies of water served both as decorative reflecting pools and as waterways for transportation, and in their midst, Olmstead placed the shady Wooded Island as a place of respite for weary fairgoers. These waterways were surrounded by fourteen main or "great" buildings, which were built in the Beaux-Arts style, with its emphasis on scale, harmony, and ensemble. The Grand Basin contained a massive gilded statue of the Republic, and was ringed by the Court of Honor Buildings. The main buildings were all monumental and classical in style, all of uniform cornice height, all decorated roughly the same, and all were covered with staff, a material composed of plaster of

Paris molded around a fibrous jute cloth. This material (along with some paint) gave the main buildings a magnificent whiteness intended to dazzle visitors who arrived at the rail terminal just outside the Fair's gates, and the fairgrounds became known as the "White City."

The stately and monumental White City stood in stark contrast to its host city, which was quickly dubbed the "Gray City." The Fair was in many ways the antithesis of the typical American metropolis. The Exposition was a well-planned and orderly enterprise with no poverty and no crime (or so the visitors were led to believe), it had state-of-the-art sanitation and transportation systems, and its visitors were awed by its beauty as well as its displays of commercial and technological

achievement. Outside the Fair's gates lay a sooty and gray city with filthy streets and poor sanitation, a city filled with ethnic and racial tension, and a city whose economic woes doomed many of its inhabitants to a life of poverty with no prospect of a better future. It was little wonder that compared to Chicago and other American cities, the White City seemed, in the words of the *Tribune*, to be "a realization of Utopia."

The Fair's design had a profound influence on American taste in architecture for at least the next twenty years, although it was not without its detractors. Chicago architect Louis Sullivan, for example, who had designed the Fair's Transportation Building, thought that the Fair was an "appalling calamity" architecturally, and that the reliance on European forms and the monumental idiom would set American architecture back "half a century." Nevertheless, the White City soon served as the model for the "City Beautiful" movement in the United States.

The City Beautiful movement sought to improve life in American cities through beautification in architecture, landscaping, and city planning, and its projects typically included broad, tree-lined boulevards, public parks, and a core of monumental but low-slung civic buildings (the "civic center"). Its proponents thought that the movement would have a number of beneficial effects. First, it would bring American cities into a cultural parity with European cities through its use of the Beaux-Arts idiom. Second, an inviting civic center would bring the upper classes back, if not to live, to at least work and spend money in the urban environment. Third, and most importantly, the beautification of American cities was seen as a way to cure the social ills of the time, as the beauty of the city would inspire civic loyalty and moral rectitude in the impoverished. In this sense, the Columbian Exposition embodied the Progressive dream that America's social problems could be solved simply by building and planning, and without a redistribution of wealth.

Many other themes introduced at the Fair still play an important role in American life: the idea that progress is measured by technological advancement; the predominance of corporations and the professional class in the power structure of the country; the triumph of the consumer culture; and the equation of European forms with "high culture." The Fair's more pedestrian legacy includes the Ferris Wheel, Cracker Jacks, Juicy Fruit Gum, Pabst Blue Ribbon beer, ragtime music, diet soda pop, and Quaker Oats. Today, two structures remain as impressive symbols of the Exposition. The "Golden Lady" sculpture is a smaller version of Daniel Chester French's Statue of the Republic that originally stood at the foot of the Court of Honor. The original Fine Arts Palace now houses Chicago's Museum of Science and Industry.

This beautiful bird's-eye view of the fairgrounds was one of many maps and guidebooks of the Fair, a good number of which were represented as the "Official Guidebook of the Columbian Exposition." Besides the White City, this map shows the three main entrances to the fairgrounds: the railway terminal located southwest of the grounds, the Lake Michigan pier with its moveable sidewalk to the east, and the street entrance from the Midway.

BIRD'S-

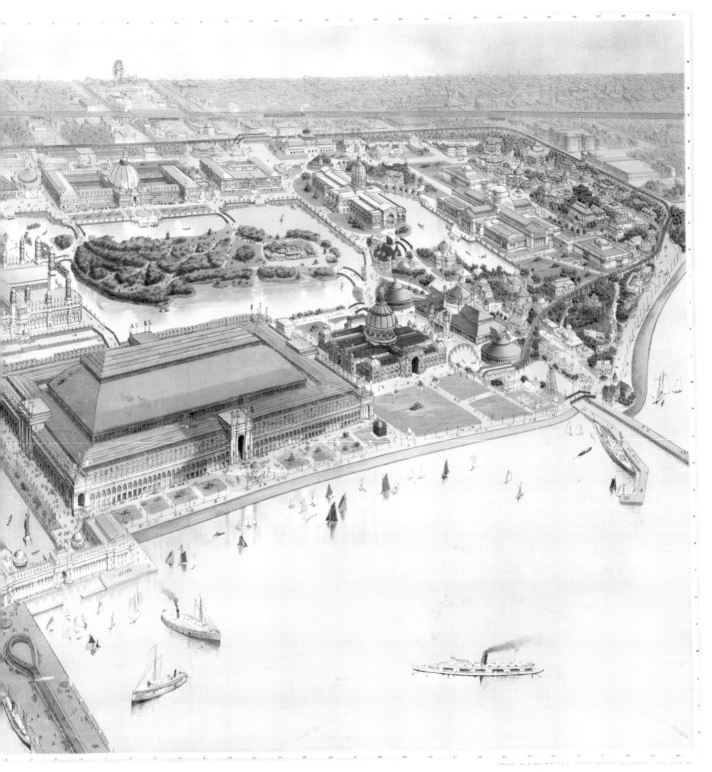

F THE WORLD'S COLUMBIAN EXPOSITION, CHICAGO, 1893.

THE BURNHAM PLAN

The Great Harbor Plan

Title: Bird's-Eye View of Grant Park at Night
Date Issued: 1909
Cartographer: Jules Guerin
Published: *Plan of Chicago prepared under the direction of the*
Commercial Club during the years MCMVI, MCMVII, and MCMVIII (Chicago)
Pencil, Watercolor, and Tempura, 80 x 114.3 cm
Chicago Historical Society, ICHi-03550

Shortly after the Columbian Exposition closed, Daniel Burnham began to publicly suggest that the design concepts behind the exposition's "White City" should be applied to the city of Chicago. Many of Chicago's prominent citizens agreed that the city was in dire need of better and greater planning, for after the Great Fire much of the city had been haphazardly rebuilt and the result was a rather inefficient infrastructure. In 1906, two of Chicago's most prestigious civic clubs, the Merchant's Club and the Commercial Club (of which Burnham was a member), formed committees to appraise the physical conditions of the city and to discover how these conditions might be improved. In spite of Burnham's membership in the Commercial Club, it was the Merchant's

Club of Chicago that officially engaged Burnham and Edward H. Bennett to undertake "for the city of Chicago and its environs a comprehensive and logical plan, indicating those lines of convenience and beauty along which the city should develop in the decades to come." After less than a year, the two civic clubs merged in recognition of the importance of the project, and took the name of the older and more established Commercial Club.

Burnham and Bennett spent three years preparing the plan, with the extensive involvement of various committees of the newly reorganized Commercial Club. Before the plan was completed, there had been ninety-two official committee meetings and hundreds of meetings with city officials and private consultants. The

final plan was presented to the public as the *Plan of Chicago* on the Fourth of July, 1909. Although the final plan was the result of a committee process, there was no doubt that Daniel Burnham was its principal author, and the plan soon became known as the "Burnham Plan." Burnham's plan was not only to influence much of the future growth of Chicago; it set new standards of development and principles of city planning.

The success of Burnham's plan hinged on its practical approach to the pressing needs of a city that was recognized to be "a center of industry and traffic." In the words of the authors, attention was paid to "the betterment of commercial facilities; to methods of transportation for persons and for goods; to removing the obstacles which prevent or obstruct circulation; and to the increase of convenience." The plan had been commissioned by commercial interests, after all, and its adoption rested on the satisfaction of those interests. On the other hand, the Burnham Plan had its roots in the City Beautiful movement, and this movement's principles directed the satisfaction of these interests.

The *Plan of Chicago* moved the industrial use of land away from the city center and the lakefront to surrounding accessible areas. The city had a "dignity to maintain," and its center was to be a place of "impressive groupings of buildings," while the lakefront would become fronted by parks and beaches. The plan proposed high-density inner city development that was oriented to transit stations, neighborhoods that were connected by pedestrian pathways, and a network of boulevards that linked open spaces and parks. It recommended a greenbelt of forest preserves surrounding the city, and identified other sensitive landscapes as areas to be protected. Outside the city, communities were envisioned as railroad suburbs in which most people could live within walking distance of a train station.

The *Plan of Chicago* has subsequently guided much of Chicago's development. Indeed, although some of its recommendations proved too ambitious, it to this day influences many civic improvements. "Make no little plans," Burnham advised. "They have no magic to stir men's blood and probably themselves will not be realized. Make big plans; aim high in hope and work, remembering that a noble logical diagram once recorded will never die but long after we are gone will be a living thing, asserting with growing intensity."

The *Plan of Chicago* contains 164 pages, and 143 visionary illustrations. Among the latter were eleven maps prepared by Jules Guerin, including the one presented here. Prepared by Guerin in late 1907 and early 1908 at his New York studio, these maps were the great splendor of the *Plan of Chicago*. Burnham or Bennett would have proposed their general layout, and prepared small sketches that were sent to draftsmen to render into large-scale pencil layouts. These were then sent to Guerin to convert into his watercolor scenes. As seen in the map here, Burnham proposed a great harbor off Grant Park. This harbor, framed by a northern pier with a lighthouse at Chicago Avenue and a southern pier at Roosevelt Avenue, was to be the centerpiece of a chain of lakeside parks running the length of the city. This great harbor was never built, nor was the smaller harbor from Lake Street on the north and Twelfth Street on the south. Instead, Chicago built the 3000-foot-long Municipal Pier to the north at Grand Avenue.

This pier, which was built between 1914 and 1916, is now known as Navy Pier. The southern pier was never built. Navy Pier thrived between the years 1918 and 1930, when it combined the business of shipping with public entertainment (such as concerts and dances). During the Depression, the pier's shipping traffic declined, although it was still used for cultural events. In the days of World War II, it served as a naval aviator training station. After the Navy moved out, it became the home of the Chicago branch of the University of Illinois for the years from 1947 to 1965. In the 1990s, the pier was completely renovated, and today it is one of Chicago's premier entertainment destinations. Among its attractions are: a 148-foot-tall replica of the Ferris Wheel that was built for the 1893 World's Columbian Exposition; a forty-four-foot-tall carousel; the Skyline Stage, which is a one-hundred-foot-high vaulted structure that is used as a 1500-seat theater in the summer and an ice-skating rink in the winter; a children's museum; a stained glass museum; and the Shakespeare Repertory Theater, which was modeled after London's Swan Theater. The pier is also home to numerous restaurants and shops, a movie theater, and is the starting point of many boat tours.

THE UNION STOCK YARDS

The Rossiter Map

Title: Map of the Union Stock Yards of Chicago showing railroads & connections
Date Drawn: 1891
Cartographer: F. C. Rossiter
Published: Separately
Lithograph, 106 x 71.8 cm
Chicago HIstorical Society, ICHi-27741

For about a century, the Union Stock Yards was one of Chicago's world-famous wonders, and one of the city's largest tourist attractions. "Not to see the Yards is to miss seeing Chicago," noted one guidebook. An elaborate and sprawling complex of animal pens, slaughterhouses, and packinghouses, the stockyards would assault the visitor's senses. Approaching, one could see smoke rising from the packinghouses; then would come the smell—a sickening stench of animal manure, urine, blood, and death. Inside the Yards, there were bellows of doomed cattle, squeals of hogs about to be slaughtered, bleats of sheep, and the crack of the whip of wranglers on horseback. "You shall find them about six miles from the city," wrote Rudyard Kipling of the stockyards, "and once having seen them you will never forget the sight."

In the early 1850s, Chicago was primarily a connection point for transporting livestock from the West to the rest of the country, and small stockyards, such as Lake Shore Yard and Cottage Grove Yard, dotted the city along various rail lines. The meatpacking industry at the time was centered in the cities of Cincinnati and St. Louis, whose river locations gave them the competitive advantage of easy transportation. Chicago's emergence as a major railroad hub overcame this advantage, however, as transportation by train was both faster and less expensive than by water. Then came the Civil War, halting all barge traffic down the Mississippi River; Chicago's meatpacking industry boomed as it worked to meet the Union Army's demand.

Chicago's scattered stockyards, many of which had been surrounded by residential housing in the growing city, could not handle the exponential growth of the city's meatpacking industry. In 1863, the city had at least forty-five packinghouses and the railroads agreed to meet the growing demand for centralization by building the Union Stock Yards in a marshy site outside the city limits. Financed by nine railroad companies, the Union Stock Yard and Transit Company began construction in June 1865. To make the tract of swampland usable, one thousand men dug thirty miles of ditches and drains that emptied into a a fork of the Chicago River, later to become known as "Bubbly Creek" as its waters thickened with pungent slaughterhouse offal. Designed by civil engineer Octave Chanute, the Union Stock Yards officially opened on Christmas Day, 1865.

By the late 1860s, the Union Stock Yards included enough animal pens and sheds to hold 25,000 head of cattle, 80,000 hogs, and 25,000 sheep, all at the same time. In 1879, an elaborate limestone gate, designed by the architectural firm of Burnham & Root, was built to mark the front entrance to the Stock Yards. The gate included a large central arch for livestock and wagons, flanked by smaller arches for pedestrians, and a security office on the side. A limestone steer head over the central arch is traditionally thought to represent

"Sherman," a prize-winning bull named after John B. Sherman, one of the founders of the Union Stock Yard and Transit Company.

Soon after the creation of the Union Stock Yards, Chicago's meatpacking companies began to establish operations around the yards. One of the first to move into the area was Phillip Armour's plant in 1867. Since there was no refrigeration at the time, meatpacking was limited to cold weather months. In 1872, however, Armour began using newly invented ice-cooled units to preserve meat, which allowed his meatpacking operations to continue year-round. Americans at the time were used to pork in packed form—be it ham, bacon, or sausage—but they had always eaten beef fresh. In fact, in its

early years, the Stock Yards was merely a way station for cattle intended to be marketed as fresh meat. After being sold in Chicago, the cattle would be shipped in railcars to New York, Boston, and other cities.

In 1882, Gustavus Swift developed the first refrigerated railroad car, thus making it possible to ship processed meat instead of live animals to America's eastern markets. Chicago's meatpacking industry again boomed, and at the turn of the century, it employed more than twenty-five thousand people and produced eighty-two percent of the meat consumed in the United States. In addition to processing meat, the packinghouses made creative and lucrative use of slaughterhouse by-products, and factories were built to

manufacture such items as leather, soap, fertilizer, glue, imitation ivory, gelatin, shoe polish, buttons, perfume, and violin strings. A common expression was that "Chicago packers used every part of the hog but the squeal."

By 1900, the stockyard grew to 475 acres, contained fifty miles of road, and had 130 miles of track along its perimeter. During the peak days of World War I, fifteen million animals moved through Chicago annually, and the city's meatpackers processed almost nine million pounds of meat per day. After World War II, however, the days of the Union Stock Yards were numbered. Refrigerated trucks and the interstate highway system allowed packinghouses to move out of the city that they had once relied upon for railroad access. Meatpackers also began

conducting business directly with farmers, making stockyards obsolete. In 1955, the first major meatpacker, Wilson & Company, quit its Chicago base of operations. Others quickly followed suit, and in 1971, the Union Stock Yard & Transit Company closed forever. The area has since become an industrial park that houses various small factories, none involved in the meatpacking industry. Nothing remains of Chicago's world-famous wonder except for the giant limestone arch, now a city landmark, which once marked the entrance to the stockyards.

This 1891 view of the stockyards provides a good sense of the fact that the Yards was almost a city unto itself: laid out on a gird pattern, its streets had whimsical names such as "Packers Avenue" and "Broadway"; the Yards

had its own water and electrical systems, a hotel (The Transit House), and even its own daily newspaper, *The Drover's Journal*. The stockyards themselves are divided into four divisions, lettered A to D. The numerous branches of the consortium of nine railroads that built the Yards are a prominent feature, and a canal—the Stock Yards Slip—connects the Yards to the river.

MAP OF SIN

The W. T. Stead Map

Title: Nineteenth district, first ward
Date Drawn: 1894
Cartographer: W. T. Stead
Published: *If Christ came to Chicago: A Plea for the union of*
all who love in the service of all who suffer. Laird & Lee (Chicago)
Folded Sheet, 14 x 23 cm
Newberry Library, Case oF 548.5 S8 1894

William T. Stead, a well-known and scholarly British journalist and minister, had come to America in 1893 to study its newspapers. His stop in Chicago changed his plans. He found Chicago the most interesting city in the United States, and wrote that "it is the only city which has had anything romantic about its recent history. The building of the city, and still more its rebuilding, are one of the romances which light up the somewhat monotonous materialism of Modern America."

Stead was impressed by Chicago's potential, but dismayed by its social problems. Earlier in the year, a depression had swept over most of the country, but Chicago, thus far, had been insulated from the worst by the success of the World's Columbian Exposition. When it closed, however, the bottom fell out of the local economy. The thousands of people who had built and run the fair had nowhere to go; as winter set in, over twenty percent of the city's workforce was laid off and at least ten percent of the population faced starvation on a daily basis.

On November 12, 1893, Stead, at his own expense, convened a civic meeting to discuss the question, "Whether if Christ came to Chicago he wouldn't find anything in Chicago he would have altered?" Attendees of the meeting, each invited by Stead, included a cross section of all of Chicago—there were corporate titans, judges, labor leaders, women temperance reformers, saloonkeepers, gambling bosses, madams, and matrons of distinguished families. At the meeting, Stead attacked the city's powerful persons and institutions, and its churches and temperance groups. What is wrong, he asked, with a city where a homeless wanderer would rather take his "chances" with saloonkeepers and madams than with the people in its churches and chapels?

The outcome of the meeting was the formation of a committee to form a Civic Federation, the purpose of which would be to "drive Satan from Chicago." Stead also mentioned at the meeting the need for "a comprehensive report of the condition of evil in Chicago," which would serve as the platform for the new civic coalition. By February of 1894, he had finished the bill of

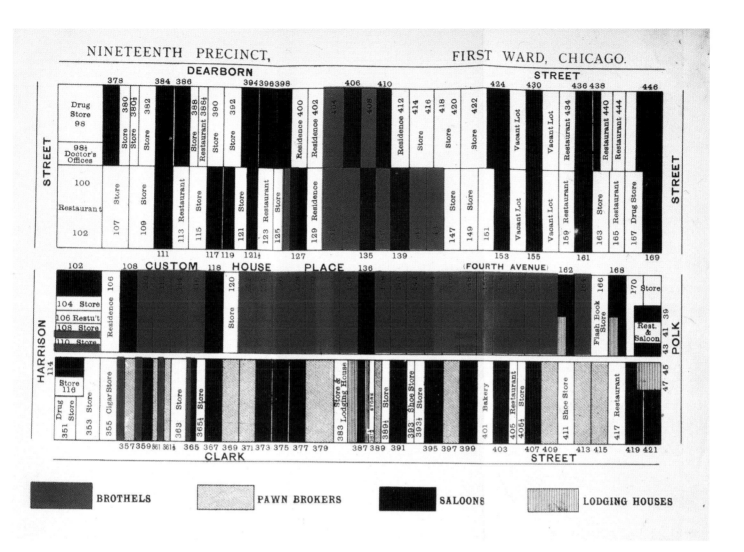

indictment, which he entitled, *If Christ Came to Chicago!*

Its publication shook the city. "Existing evils are exposed," exclaimed the *New York World*, "and the chief abettors are named without regard to persons or consequence." Its controversial cover was a reproduction of a painting of an angry Jesus driving the money changers from the temple. The original faces of the money changers, however, were now caricatures of some of the biggest political and business leaders of Chicago. To fuel public outrage, the frontispiece of the book was this map of the Levee District, color-coded to indicate saloons, pawnbrokers, and brothels.

The Levee was Chicago's major vice district, and was located in an area just south of the Loop. It took its name from the influx of Southern gamblers to the area ("Levee" often being the designation for the raunchiest part of southern river towns). Here one could find saloons, bordellos, gambling parlors, opium dens, and almost any other vice imaginable. Fair-goers found the heart of the district crowded, gaslit and well patrolled by police—as both the city and its vice lords were concerned with keeping the area safe for out-of-towners. The appendix of Stead's book listed the addresses, proprietors, and tax-paying owners of the properties in the district used for indecent purposes. News of the book's cover, its "map of sin," and its list of vice landlords swept through the city in days before its publication "like another Chicago fire."

HULL-HOUSE MAPS

The Wage and Nationality Maps

Title: Wage map no. 1, Polk to Twelfth
Date Issued: 1895
Cartographer: Samuel Sewell Greeley
Published: *Hull-House Maps and Papers: A Presentation of Nationalities and Wages in a Congested District of Chicago, Together with Comments and Essays on Problems Growing Out of the Social Conditions.* Thomas Y. Crowell (New York)
Colored Sheet, 36 x 112 cm
Newberry Library, Map 6F G4104.C6 E2 1897. G7 Wage

Title: Nationalities map no. 1, Polk to Twelfth
Date Issued: 1895
Cartorapher: Samuel Sewell Greeley
Published: *Hull-House Maps and Papers: A Presentation of Nationalities and Wages in a Congested District of Chicago, Together with comments and Essays on Problems Growing Out of the Social Conditions.* Thomas Y. Crowell (New York)
Colored Sheet, 36 x 112 cm
Newberry Library, Map 6F G4104.C6 E2 1895.G7 Nationalities

In 1889, Jane Addams and Ellen Gates Starr rented a house that had been built by Charles G. Hull at 800 South Halsted Street. There they opened Hull-House, one of the first settlement houses in North America. The settlement movement had begun with Toynebee Hall in London, and its main purpose was to develop and improve life in a neighborhood as a whole (as opposed to providing selected services to the people in a neighborhood).

Addams and Starr first set out to better the lives of the many immigrants in their Halsted Street neighborhood by opening a kindergarten, which soon was expanded to include a day nursery and infant care center. Eventually Hull-House would provide secondary and college-level extension classes, as well as evening classes on civil rights and civil duties. As word of the work at Hull-House spread, donations began to pour in and additional buildings were purchased. Hull-House developed into a complex that covered half a city block and included a gymnasium, social and cooperative clubs, shops, housing for children, and playgrounds.

Addams, Starr, and other Hull-House associates were instrumental in the enactment of state child labor laws, and in the establishment of juvenile courts and juvenile protection agencies. They contributed to the women's suffrage and the international peace movements, and assisted in the development of local trade union organizations, social welfare programs, and adult education classes. Hull-House activists were also firmly convinced that once the overwhelming suffering of the poor was publicized, meaningful reforms would be quickly put into place.

Although this assumption proved to be overly optimistic, the associates of Hull-House established a reputation as dedicated investigators unafraid to venture into some of Chicago's poorest neighborhoods. In 1893, Congress commissioned a nationwide survey, *A Special Investigation of the Slums of Great*

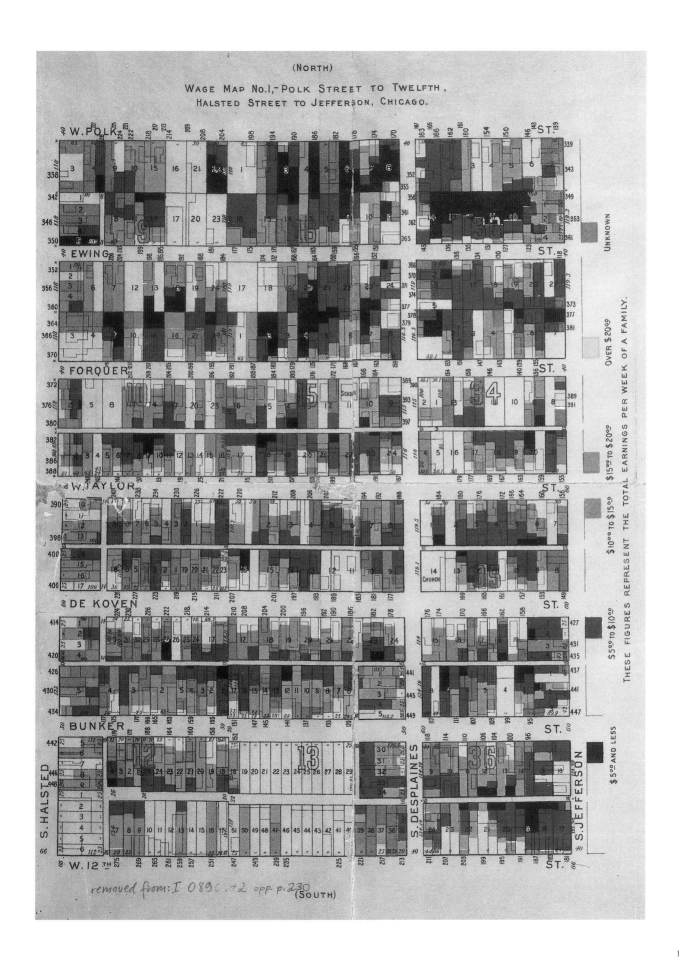

WAGE MAP No.I,–POLK STREET TO TWELFTH,
HALSTED STREET TO JEFFERSON, CHICAGO.

THESE FIGURES REPRESENT THE TOTAL EARNINGS PER WEEK OF A FAMILY.

UNKNOWN

OVER $20.00

$15.00 TO $20.00

$10.00 TO $15.00

$5.00 TO $10.00

$5.00 AND LESS

removed from: I 0890.42 opp. p. 230

(SOUTH)

161

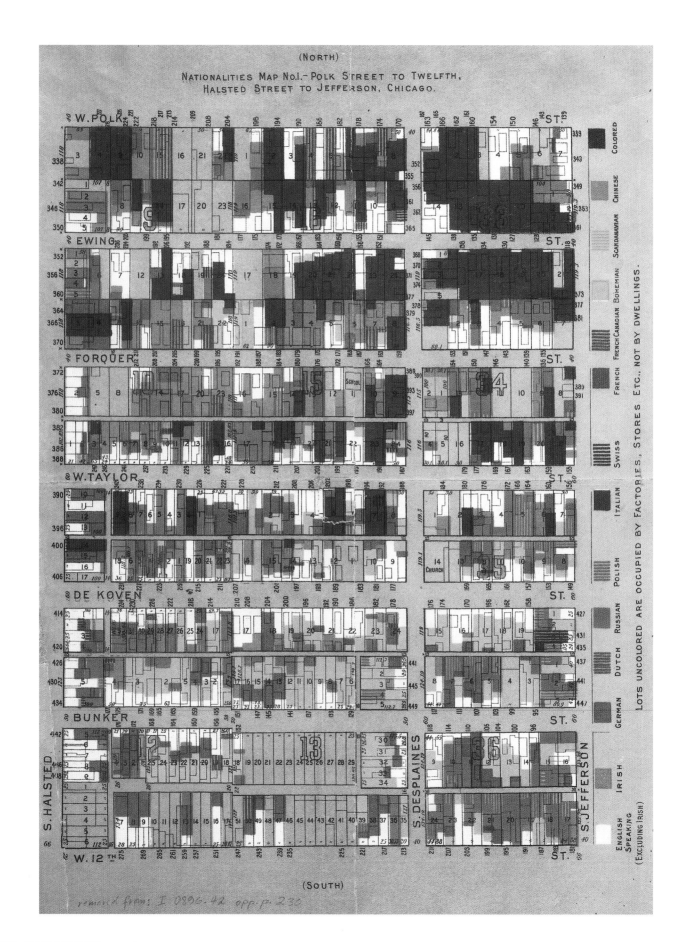

Cities, to assess the extent of poverty in urban areas. When Hull-House resident Florence Kelley was selected to lead the survey effort in Chicago, she and her fellow residents took it upon themselves to extend the project: they set out to create a series of maps documenting poverty in Chicago (using Charles Booth's maps of poverty in London as their model).

During the spring and summer of 1893, Hull-House associates administered an extensive survey to every house, tenement and room in their surrounding neighborhood (an area bounded by Halsted Street on the west, State Street on the east, Polk Street on the north, and Twelfth Street on the south). They represented their findings on street maps of the area, documenting the nationality, wages, and employment history of each resident. On the maps, each house in the neighborhood is colored to reflect the birthplace of the head of the household and the family's wages. In those cases where multiple families with different nationalities or wages occupied the same housing unit, Kelley and her group created cartograms, allocating space on the map in proportion to the number of individuals in each nationality or wage group.

The two maps shown here are sheets 1 (of four) of the Wage and Nationality maps published by Hull-House. The color coding for the Wage Maps represents household weekly earnings as follows: Black = $5 and less, Blue = $5–$10, Red = $10–$15, Green = $15–$20, Yellow = over $20, and Purple = unknown. The Nationality Maps illustrate the following ethnic and racial diversity in the neighborhood: White = English Speaking (excluding Irish), Green = Irish, Dark Green = Greek, Green Stripes = Syrian, Purple = German, Purple Stripes = Dutch, Red = Russian, Red Stripes = Polish, Blue = Italian, Blue Stripes = Swiss, Brown = French, Brown Stripes = French Canadian, Orange = Chinese, Yellow Stripes = Scandinavian, and Black = Colored.

GANGLAND MAP

The Bruce-Roberts Map

Title: A Map of Chicago's gangland from authentic sources: designed to inculcate the most important principles of piety and virtue in young persons, and graphically portray the evils and sin of large cities
Date Issued: 1931
Cartographer: Bruce-Roberts, Inc.
Published: Bruce-Roberts, Inc. (Chicago)
Lithograph, 48 x 62 cm
Newberry Library, Map +G 10896.548

During the Prohibition Era, Chicago developed a worldwide reputation as a haven for underworld figures. Although only partially deserved, this reputation was perpetuated by popular literature, Hollywood films, and maps such as this one. This publicity helped turned many Chicago "Gangster Era" figures into celebrities, including "Baby Face" Nelson, George "Machine Gun" Kelly, John Dillinger, "Pretty Boy" Floyd, and the most notorious of them all, Al "Scarface" Capone.

Al Capone came to Chicago in 1920 from Brooklyn to work for Johnny Torrio. Torrio, who had also come to Chicago from Brooklyn, was there to help run the business affairs of his relative, "Big Jim" Colosimo. At the time, the politically connected Colosimo was the kingpin of Chicago's flesh trade, and operated one of the city's most popular nightclubs, the Colosimo Café. Despite his profession, Colosimo socialized with the rich and famous, and regulars at his nightclub included Enrico Caruso and Clarence Darrow. Often called "Diamond Jim"—he wore diamond rings on all his fingers, as well as diamond-studded belts and buckles—Colosimo built the first truly organized crime syndicate in Chicago.

Big Jim's interest in the business began to wane after he married a young singer that worked in his nightclub. When Torrio pressed him to build a liquor syndicate after the onset of Prohibition, Big Jim resisted. Torrio, who recognized the potential of bootlegging, was loath to stand by as other gangs divided Chicago into liquor distribution territories. On May 11, 1920, while waiting for two truckloads of liquor at his club, Big Jim was murdered. His funeral was the first of many great Chicago gangster memorials, and as described by Laurence Bergreen, was "a gaudy demonstration more appropriate to . . . a powerful political figure or popular entertainer ... an event that priests and police captains alike attended to pay their last respects to the sort of man they were supposed to condemn. Colosimo was universally recognized as Chicago's premier pimp, yet his honorary pallbearers included three judges, a congressman, an assistant state attorney, and no less than nine Chicago aldermen."

Torrio quickly extended the late Colosimo's empire into the bootlegging business. His syndicate already had the political connections necessary to thwart interference from the police, and the production and distribution of beer and whisky proved to be an immensely profitable enterprise. In fact, it was so profitable that Torrio is believed to have approached the leaders of Chicago's top criminal gangs and suggested that there was enough money to be made for everyone. All that was needed, he argued, was for each gang to maintain territorial sovereignty. He urged each gang to focus its efforts on the control of liquor distribution in its own area, and to not encroach upon the terrain of others.

At the time, the distribution of liquor in Chicago was divided among the following gangs: The Johnny Torrio/Al Capone Gang controlled the Loop and near south side, Dion O'Banion and his associates the near north side, and Klondike O'Donnell and his brothers the near northwest side. Roger Touhy, who claimed only to be a bootlegger and not involved in vice, worked the far northwest side. The "Terrible" Genna brothers reigned over the near west side Taylor Street area. The far west side was controlled by Terry Druggan and Frankie Lake and their Valley Gang. On the southwest side, both the O'Donnell brothers and the Frankie Saltis/Joe McErland Gang were active in bootlegging. These various gangs adopted Torrio's plan, and their coalition ran smoothly—at least for a while.

In 1923, reform candidate William Dever was elected mayor of Chicago, and he immediately had police clamp down on the city's speakeasies. His reforms soon forced the Torrio Syndicate to relocate operations to the town of Cicero, where an alliance was quickly formed with that city's politicians. In particular, the syndicate—with Al Capone now assuming more of a leadership role—helped carry the election for Cicero's Republican Party; in return, the gang was given free reign to sell liquor in the town. Chicago's gangs, which were usually centered in immigrant areas, worked in the same manner. In exchange for delivering the vote, their criminal enterprise would be allowed to flourish, with the understanding that at least part of the proceeds would be delivered to the local political organization.

The alliance of Chicago's various gangs began to unravel as stepped-up pressure by the Dever administration caused liquor sales to dwindle. This forced Chicago's bootleggers into direct competition with one other, and territorial encroachments soon followed. The worst problem was the antagonism between Dion O'Banion and the Genna brothers. The Genna brothers had begun selling liquor in O'Banion territory, and O'Banion retaliated by high-jacking Genna trucks. Torrio worked as a conciliator, and O'Banion offered him a way to maintain the peace. O'Banion would retire to Colorado if Torrio bought out his interest in the Sieben brewery, which was located at 1464 North Larrabee Street. Torrio accepted the offer, but it was a set-up: O'Banion had prior knowledge that the brewery was about to be raided, and when it was, thirty-one bootleggers, including Torrio, were arrested. Not only did Torrio end up in jail, O'Banion refused to return the money he had received for the now padlocked brewery. O'Banion sealed his own fate by bragging about how he had scammed Torrio. At noon on November 10, 1924, O'Banion was gunned down in his floral shop.

Although the police were unable to solve O'Banion's murder, his associates knew full well who was responsible and they vowed revenge. From that day on, Torrio and Capone were constantly on guard. In January of the following year, Torrio was shot by two O'Banion Gang members, "Hymie" Weiss and "Bugs" Moran.

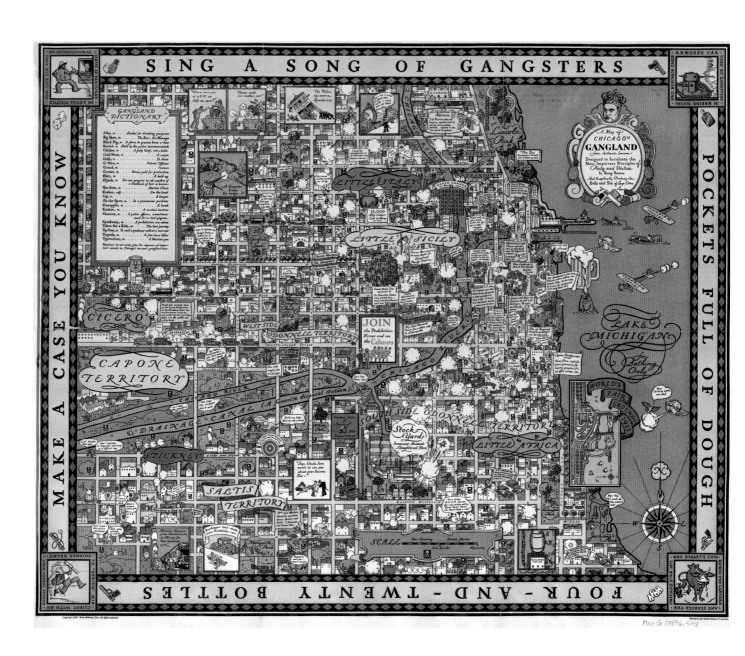

Torrio recovered from his wounds and a short time later entered the Lake County jail to serve out a nine-month sentence stemming from the Sieben's brewery incident. While in jail, Torrio decided that he had had enough, and called Capone to his cell. He was retiring from the Chicago rackets, he told Capone, and was turning over his entire operation to Al. It was quite a legacy, and included nightclubs, whorehouses, gambling joints, breweries and speakeasies. Within two years, Capone was earning $60 million a year from alcohol sales alone; other rackets earned him an additional $45 million a year.

The collapse of the Torrio coalition meant that Capone faced war with other Chicago gangs—and the result was the so-called "Beer Wars" of the late 1920s. During this period, the gangs generally aligned themselves according to ethnic ties. The Irish, Polish, and Jewish gangsters, such as the west side O'Donnells and the Saltis-McErlane Gang, joined forces with O'Banion's successor, Hymie Weiss. The Sicilians, notably the Gennas and most other Italians, stuck with Capone. So did Druggan and Lake, whose Valley Gang was headquartered in the near west side Maxwell Street area immediately adjacent to the Taylor Street Italian stronghold.

After over two hundred gangland slayings, the war culminated on February 14, 1929 in the S.M.C. Cartage garage at 2122 N. Clark. In what became known as the St. Valentine's Day Massacre, seven members of the old O'Banion Gang, now led by Bugs Moran, were machine-gunned to death by forces loyal to Capone. The St. Valentine's Day Massacre established the supremacy of the Capone mob as the leading force in Chicago's underworld and catapulted Capone into the national limelight. By 1930, Al Capone, then only thirty-one years of age, became the supreme overlord of crime in Chicago, and as estimated by the *Chicago Daily News*, controlled 6,000 speakeasies and 2,000 handbooks for betting on horse races. The combined revenue from these activities plus prostitution and racketeering was calculated to be $6,260,000 a week.

This *Map of Chicago's Gangland* pays homage to Capone by placing a crown on his portrait of at the top of its cartouche. Although it is a tongue-in-cheek map for tourists, it does give an accurate representation of the history of Chicago's gangs in the 1920s. Numbers in red circles give a sequence of important events in Chicago's ten-year gangland war, starting with the killing of Big Jim Colosimo. The next

is the shooting of Dion O'Banion, and then a series of events leads up to the St. Valentine's Day Massacre, and ends with what is labeled the "Gangster's Waterloo"—the shooting of *Tribune* reporter Alfred "Jake" Lingle. The location of various gang territories and warehouses are indicated, the county morgue is located, and skull and crossbones mark the reputed locations of gangland slayings.

CHICAGO'S JAZZ SPOTS

The Esquire Map

Title: Chicago Jazz Spots 1914–1928
Date Issued: 1946
Cartographer: Paul Eduard Miller & Richard M. Jones
Published: *Esquire's 1946 Jazz Collection* (New York)
Folded Sheet, 43 x 51 cm
Author's Collection

By the early 1920s, Chicago had become the focal point for America's only indigenous art form—jazz. Although this development is often attributed to musicians finding their way north after New Orleans's Storyville district was closed in 1917, the story is not quite that simple. For in the early decades of the twentieth century there began a "Great Migration" of African Americans from the South to the North. These migrants came north in search of a more promising future, and Chicago was their Mecca. During World War I, the *Chicago Defender* encouraged migration from the South to Chicago and often listed churches and other organizations that would be there to help. And there was

the Illinois Central Railway, which led directly from the Mississippi Delta to Chicago, where factories needed workers and paid decent wages.

The African-American population in Chicago tripled in the teenage years of the twentieth century, and most of the immigrants found their way to an already thriving community on the South Side of Chicago. Known at the time as the "Black Belt," the center of this neighborhood was a stretch of State Street from Thirty-First Street to Thirty-Fifth Street called "The Stroll." The Stroll was a flourishing business district by day and an entertainment hub by night. It was, according to the *Chicago Whip*, "the Bohemia of the Colored Folks," where the shops and

restaurants never closed their doors. When Langston Hughes visited in 1918, he reported that there was "excitement from noon to noon," and that "midnight was like day. The street was full of workers and gamblers, prostitutes and pimps, church goers and sinners." There were clubs that catered to blacks only, and others, called "black-and-tans," that welcomed both blacks and whites.

For a jazz musician stepping off the train at Chicago's Twelfth Street Station, here was the Promised Land—there was plenty of work and good pay. (Louis Armstrong, for example, received $1.50 a day for work in New Orleans; in Chicago, his pay was $52.50 a week.) It was a time, band leader Eddie Condon would later claim, that a trumpet held up in the air along State Street would play itself. This is not to say, of course, that there was no jazz in Chicago before Storyville closed. Indeed, Chicago boasted major musical talent and famous venues well before then. The Pekin Theater at 2700 South State Street was active as early as 1904; the future leader of the Vendome Orchestra, Erskine Tate, played his first violin recital in Chicago in 1910; Wilbur Sweatman was in Chicago playing clarinet in 1906; and Jelly Roll Morton led a band at the Richelieu starting in 1914 and also appeared at the DeLuxe and Elite #2 Cafes during the years 1914 and 1915. Although various New Orleans musicians had already been north before 1917, Tom Brown's Ragtime Band (a white band) is generally recognized as the first band to come north, in 1915.

Soon Chicago had an unprecedented gathering of jazz talent, including names like King Oliver, Freddie Keppard, Louis Armstrong, Earl Hines, Jelly Roll Morton, Jimmie Noone, Sidney Bechet, Kid Ory, Lee Collins, and Johnny Dodds. The Stroll also attracted white musicians, who would head south from their north side gigs to listen and learn from the city's new arrivals. Among them were five graduates from

Austin High School on the city's west side: Jimmy and Dick McPartland, Bud Freeman, Frank Teschemacher, and Jim Lannigan. Dave Tough, Gene Krupa, Muggsy Spanier, and Eddie Condon would also become well-known Chicago musicians, and collectively these white musicians are credited with the creation of the "Chicago" jazz style of the 1920s.

This *Map of Chicago Jazz Spots* was prepared for *Esquire's Jazz Book*, which was published annually for three years, beginning in 1944. The 1945 edition contains a chapter devoted to the history of New Orleans Jazz, along with a map of the Storyville District. This map is from the 1946 edition, which devoted several chapters to the Chicago period of jazz. The map locates jazz clubs around the city (as well as various other city landmarks) during the years 1914–28, and is divided into three sections.

The first section takes up the left portion of the map, and shows the South Side from Twenty-Sixth Street on the north to Sixty-Third Street on the south, and from Dearborn Street on the west to Cottage Grove Avenue on the east. Two insets detail the businesses on each end of The Stroll, the top one showing the intersection of Thirty-First and South State, the bottom one the intersection of Thirty-

Fifth and State. This area of the city contained the greatest number of jazz venues, which were particularly dense along The Stroll. Places like the Grand and Vendome Theaters, the Dreamland Café, the Panama Club, the Fiume Café, the Plantation, the Monogram Theater, the Royal Gardens, the Sunset Café and dozens of other small spots could all be found in this four-block long section of South State Street.

The second section takes up most of the right half of the map, and pictures the Loop and the near south side. Its borders are Chicago Avenue on the north and Twenty-Second Street on south; Clark Street on the west, and Michigan Avenue on the east. Directly below this section (under the three horizontal lines) a small strip directly west of the Loop is depicted. This area's borders are Halsted Street on the east, Western Avenue on the west, Madison Avenue on the north, and Van Buren on the south. Jazz venues were more scattered in these two areas, and some are depicted more for their general interest rather than for their association with jazz (although most of them featured dance bands).

Fifty-two jazz spots are numbered on this map, beginning with the Pekin Theater (1). This was the most important site for entertainment before the arrival of New Orleans jazzmen in Chicago, and featured theater, stock productions, vaudeville, and a cabaret for dancing. Prior to World War I, the Big Grand Theater (5) played weekly runs of vaudeville acts, both black and white. Almost every singer who made a record during the 1920s appeared at the Grand, and the Original Creole Band played there while on a national tour in 1912. The Original Creole Band was also the first African-American band to play in the Loop when it performed at the North American Restaurant (37) in 1913. Two famous homes of white jazz were the Friar's Inn (46), where The New Orleans Rhythm Kings produced New Orleans style jazz, and the White City Ballroom (25), named after the 1893 Columbian Exposition.

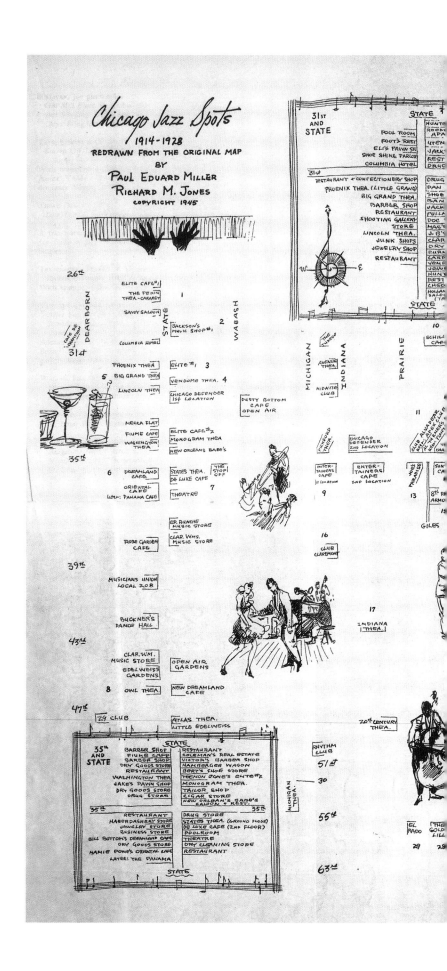

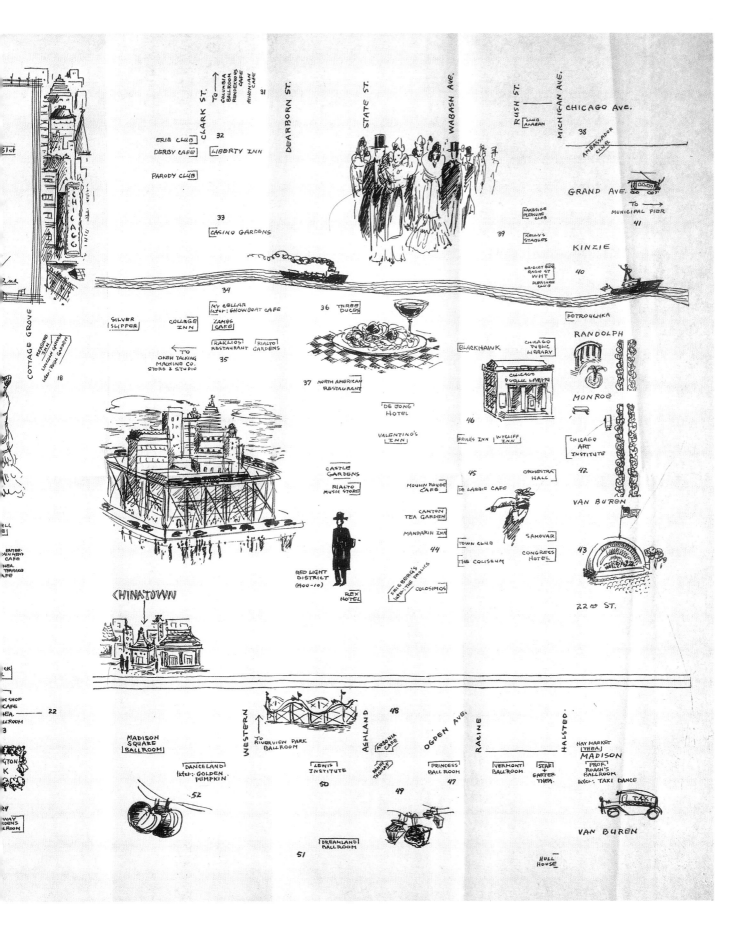

ETHNIC NEIGHBORHOOD MAP

The Grossman Map

Title: Chicago: its people and neighborhoods
Date Issued: 1982
Cartographer: Ron Grossman and William O. Neebe (designer)
Published: *Chicago Magazine* (Chicago)
Colored Sheet, 49 x 43 cm
Chicago Historical Society, ICHi-37868

Chicago has always been ethically diverse. Its earliest settlers included French traders, Native Americans, and a man of mixed French and Haitian ancestry. By the time the settlement organized into a town, the French had been displaced by Anglo-American settlers, and in 1836, Native Americans quit the area altogether. Harbor improvements and the prospects of the Illinois and Michigan Canal quickly stimulated the area's economy, and in 1837, when Chicago's population reached 4,000, the community was incorporated as a city.

As the city began to flourish, its industrial base grew, and so did its need for cheap, unskilled labor. Foreign-born immigrants supplied this demand, and most arrived in this country poor and ill-equipped for life in a bustling conurbation. Thus, they tended to seek support and companionship from others like themselves by forming social organizations, and would often settle together in large groups. As a result, ethnic enclaves could be found scattered throughout the city.

The Irish were the first foreigners to settle in Chicago in large numbers, arriving in the late 1830s to work on the Illinois and Michigan Canal. By 1850, when the population of Chicago numbered nearly 30,000, over twenty percent of the city was Irish (and thirty-nine percent of the city's foreign-born population). The Irish settled in Bridgeport on the south side, and on the north side near the river. There was also a considerable west side Irish population congregated in a squalid shantytown known as Conley's Patch.

In 1850, the English were Chicago's next largest immigrant group, and together with the Scottish and Welsh, made up twenty-nine percent of the city's total population and fifty-five percent of the foreign born. These immigrants from the United Kingdom were culturally similar to Chicago's Yankee settlers, and this made for their rapid assimilation into the city's growing middle class. Despite this fact, they still felt the need to associate with one another, and quickly formed their own fraternal organizations. Besides creating social outlets, these organizations lent aid to impoverished immigrants and to the children and widows of their deceased nationals.

The Germans were soon to become Chicago's largest immigrant group. In 1850, they already constituted seventeen percent of the city's population; twenty years later, they would grow to over twenty percent. The Germans settled throughout the city, but their largest concentration was on the north side, particularly on Clark Street and on Lincoln Avenue. Many also joined the Irish in Bridgeport, as the nearby stockyards attracted skilled German and Bohemian butchers to the area. Another neighborhood that was distinctly Irish and German was the Back of the Yards, which was adjacent to the Union Stock Yards; this area would later come to be dominated by people of Slavic origin.

The Scandinavian nations and the Netherlands also contributed many of Chicago's early residents, and by 1890, Swedes comprised the city's third-largest immigrant group. In 1900, Chicago was—after Stockholm—the world's largest "Swedish" city. The Scandinavians tended to gather on the near North Side near the old German settlements around Chicago Avenue just west of Wells Street, and like the Irish lived in some of the city's poorer districts. Gradually, many moved to the south side, especially to Englewood, while others trekked northward, and were replaced in the older districts by newer groups of immigrants.

Although the French played an important part in the early development of Chicago, they played virtually no role in the city's later development. In 1870, the French community numbered only 1,418, making them less than one percent of the total population. Other groups that would later play an important role in the history of the city were either very small or nonexistent in 1850. At that time, there were only 323 African Americans in Chicago; by 1870, this number swelled to 3,691. At this early date, African Americans were already segregated from the rest of the city's population—over eighty percent of the city's African Americans lived on the near south side.

By 1890, Chicago's population exceeded the one million mark, and nearly seventy-eight percent were either foreign-born or children of the foreign-born. The city that had started as a port and trading center for raw materials from the Midwest and finished goods from the East, was now the nation's railroad hub and an important manufacturing center. As it continued to prosper and grow, waves of immigrants, including Poles, Jews from many countries, Serbs, Russians, Czechs, Lithuanians, Italians, and Greeks, arrived in the city.

As the city expanded to accommodate its new arrivals, many older residents moved outward, the central areas quickly filling with newcomers. As a result, the ethnic makeup of Chicago's neighborhoods shifted over time: the city's growth went hand-in-hand with ethnic change. A substantial number of immigrants around the turn of the century came from Poland, and most settled in the northwestern sector of the city bounded by Chicago Avenue, Clybourn Avenue, and Carpenter Street. A significant number of Czechs also arrived at the end of the nineteenth century, and soon formed a colony called Pilsen between Halsted Street and Ashland Avenue south of Sixteenth Street. This area is now primarily inhabited by people of Mexican descent. Italian arrivals settled along Grand Avenue west of the river, in an area that had been previously occupied by Germans, Irish, and Scandinavians. Eastern European Jews flocked to an area on the west side bounded by Polk Street on the north, Blue Island Avenue on the west, Fifteenth Street on the south, and Stewart Avenue on the east.

There was a glaring exception to mobility of Chicago's immigrant groups. In the early decades of the twentieth century, a large number of African Americans migrated to Chicago from the South, and settled primarily on the city's south side. Once there, the new arrivals found that they

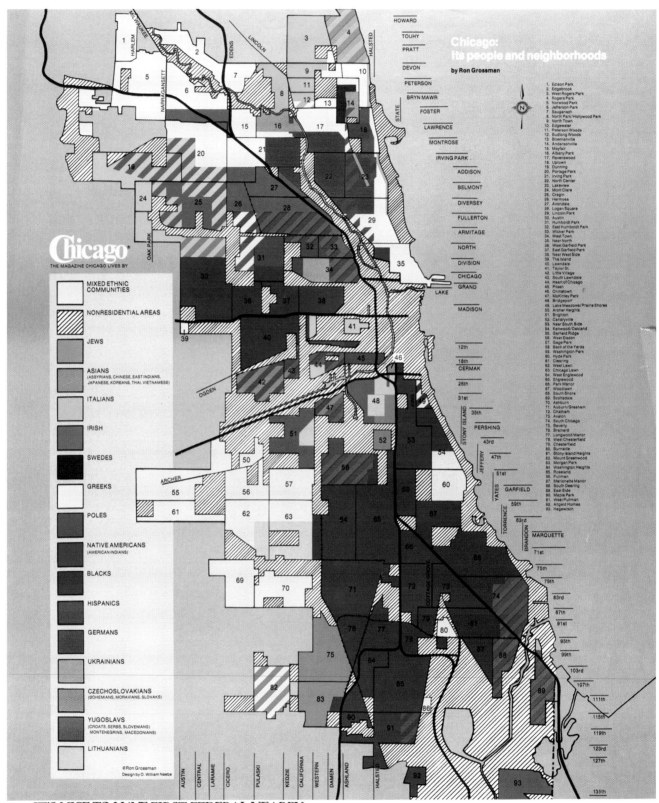

Chicago:
Its people and neighborhoods
by Ron Grossman

1. Edison Park
2. Edgebrook
3. West Rogers Park
4. Rogers Park
5. Norwood Park
6. Jefferson Park
7. Sauganash
8. North Park/Hollywood Park
9. North Town
10. Edgewater
11. Peterson Woods
12. Budlong Woods
13. Bowmanville
14. Andersonville
15. Mayfair
16. Albany Park
17. Ravenswood
18. Uptown
19. Dunning
20. Portage Park
21. Irving Park
22. North Center
23. Lakeview
24. Mont Clare
25. Cragin
26. Hermosa
27. Avondale
28. Logan Square
29. Lincoln Park
30. Austin
31. Humboldt Park
32. East Humboldt Park
33. Wicker Park
34. West Town
35. Near North
36. West Garfield Park
37. East Garfield Park
38. Near West Side
39. The Island
40. Lawndale
41. Taylor St.
42. Little Village
43. South Lawndale
44. Heart of Chicago
45. Pilsen
46. Chinatown
47. McKinley Park
48. Bridgeport
49. Lake Meadows/Prairie Shores
50. Archer Heights
51. Brighton
52. Canaryville
53. Near South Side
54. Kenwood/Oakland
55. Garfield Ridge
56. West Elsdon
57. Gage Park
58. Back of the Yards
59. Washington Park
60. Hyde Park
61. Clearing
62. West Lawn
63. Chicago Lawn
64. West Englewood
65. Englewood
66. Park Manor
67. Woodlawn
68. South Shore
69. Scottsdale
70. Ashburn
71. Auburn/Gresham
72. Chatham
73. Avalon
74. South Chicago
75. Beverly
76. Brainerd
77. Longwood Manor
78. West Chesterfield
79. Chesterfield
80. Burnside
81. Stony Island Heights
82. Mount Greenwood
83. Morgan Park
84. Washington Heights
85. Roseland
86. Pullman
87. Marionette Manor
88. South Deering
89. East Side
90. Maple Park
91. West Pullman
92. Altgeld Homes
93. Hegewisch

Chicago
THE MAGAZINE CHICAGO LIVES BY

MIXED ETHNIC COMMUNITIES

NONRESIDENTIAL AREAS

JEWS

ASIANS
(ASSYRIANS, CHINESE, EAST INDIANS, JAPANESE, KOREANS, THAI, VIETNAMESE)

ITALIANS

IRISH

SWEDES

GREEKS

POLES

NATIVE AMERICANS
(AMERICAN INDIANS)

BLACKS

HISPANICS

GERMANS

UKRAINIANS

CZECHOSLOVAKIANS
(BOHEMIANS, MORAVIANS, SLOVAKS)

YUGOSLAVS
(CROATS, SERBS, SLOVENIANS)
(MONTENEGRINS, MACEDONIANS)

LITHUANIANS

©Ron Grossman
Design by O. William Neebe

IT'S NICE TO HAVE FIRST FEDERAL NEARBY.

did not have the same housing opportunities as those immigrants that had arrived from abroad. Although most foreign immigrants found their first residence near the center of the city, typically amid conditions of squalor and deprivation, it was possible for those that found jobs and thrived in their new city to find better accommodations—if not the first generation, then at least the next. African Americans were not given the same opportunity, for no matter how successful they became, they were not free to relocate outside their established neighborhood.

Today, Chicago is one of the most ethnically, racially, and religiously diverse cities in the world. In 2000, more people claimed Polish ancestry in Chicago than any other ancestry, followed by Irish and German. At least forty-six percent of the more than 629,000 foreign-born people now living in Chicago entered the United States between 1990 and 2000. Spanish and Polish are the two most common languages spoken at home other than English.

The map shown here divides Chicago into ninety-three neighborhoods and shows the distribution of fifteen ethnic groups among these communities. Originally published in *Chicago Magazine*, it was later reproduced by a local savings and loan. The reverse side of the map describes eight ethnic Chicago neighborhood tours that one could take in the year 1982.

One must keep in mind, of course, that people of all ethnic backgrounds are spread out throughout the city (note, however, the distribution of "mixed ethnic" peoples). That being said, it is still possible to find people of similar ethnic backgrounds grouped together in various Chicago neighborhoods. Chicago's original immigrants, the Irish, are the most prominent ethnic group in the south side communities of Beverley, Morgan Park, Mount Greenwood, Canaryville, and Bridgeport. Germans remain concentrated in the north side communities of North Center, Ravenswood, Irving Park and Lincoln Park. Native Americans have returned to Chicago and live primarily in the Uptown neighborhood. Chicago's Polish population is spread out across the city in the communities of Avondale, Logan Square, Hermosa, Cragin, the Near South Side, Bridgeport, Brighton, and Hegewich. Perhaps the most striking feature of this map is its depiction of the continued segregation of Chicago's African Americans, who live primarily on the city's south side and in a strip of land that stretches from the near west side to the city's far west Austin neighborhood. neighborhood.

GRACELAND CEMETERY

The Rascher Map

Title: Map of Graceland Cemetery
Date Issued: c. 1876
Cartographer: Charles Rascher
Published: Separately
Folded Sheet, 53 x 87 cm
Newberry Library, map6F oG4104.C6:2G7 1861 .R3

Graceland Cemetery is one of Chicago's best-known and most historic cemeteries. It was established in 1860, and in 1861 received a perpetual charter from the State of Illinois. Originally located on eighty acres of land in the town of Lakeview, its southern boundary (now Irving Park Road) was two miles outside city limits. Its western boundary (now Clark Street) was Green Bay Road, an old Native American trail that followed a natural ridge—that is, high ground appropriate for a burial place.

The landscape architect H.W.S. Cleveland was responsible for much of the early design of Graceland. In the 1870s, in accordance with Cleveland's plan, sod was laid over the paths as well as the plots of the cemetery to produce a uniform surface, and the traditional marking of plot boundaries with low fences or with coping (stone curbing) was prohibited. After its expansion, the cemetery hired Ossian Cole Simonds to work out a more innovative plan for Graceland.

The partnership between Graceland and Simonds would prove to be a lasting one, and would make both internationally famous. At the time, Simonds had worked as a consulting landscape designer for the Lincoln Park Commission, and was a founder and partner of the architectural firm of Holabird, Simonds & Roche. It was also a time when it was fashionable for landscapers to lay out "showy" foreign plants in formal arrangements without any regard to the existing environment. Simonds rejected this trend, and along with fellow Chicago landscape architect Jens Jensen, began to develop a new regional school of landscape design that focused on the use of native plants and respected the existing terrain. This style was later called the "Prairie" or "Midwestern" style of landscape design.

At Graceland, Simonds sought to create a parklike setting consisting of a restful network of country lanes. Eventually, he withdrew from his architectural firm and began a lifelong association with Graceland. As the cemetery's superintendent, he had full authority for the development of its grounds and buildings. Simonds used thickets of native shrubs and trees with gently sculpted landforms and bodies of water in his attempt to make Graceland a quiet, restful image of the Midwestern landscape.

Simonds became so well known for his work at Graceland that Chicago's wealthiest families demanded his services to design the grounds for their estates. And it was Graceland Cemetery that many of these same people chose as their final resting place.

John Kinzie, one of Chicago's earliest settlers, was buried here when Graceland, along with Rosehill and Oak Woods Cemeteries, received bodies from the condemned Chicago City Cemetery. State Street developer Potter Palmer, railroad car manufacturer George Pullman, and Cyrus Hall McCormick, inventor of the mechanized reaper, are all interred here. Other Chicago "giants" buried here include civic planners and builders Daniel Burnham and Charles Wacker; Marshall Field, the retailing

genius; Martin Ryerson, a lumber merchant and developer; newspaper publisher Victor Lawson; Joseph Medill, a founder of the Republican party and part owner of the *Chicago Tribune*; meatpacker Phillip D. Amour; and Carter H. Harrison, Sr., a five-term mayor of Chicago. World-famous Chicago architects such as John Root, William Holabird, Louis Sullivan, David Adler, Howard Van Doren Shaw, and Mies Van der Rohe all lie in Graceland.

Graceland is distinguished by its monuments and mausoleums, many of which are works by Chicago's greatest artists and architects (many of whom are also interred here). Sculptor Daniel Chester French designed the monument titled "Memory" for Marshall Field's tomb;

Lorado Taft's "Silence" marks pioneer Chicagoan Dexter Graves's site, and Louis Sullivan's tomb for the Getty family is justly celebrated for his characteristic fecundity of ornament balanced with classical proportions that presage Modernism.

This beautiful map gives a sense of the park-like environment Simonds created, and lists the names of plot owners in the cemetery. Originally folded into a cover entitled "Graceland Cemetery," its exact date of publication is not known, although there is some evidence that indicates the year 1876.

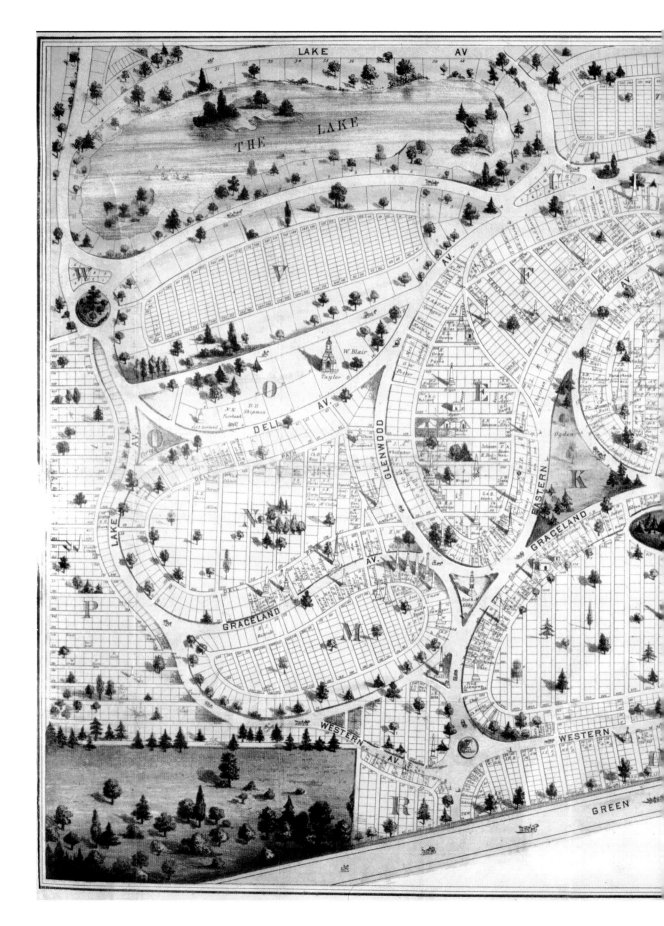

MAP
OF
GRACELAND
CEMETERY.
CHICAGO.

CHICAGO'S FREIGHT TUNNELS

The Chicago Tunnel Company Map

Title: Map showing tunnels and connections
Date Issued: 1928
Cartographer: Chicago Tunnel Company / Chicago Warehouse & Terminal Company
Published: *The Chicago Freight Tunnels* (Chicago)
Colored Sheet, 27.9 x 43.2 cm
Chicago Historical Society, ICHi-38517

Chicago has a unique, and once relatively unknown, system of freight tunnels lying forty feet below its downtown streets. The story of the tunnels begins in 1899, when the City of Chicago granted a thirty-year franchise to the Illinois Telephone and Telegraph Company (IT&T) for an underground telephone system in an area bounded by Fullerton Avenue, Western Avenue, Twenty-Second Street, Halsted Street, Fifty-Fifth Street, and Lake Michigan. Shortly thereafter, construction began on a tunnel system purportedly for the purpose of carrying telephone wires and cables.

In the summer of 1900, construction was halted because, the company claimed, inaccuracies had been discovered in city maps and additional surveying would be required before construction could resume. Promoters of the fledgling company used this downtime to surreptitiously increase their corporate powers to include the use of their tunnels for the handling of merchandise, mail, and other freight. From this point on, the primary focus of the corporation was on the construction and operation of an underground railway, with the business of a telephone company playing a secondary role.

In 1903, the city granted IT&T an amended franchise that legalized the use of the tunnels for the transport of freight. Construction was accelerated, but after the completion of about twenty miles of tunnels, the company had exhausted its funds and credit. Investors quickly incorporated a new company, the Illinois Tunnel Company, with broader powers and a larger authorized capital structure than IT&T. Construction of the underground railroad began anew, and in January of 1904, with about twenty miles of the two-foot-gauge system completed, test runs of the railway began.

The company planned to ferry packages and merchandise between stores, warehouses and other delivery points, and had a railway to do so. There remained, however, a problem: the rail system had no access to the ground level buildings and delivery points. The company's promoters were unable to raise the money needed for further construction, and a holding corporation, The Chicago Subway Company, was formed to recapitalize the project. This company immediately proceeded not only to finish a comprehensive system of railway tunnels, but to organize a subsidiary company, the Chicago Warehouse and Terminal Company, whose function was to build tunnels under railroad and private property with connecting shafts and elevators to buildings, railroad freight houses, shippers' premises and universal freight stations.

In August of 1906, the railway began revenue operations over about forty-five miles of completed track. A large part of its business was the transport of coal and cinder; it also delivered mail, packages, railroad baggage, raw materials, and finished goods. Revenues were not sufficient to pay the interest on its debts, however, and both the Illinois Tunnel Company and the Chicago Warehouse and Terminal Company were forced into receivership by the end of 1909. While in receivership, the railway did turn a modest profit, and the receivers continued to make capital improvements to the system. The telephone portion of the business was never profitable.

Reorganized in 1912 as the Chicago Tunnel Company, the railway continued to excavate new tunnels, which provided landfill for over one hundred acres of Grant and Burnham Parks along the lakefront (the Field Museum, Soldier Field, and McCormack Place all stand on top of tunnel excavations). When completed, the railway system had approximately sixty-two miles of tunnels and connections running forty feet beneath most of the downtown streets, all equipped with track of two-foot gauge and overhead trolley wire for the use of electric locomotives. The finished tunnels were roughly six feet wide by seven and a half feet high, and were lined with non-reinforced concrete about one foot thick. The system included eleven tunnels or "drifts" that passed under the Chicago River to reach North Side and West Side customers. Service was provided with 149 four-wheeled electric locomotives of various capacities, and over three thousand double-truck freight cars including flat cars, merchandise cars, coal cars, and ash cars.

From a public relations perspective, the idea of removing freight shipments from overcrowded city streets and transporting them via an underground railway system seemed like a good idea; logistically, it did not fare as well. The time and expense required to load a car at a surface station, send it down an elevator, add it to a train, and then reverse the procedure at its destination, meant that the railway could work, at best, on a small profit margin. A number of other factors would lead to the railway's eventual demise. The system was hampered by narrow tunnel clearances and limited operating areas, and trucks began to prove to be an inexpensive alternative to the tunnel service. Trucks could not only handle bulky and large articles that could not fit through the tunnels, they could deposit coal shipments directly into a building's bins. Then, in 1938, the city began digging the State Street Subway, which displaced the company's connections to many of its best customers. In the 1950s the Post Office was interested in using the railway to transport mail, but several test runs failed to convince postal officials of its efficiency. By this time, the railroad's business was primarily ash removal, and deferred maintenance had left its most of its equipment unusable. When it ceased operations in June of 1959, ninety-eight cars loaded with ashes were left stranded throughout the system.

Later that year, the system began to be dismantled, and salvagers removed the copper trolley wire, the lead-lined feeder cable, twenty-five elevators, the steel freight cars, two locomotives, and other scrap—including the watertight doors at each end of the eleven drifts under the Chicago River. The tracks, which are embedded in concrete, remained, as did the abandoned ash-filled cars. Over the years, the tunnels under City Hall were made into fallout shelters, Commonwealth Edison has used some tunnels for power lines, and other tunnels have been used by telecommunications companies to run cables (thus returning some of the tunnels to their original intended use).

In 1992, in one of Chicago's most unusual accidents, a wooden piling being driven into the Chicago River bottom breached one of the tunnel system's drifts, which began to leak. The leak was allowed to continue for several months without repair, which caused the wall of the drift to collapse, and the river rushed into the entire tunnel system. Many subbasements in the Loop were still connected to the system, and these also flooded. The flood disrupted utility service throughout the Loop, which was shut down for several days until government agencies emptied the tunnels of water. The subsequent loss of millions of dollars of business probably could have been prevented if the water tight doors had been left in place and maintained. Also probably lost in the torrent of flood water, silt, and debris were most of the remaining Chicago Tunnel Company freight cars and artifacts. One thing was for certain: the existence of Chicago's underground freight tunnels was now well-known.

From the beginning of its operations and through the 1920s, the railway's various corporate incarnations published promotional booklets and pamphlets describing the system and touting its valuable service to the city. In 1928, the Chicago Tunnel Company published a booklet that contained a history and detailed description of the narrow-gauge freight tunnel railroad system. It was illustrated by photographs, numerous small drawings, a picture of the loop with the tunnels superimposed on it, and the large map of the tunnel system presented here.

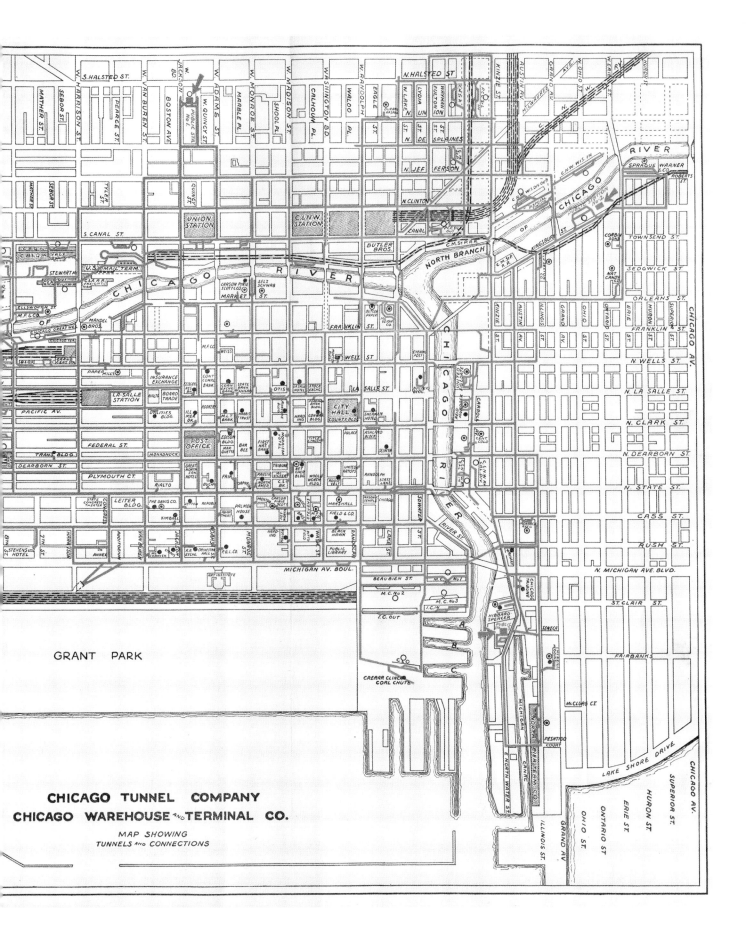

CHICAGO TUNNEL COMPANY
CHICAGO WAREHOUSE AND TERMINAL CO.

MAP SHOWING
TUNNELS AND CONNECTIONS

THE MATURE CITY

The Poole Brothers View

Title: Bird's-eye View of the Business District of Chicago
Date Issued: 1898
Cartographer: Poole Brothers
Published: Poole Brothers (Chicago)
Lithograph, 4 sheets, 55 x 77 cm
Chicago Historical Society, ICHi-14892

This beautiful map of Chicago's business district at the turn of the century documents what is now a well-established and mature city. To be sure, Chicago had not finished growing. At the time this map was published, Chicago had a population of almost 1.7 million—nearly five times as many people as lived in the city before the Great Fire. By 1930 this figure would be doubled, and in 1950, Chicago's population would peak at over 3.6 million. Nevertheless, by 1893 the post-fire city's downtown had been twice rebuilt, and it was now what every American city or town that aspired to be a metropolis could hope to be— that is, a vertical city, a city of skyscrapers.

Some elements of the old downtown still remained. Michigan Avenue still ended on the south bank of the river, the nearest access across the river to the north being the swing bridge at Rush Street. The swing bridges across the river, which had been built in the 1860s on what amounted to islands in the middle of the river, continued to be a major impediment to river traffic. Grain elevators remained fixtures on Chicago's skyline, although they now vied with buildings as the city's tallest structures. The tracks of the Illinois Central still cut across the lakefront, and tracks from two other railways can be seen entering the city from the south. On the north bank of the river (close to where the Merchandise Mart now stands) was the enormous Chicago and Northwestern station.

These remnants could not disguise the fact that Chicago's downtown was no longer a center of industry, but a commercial center filled with tall buildings. And unlike New York, Boston, or Philadelphia, whose downtowns served as cultural and financial centers, Chicago's downtown was oriented to no other purpose than that of making money. There were exceptions, of course, and both the Chicago Public Library and the Art Institute appear on this map. They are located, however, just outside the Loop—inside the Loop was strictly for business.

Developments in Chicago's system of mass transit can readily be seen on this map. The elevated trains making the circuit that defines the Loop and their downtown stations are

BIRD'S-EYE VIEW OF THE BUSINESS DISTRICT OF GHIGAGO

prominently depicted. Most of these stations remain unchanged today. The automobile was yet to invade the center of the city; this was the age of the streetcar, and streetcar lines are clearly illustrated on the downtown streets. The lower border of the map provides a location index for public buildings, blocks, and halls; hotels; theaters; banks; railway depots; elevated railway stations; some prominent business houses; and some "miscellaneous" clubs, schools, and associations.

This map is another example of the panoramic or "bird's-eye view" maps that were popular in the late nineteenth and early twentieth centuries. By using an elevated perspective, these maps could portray the underlying grid of the often confusing maze of city streets and buildings in America's rapidly growing cities. And, as in the case at hand, these views could also depict a city's vertical growth occasioned by the construction of multi-story buildings. Many of the

nineteenth-century panoramas were motivated by civic pride and a city's desire to encourage commercial growth. They were often prepared for chambers of commerce and other civic organizations, which would use them to advertise a city's commercial and residential potential.

THE ELEVATED RAILROAD SYSTEM

The McComber View

Title: Bird's-eye view of the elevated railroads, parks, and boulevards of Chicago
Date Issued: ca. 1910
Cartographer: Joseph McComber
Published: Supplement to the J. B. McComber's *Elevated railroad directory* (Chicago)
Lithograph, 43 x 78 cm
Newberry Library, map4F oG4104.C6P34 1910 .M3

Chicago has long been closely identified with its elevated railroad system, which is known as the "L." This map depicts Chicago's four original elevated lines, along with their famous "Loop" around the city's central business district.

Between 1869 and 1900, over seventy companies were incorporated in Chicago for the purpose of running an elevated railway system. The first to actually open a transit line was the Chicago and South Side Transit Company, which operated the South Side Elevated (shown here in red). When the South Side Rapid Transit line opened in 1892, it went from a terminal at Congress Street to Thirty-Ninth Street, a distance of 3.6 miles, all in a straight line. This was accomplished by one of the railway's most unique features: its route ran completely through city-owned alleys, which earned it the nickname "Alley L." This route circumvented the difficulty of obtaining consent signatures from the property owners along the streets, something required by the Cities and Villages Act of 1872. When it first opened, the South Side Elevated operated with steam locomotives; they were replaced by electric trains that ran from a "third rail" in 1898.

To accommodate the World's Columbian Exposition, the Alley L was extended east and south to Jackson Park in time for the 1893 fair. Other extensions soon followed. In 1905, the south side L began service to the growing Englewood neighborhood along the South Englewood Branch. A short line, called the Normal Park Branch, was built off the Englewood Branch to serve real estate development needs. The line opened in 1907 and was abandoned in 1954. The Stock Yards Branch was built to replace a grade-level train run by the Stock Yards. It made a circuit around "Packingtown," and was created for Stock Yards employees who commuted from their south side homes. Another line, the Kenwood Branch, was built directly to the east, and this neighborhood was soon settled by Stock Yards workers. The Stock Yards branch was opened in 1908, the Kenwood line in 1907; both were abandoned when their need was gone.

Chicago's second elevated railway was operated by the Lake Street Elevated Railway Company. This company was originally owned by

Michael C. McDonald, a gambler nicknamed "King Mike," who had earned a fortune in the vice trades. Chartered the same year as the Chicago and South Side Transit Company (1888), the Lake Street Elevated began operations with steam locomotives in 1893, the year after its south side counterpart. Later to become the Chicago and Oak Park Elevated (shown here in maroon), the line originally ran from Fifty-Second Avenue (Laramie Avenue) on the city's western limits to Market and Madison Streets on the edge of the central business district. Thus, the Lake Street Elevated faced a problem that it shared with the South Side Elevated: neither had direct access to downtown, and so they were forced to deposit passengers on the outskirts of the business district.

The Metropolitan West Side Elevated was Chicago's third L (shown here in blue), and the first to operate an elevated train using electric traction technology. The main line began at a Franklin Street terminal and went west until it split into three branches at Marshfield Avenue: Garfield Park directly west, Douglas Park to the southwest and Logan Square to the northwest. At Robey (Damen) Street, a line came off the Logan Square branch, going due west a short distance to Humboldt Park. The "Met" or "Polly"—both nicknames of the period for the

Metropolitan—was soon extended to Oak Park via the Douglas Park branch and to Forest Park via the Garfield Park branch. Other extensions would be added later. A more pressing issue was that of downtown access: the Met, like the South Side and Lake Street Lines, ended just outside the business district. As one reporter noted, "[The Met] practically begins and ends nowhere."

The lack of a true downtown terminal prevented efficient elevated service, as passengers were not only forced to walk from train terminals into the business district, they could not easily transfer between two elevated lines; this meant that the L could not boast a marketable advantage over streetcars. What was needed was a common downtown terminal that served all the elevated lines. This was problematic, however, since an elevated railroad needed consent from the majority of property owners along each mile of a street where it planned to build. This seemed unlikely along downtown streets, which were already lined with upscale stores, and whose owners feared that the looming shadows of the hulking elevated structure would bring lowered property values. It took Charles Tyson Yerkes to overcome these obstacles and build a structure that today is one of the most defining elements of Chicago's central business district: the Loop.

Yerkes had enough political power and deftness to convince store owners to sign consent forms allowing construction of the overhead structures on their streets; when needed, Yerkes also relied on duplicity. The northern leg of the Loop (completed in 1895) would run along Lake Street to Wabash Avenue, and accommodated the entrance of the Lake Street Elevated (now owned by Yerkes) into downtown. Yerkes used a great deal of political and corporate maneuvering to obtain his franchises, and often would obtain a franchise for one company in the name of another. So it was that the eastern leg of the Loop was awarded in the name of the Union Elevated Railroad Company, and what is simply referred to today as the "Loop" was originally known as the "Union Loop." This leg, which runs along Wabash Avenue, was placed in service late in 1896.

Yerkes obtained the franchise for the western leg of the Loop in the name of his as-yet-unbuilt Northwestern Elevated Railroad. Construction on this leg, which runs along Wells Street, began in 1895. By the end of this year, the only section of the Union Loop without a franchise was the southern leg. Harrison Street was originally considered for this leg, but the Metropolitan West Side Elevated protested that this would subject its riders to a lengthy delay and detour.

Accordingly, Yerkes set his sights on a leg that ran along Van Buren Street from Wabash to Wells.

Here Yerkes encountered a problem by the name of Levi Z. Leiter. Leiter owned much of the Loop property along Van Buren Street and strenuously objected to the idea of having an elevated train built along the street. A bitter war of words ensued between Yerkes and Leiter in the newspapers, which appeared to end in a stalemate between the powerful businessman and the incensed property owner. Yerkes was not finished, however, and soon devised one of his most cunning and duplicitous schemes. He created a new company, the Union Consolidated Railroad, for the purpose of building an elevated line along Van Buren Street from Wabash Avenue to Halsted Street, a distance of one mile. The western half of this stretch consisted mainly of warehouses and industry, the owners of which were at worst indifferent to the presence of an elevated along the street. Yerkes was easily able to gain their consent signatures, which along with those he had already obtained east of Market Street (the access point of the Metropolitan Line to the Loop), were all he needed to proceed. Of course, he never intended to actually build the structure all the way to Halsted Street; construction of the southern leg of the Loop began east of Wells Street in late 1896.

The Lake Street Elevated made the first full circuit around the Union Loop in 1897. Chicagoans could now be deposited in the heart of the city's central business district and could directly change to another line's train. There were also direct entrances to various buildings, most notably the Carson Pirie Scott & Company's department store. The public was quick to take advantage of the new

facilities, and every elevated company had significant gains in their number of riders after the Loop's completion. The Metropolitan, for instance, experienced a fifty percent increase, its number of riders quickly climbing from 40,000 to 60,000.

The last of the major L companies to be created was the Northwestern Elevated Railroad Company. Incorporated in 1893, the

company was backed by transit magnate Yerkes, but did not begin full service until 1900. When it opened, the Northwestern Elevated (shown here in orange) connected to the Loop at Fifth (Wells) and Lake Streets, then wound northward to a terminal at Wilson Avenue. In 1907, the Ravenswood Branch was put into service, and soon thereafter the Northwestern began running to Central Street in north Evanston. By 1908, service demands in the northern suburb were so great that the Central Street terminal and yards were insufficient to handle the load. To handle this demand, the Northwestern was extended even further north along the tracks of the Chicago North Shore and Milwaukee Railroad's tracks to a new terminal at Linden Avenue in the suburb of Wilmette.

By 1909 (the year before this map was published), the city of Chicago enjoyed one of the best rapid transit systems in the world; it would remain largely as depicted on this map for over sixty years. This system provided reliable and unified service to outlying communities and neighborhoods, and in some cases—most notably on the North Side above Wilson Avenue, an area that was still an open prairie land—provided the stimulus for further real estate development in the city.

Note that this map also depicts the city's parks and boulevards, which are shaded in green. When first laid out, most of these parks were located too far from working-class neighborhoods to provide an escape from the grime of the city for anyone but the privileged. With the arrival of the L system, the parks could now easily be reached by skilled laborers, clerks, and their families. The parks would still remain alien territory, however, to the city's unskilled labor force—primarily those in the city's immigrant neighborhoods—for whom a family train ride might eat up half a day's wages. It is interesting to note that the city's many cemeteries are also shaded in the park-designating green color, a reference perhaps, to the fact that many turn-of-the-century Chicagoans continued a practice begun before the advent of a city park system—using cemeteries as picnic grounds.

BIRDS - EYE
VIEW
OF THE
ELEVATED RAILROADS
PARKS AND BOULEVARDS
OF
CHICAGO

Showing: METROPOLITAN W.S. ELEVATED
SOUTH SIDE ELEVATED
NORTH WESTERN ELEVATED
CHICAGO & OAK PARK ELEVATED
UNION LOOP ELEVATED

SUPPLEMENT
TO THE
ELEVATED RAILROAD DIRECTORY.
PUBLISHED BY
J.B. McCOMBER CHICAGO, ILLS.

AUTO TRAILS

The Rand McNally Map

Title: Rand McNally Official Auto Trails, Southern Wisconsin, Northern Illinois
Date Issued: 1917
Cartographer: Rand McNally
Published: Rand McNally & Co. (Chicago)
Wax Engraving, 85.5 x 50.5 cm
Newberry Library, Rd McN 6F 9 4

Although the automobile was first introduced to the American public in 1896, the age of the automobile in America would not begin until 1908. This was the year the first affordable car appeared on the market—Ford's Model T. Thereafter, automobile sales soared: by 1916, Americans owned 3.3 million automobiles; by 1929, there were 29 million cars on the road, or roughly one for every four Americans. While today the automobile is regarded as a necessity by most Americans, in the early decades of the twentieth century, motoring was considered a leisure activity. The automobile offered—or at least was advertised to offer—freedom and adventure, as it gave city-dwelling

motorists a chance to take to the road to explore and rediscover the wilds of nature. Automobiles were first used for weekend jaunts in the country; by the 1920s, however, millions of Americans began taking trips that covered longer and longer distances.

These early motorists encountered two problems. The first was the poor condition of most of America's roadways. In 1914, the United States had only 29,000 miles of paved roads, most of which were concentrated around major cities. The second problem was navigational—the nation's roads were poorly marked, and it was easy to lose one's way. Although rural roads usually suffered from both of these problems, even well-marked roads were occasionally impassable.

These problems were first addressed by the nation's pioneer automobile clubs and highway associations. Although these groups may have been formed as social clubs for those interested in motoring and motor racing, they soon began to actively promote highway construction and safety. Some set aside money for road improvements, and many lobbied for legislation and programs in the interests of motorists. Results of their efforts began to appear in the later 1910s and early 1920s, as road conditions slowly improved. In 1916 and 1921, the first Federal road aid laws were passed, providing federal funds to support the construction of post roads (roads maintained for the transport of mail) and "interstate" highways.

Automobile clubs were also instrumental in helping motorists find their way on the nation's roadways. They began identifying important cross-country and regional "trails," to which they gave colorful or historical names, such as the Abe Lincoln Highway, the Midland Trail, the Yellowstone Trail, and the Dixie Highway, and then offered touring guides to help motorists navigate their way along these trails. The American Automobile Association, which was established in 1902 as a consolidation of nine earlier clubs, was one of the standard bearers in this endeavor. It began to collect information on America's major roadways in 1907, which was published by the Automobile Blue Book Publishing Company. These bulky "blue books" contained route "logs" that carefully guided motorists from one place to the next, noting each turn, fork, or crossroad, landmark, and the miles between each feature.

In 1917, Wisconsin became the first state to legislate the numbering—as opposed to naming—of its roads; by the early 1920s, several other states had soon followed suit. In 1925, a federal law was passed creating a national system of numbered federal highways. This 1918 map of the road system between Chicago and Milwaukee shows the numbering system Wisconsin employed for its roads in the southeastern section of the state. In the absence of an official numbering scheme for the roads in Illinois, Rand McNally assigned their own numbers to the thirty-six different Illinois roadways shown here.

Founded in 1856 as the printing office of the *Chicago Tribune*, Rand McNally had established itself, by the time of the automobile, as the leading publisher of maps and atlases in the United States. The first Rand McNally road map (of greater New York City) was published in 1904; and in 1917, the firm launched its series of *Auto Trails* maps, of which this is an example.

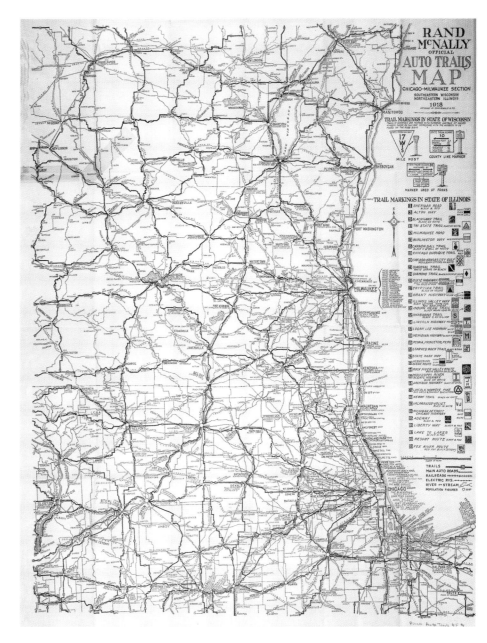

CHICAGO MOTOR COACH COMPANY MAP

A Pictorial Map and Guide to Chicago

Title: Pictorial Map and Guide to Chicago
Date Issued: c. 1926
Cartographer: Chicago Motor Coach Company
Published: Clason Publishing Company (Denver, Chicago)
Folded Sheet, 55.8 x 64.4 cm
Author's Collection

By the mid-1920s, three companies controlled Chicago's mass transportation —that is, its streetcar, elevated and bus lines. These companies were regulated by the state as public utilities. In 1945, the Chicago Transit Authority (CTA) was established and empowered to acquire and operate public transportation in the city and nearby suburbs; as an independent government agency, it was freed from regulation as a utility. In 1947, the CTA purchased the properties of the Chicago Surface Lines and the Chicago Rapid Transit Company, and began operating the city's streetcars and elevated trains. In 1952, the Chicago Transit Authority purchased the Chicago Motor Coach Company, and was now owner and operator of all three branches of city's mass transportation system—lines of transit that for years had operated as separate, competing companies.

This pictorial map of Chicago was distributed compliments of the Chicago Motor Coach Company, which ran Chicago's bus service. The map was billed as "the first of its kind of any American city," and gives a comprehensive view of Chicago in the mid-1920s. The map shows Chicago's "magnificent" park and boulevard system, its mile streets and avenues, and the city's diagonal streets; "numerous golf courses, cemeteries, amusement parks, etc. are depicted; also more than nineteen miles of superb lakefront."

What makes this map unique is its illustration of many different types of buildings throughout the city— "churches, hotels, schools, industrial plants, hospitals and other public and private institutions, etc. Some are shown because they are widely known and of public interest; some because of their beauty of architecture; many simply as being the outstanding buildings or representatives of the districts in which they are located." Each square on this map represents a square mile, so a number of interesting buildings had to be omitted for lack of space. Downtown buildings were shown on an enlarged and detailed map that appeared on the reverse side of this map.

The legend notes that the "view of each building is from the direction best illustrating architectural lines. The sites are, of course, only relatively proportional. In congested districts, where buildings are shown slightly out of position, an arrow indicates the exact location. A uniform color has been used on all buildings."

A CENTURY OF PROGRESS

The Turzak Map
The Seymour Map

Title: Chicago, U.S.A., an illustrated map of Chicago, youthful city of the big shoulders, restless, ingenious, willful, violent, proud to be alive!
Date Issued: 1931
Cartographer: Charles Turzak & Henry T. Chapman
Published: The Tudor Press (Boston)
Lithograph, 57 x 95 cm
Newberry Library, map6F oG4104.C6A3 1931 .T8

Title: Map of Chicago for the year 1933, Portraying some of its History and indicating the approximate location of Points of Historical Interest: also a few of the Present Day Institutions and Civic Improvements
Date Issued: 1932
Cartographer: Ralph Fletcher Seymour
Published: T.N.T. Company (Chicago)
Stone Lithograph, 43 x 56 cm
Newberry Library, temp map2F oG4104.C6A3 1933 .S4

As the centennial of its founding approached, there was little doubt that the last one hundred years had belonged to Chicago. Indeed, no large city had ever grown as fast as Chicago. When it incorporated as a town in 1833, Chicago was little more than a desolate trading post and fort on the northwestern frontier. By 1893, it was the world's first skyscraper city and had a population of over one million. By 1933, it had become a modern metropolis and home to nearly 3.4 million people.

To celebrate the centennial of the founding of Chicago, the idea of holding a World's Fair seemed to be a natural one. The Columbian Exposition had been an immensely popular and important event just a few decades earlier, and in many respects, was the city's first proclamation as an international center of power and culture. So it was that a corporation was formed in 1928 for the purpose of "holding a World's Fair in Chicago in the year 1933," which was given the name "Chicago's Second World's Fair Centennial Celebration." In order to

spark global interest in the fair, its name was changed in 1929 to "A Century of Progress," and the fair was billed as an "attempt to demonstrate to an international audience the nature and significance of scientific discoveries, the methods of achieving them, and the changes which their application has wrought in industry and in living conditions."

The fairgrounds covered 427 acres of Lake Michigan shoreline (much of it created by landfill) just south of downtown, from Twelfth Street to Thirty-Ninth Street (now Pershing

Road). Today the site is occupied by McCormick Place, an exposition complex, and Northerly Island, on which an airport known as Meigs Field once operated. A Century of Progress officially opened on May 27, 1933, and ran until the middle of November of that year. The Fair was originally planned to run for the 1933 season only, but was quickly extended for another year; it reopened on May 26, 1934, and closed on October 31, 1934. This extension was due in part to the Fair's public popularity, but it was primarily an effort to generate enough revenue to retire its debts.

Although inspired by the city's first World's Fair, the Century of Progress Exposition was radically different in a number of ways. Whereas the Columbian Exposition had been funded by a number of governmental agencies at the federal, state, and municipal levels, A Century of Progress was underwritten entirely by private sources—wealthy Chicago citizens and corporate sponsors. As opposed to the classical Beaux Arts architecture of the 1893 fair, the buildings of the 1933 fair were typified by the geometrical style known as art deco. And in contrast to "The White City" of the World's Columbian Exposition, A Century of Progress was dubbed the "Rainbow City" for its vibrant use of color in the decoration of its buildings. At night,

these buildings were illuminated by lights that heightened the effect.

Perhaps the most important point of demarcation between the two fairs was the perspective they created. The Columbian Exposition—with its classical buildings, conservative art, and naturalistic setting—was designed to celebrate an America of the past, and specifically, to idealize the four hundred years of expansion that began with the landing of Columbus upon its shores. A Century of Progress, by contrast, looked toward America's future. There were, of course, a handful of exhibits that recalled Chicago's frontier past, such as the recreations of the cabin of Jean Baptiste Point du Sable and of Fort Dearborn (it was, after all, a celebration of Chicago's one hundredth anniversary). The overwhelming focus, however, was on the America that was to come, and the technological wonders that promised Americans a better life. One could find, for example, an experimental kitchen full of labor-saving devices that promised trouble-free times for American homemakers—not only would food be plentiful, it would be prepared in a modern, efficient, and aesthetically pleasing environment. The imagination of fairgoers was especially captured by the potential for high-speed transportation, as evoked in displays of streamlined cars and trains. And above the crowds hovered the symbol of the fair, the Goodyear blimp.

The promise of a better life was a particularly poignant theme in 1933, as the country was in the midst of the Great Depression. By colorfully showcasing America's greatest advancements in art, literature, architecture, science, and industry, the fair served as a source of optimism for even the poorest of Americans. In particular, the fair not only illustrated that Americans had much to be proud of, it offered some much needed hope that, despite the current situation, the future of America was bright.

This promise carried over into the striking and unusual maps that were published around this time. The first map presented here is a colorful art deco bird's-eye view of Chicago just prior to the World's Fair. Created by the well-known artist Charles Turzak, along with Henry Chapman, this stone lithograph includes an index to various "points of interest" around the city and loop, including suburban towns, the city's boulevard system, parks, hospitals, universities, historical sites, theaters, airports, train stations, the stockyards, steel mills, and many other sites, including that of the upcoming World's Fair. Along with the many ships seen heading to and from the city, there are no less than eighteen airplanes seen flying around the city. During the early 1930s, it was not unusual to find crowds of people spending their weekends at airports, attracted by the speed of the airplane and its potential for limitless travel—and, perhaps, to let their minds escape the dire straits of those depressed times.

The second map was produced by Ralph Fletcher Seymour, a well-known Chicago commercial artist and publisher (among the many books he illustrated was the first edition of L. Frank Baum's *American Fairy Tales*). This panoramic map looks west over the fairgrounds from Lake Michigan. At the top of the map is an image that depicts a history of Chicago's settlement: on the right a Native American is depicted with a harvest of corn, wheat, apples, and fish; on the left is a European settler, holding the handle of a sledgehammer upon which rests a cog wheel. These figures are shown resting on a disk that contains the city motto— *Urbs in Horto* (City in a Garden).

The images on the right-hand border illustrate various episodes in Chicago's history—including Father Marquette's return (1674), the first Fort Dearborn (1803), the Chicago Fire (1871), the Northern Trust Company Branch at the World's Fair (1893), and an image of Chicago's financial center, LaSalle Street (1915). Images on the left-hand border illustrate contemporary sites, including the downtown skyscrapers or "Cathedrals of Commerce," the South Side Steel Mills, the Union Stock Yards, the University of

Chicago, and LaSalle Street and the Northern Trust Company.

It is evident that this map was commissioned by The Northern Trust Company, and served as an advertisement for that company during the fair. The map itself prominently displays the grounds of A Century of Progress extending into Lake Michigan. On the lower border there is a key to eighteen buildings on the fairgrounds. The city is depicted behind the fairgrounds: various streets are marked, sports venues are located, railroad depots are shown, and other points of historic and civic interest are noted. Although this map certainly would not have served the needs of a tourist that wished to make his or her way around the city, it does present a striking perspective of Chicago, and gives as well a good orientation of the layout of the fairgrounds.

Like those of its predecessor, the buildings erected for Chicago's second World's Fair were meant to be temporary structures; today, Balbo's Column is the only structure remaining on its original site. This column, a gift of the Italian government, was removed from the ruins of a Roman temple in Ostia. It commemorates General Balbo's trans-Atlantic flight to Chicago in 1933, and still stands, opposite Soldier Field, at 1600 South Lake Shore Drive.

WPA MAPS

Land Use in the Northeast Loop

Title: Land Use in the Northeast Loop: Chicago Avenue to Madison Street, Lake Front to State Street
Date Issued: 1942
Cartographer: Prepared by the Work Projects Administration under the Direction of Chicago Plan Commission
Published: *The Chicago Land Use Survey* (Chicago)
Colored Sheet, 30.5 x 22.9 cm
Chicago Historical Society, ICHi-38518

The Great Depression was the bleakest financial decade in U.S. history. It was ushered in by the stock market crash of 1929, and by the early 1930s worsened to the point that unemployment was a national crisis. President Franklin Roosevelt responded by initiating a series of programs to put the able-bodied unemployed to work; these programs included the Federal Emergency Relief Administration (FERA), the Public Works Administration (PWA) and the Civil Works Administration (CWA). In 1934, these "alphabet" relief programs were all replaced with an umbrella program, the WPA, or Works Progress Administration.

While the WPA was derided by critics as a device for creating a patronage army loyal to the Democratic Party, its stated purpose was to provide useful work for millions of victims of the Great Depression. It was typically defended by a twofold line of argument: first, by providing gainful employment, the program would help preserve the skills and self-respect of those who found themselves out of work; second, the program would help stimulate the economy by increasing the purchasing power of those whom it employed.

The WPA was in existence for eight years, during which it put some 8.5 million people to work (there were over eleven million unemployed in 1934). The agency's construction projects produced more than 650,000 miles of roads, 125,000 public buildings, 75,000 bridges, 8,000 parks, and 800 airports. The Federal Arts Project, Federal Writers' Project, and Federal Theater Project—all sponsored by the WPA—employed thousands of artists, writers, and actors in such cultural programs as the creation of art work for public buildings, the documentation of local life, and the organization of community theatres.

In 1939, the WPA funded a land study in the city of Chicago. Directed by the Chicago Plan Commission, the purpose of this study was "to provide an inventory of the physical, economic, and social characteristics of every use of land in the City of Chicago; to picture the pattern of land variation of these characteristics; to provide an indication of city-wide and local trends—their nature, direction and rate; to furnish a reservoir of facts which may be used in determining more precisely the fundamental principles of city growth; and finally to establish a case-record file for daily reference, for use in supplementary studies, and for the periodic measurement of trends."

The WPA employed over 1,500 census and data workers who canvassed the city recording information on Chicago's built environment; during its peak period, this number increased to 3,000. The study, which was the first in the country to tabulate and map land use by individual parcels, remains one of the most exhaustive portraits of a major urban center ever produced. Its results were published in two volumes as *The Chicago Land Use Survey*.

Volume I of this publication, entitled *Residential Chicago*, summarized citywide data on residential land use and presented statistical information on the physical, social and economic character of residential properties in Chicago. Presented as graphs, pictures, maps and tables, this data includes the age, condition, number of stories, and exterior material of residential structures. Other data collected were rental values, encumbrance states, and occupancy information such as

persons per unit, tenure of occupancy, race and nativity, and average number of persons per room. The final chapter in this volume offers a report on the "evolution of Chicago's housing pattern."

Volume II of this publication is entitled *Land Use in Chicago* and contains some 475 maps that document land use on a square-mile basis. There is a citywide map of land coverage by large parks, cemeteries and industry, and a citywide square mile index map for the individual maps that follow. As of January 1, 1941, land use in Chicago was broken down as follows: 24.6 percent of the land was occupied by streets and alleys; 2.7 percent was waterways; 21.4 percent of the land was vacant; 12 percent was occupied by single-family residences; 8.8 percent had two-, three- and four-family residences; 3.3 percent was apartments; 4.6 percent was commercial; 6.9 percent industrial; 7.6 percent was used by railroads; 4.8 percent was park and playgrounds; and 3.3 percent was classified as "other public and institutional use."

The map presented here shows land use for the square mile that includes the northeastern corner of the Loop, and overall an area from Chicago Avenue to Madison Street, and from Lake Michigan to State Street. The legend lists the following types of land use: seven types of residential housing (single family detached, single family attached, two family, three and four family, apartments without business,

apartments with business, business with dwelling units); commercial; mixed commercial and industrial; industrial; railroads; parking and used car lots; other temporary business; parks and playgrounds; cemeteries; other public and institutional; streets and alleys; waterways; vacant. There is also a small girded city map that locates which square-mile section of the city is depicted by the map. The legend also notes the number of instances of each type of land use for that section of the city, as well as the area (in square feet and total percentage) of each type of land use recorded in this square mile of the city.

The most prominent feature in this area remains the Illinois Central railroad tracks and rail yard, which occupy most of the land south of the river. Navy Pier is depicted (as an insert) and marked as three thousand feet long; also shown is Ogden Slip, which is straddled by the Chicago and Northwestern tracks. Railways, in fact, cover over 19 percent of the land in this area. There is very little residential housing in this square mile— just over four percent. Streets and alleys cover 23.3 percent of the area, while parks and playgrounds (primarily Grant Park) account for ten percent of the land use. In the forthcoming decades, land use in this area was to undergo major changes as rail lines began to be replaced with commercial and residential development.

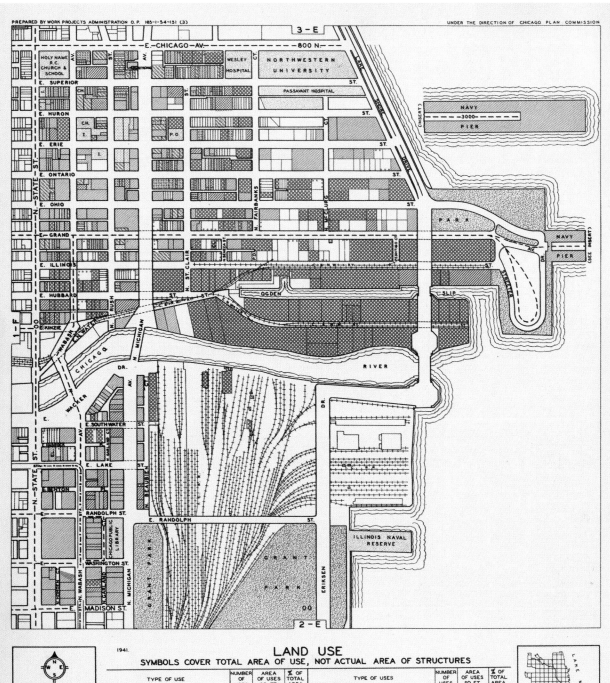

3 - E

E. CHICAGO AV.　　800 N.

HOLY NAME R.C. CHURCH & SCHOOL

WESLEY CT.

NORTHWESTERN UNIVERSITY

E. SUPERIOR ST.

PASSAVANT HOSPITAL

E. HURON

E. ERIE

P.O

E. ONTARIO

E. OHIO

E. GRAND

PARK

E. ILLINOIS

E. HUBBARD

NAVY PIER

3000

E. KINZIE

NAVY PIER

CHICAGO

OGDEN SLIP

RIVER

E. SOUTHWATER ST.

E. LAKE ST.

E. BENTON

RANDOLPH ST.

CHICAGO PUBLIC LIBRARY

E. RANDOLPH ST.

ILLINOIS NAVAL RESERVE

E. WASHINGTON ST.

GRANT PARK

ERIKSEN

E. MADISON ST.

2 - E

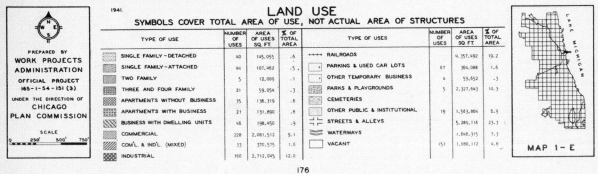

1941.

LAND USE
SYMBOLS COVER TOTAL AREA OF USE, NOT ACTUAL AREA OF STRUCTURES

TYPE OF USE	NUMBER OF USES	AREA OF USES SQ. FT.	% OF TOTAL AREA	TYPE OF USES	NUMBER OF USES	AREA OF USES SQ FT	% OF TOTAL AREA
SINGLE FAMILY - DETACHED	40	145,055	.6	RAILROADS		4,357,492	19.2
SINGLE FAMILY - ATTACHED	44	107,462	.5	PARKING & USED CAR LOTS	67	364,088	1.6
TWO FAMILY	5	12,009	.1	OTHER TEMPORARY BUSINESS	4	59,652	.3
THREE AND FOUR FAMILY	21	59,054	.3	PARKS & PLAYGROUNDS	5	2,327,643	10.3
APARTMENTS WITHOUT BUSINESS	35	136,319	.6	CEMETERIES			
APARTMENTS WITH BUSINESS	21	131,890	.6	OTHER PUBLIC & INSTITUTIONAL	19	1,563,864	6.9
BUSINESS WITH DWELLING UNITS	46	198,450	.9	STREETS & ALLEYS		5,285,116	23.3
COMMERCIAL	228	2,081,512	9.1	WATERWAYS		1,646,315	7.3
COM'L. & IND'L. (MIXED)	33	370,575	1.6	VACANT	151	1,080,112	4.8
INDUSTRIAL	160	2,712,045	12.0				

MAP 1 - E

LAKE MICHIGAN

176

USGS MAPS

The Metro Survey of 1963

Title: Chicago Loop Quadrangle, Illinois—Cook Co., 1963: 7.5 minute series (topographic)
Date Issued: 1964
Cartographer: United States Geological Survey
Published: United States Department of Interior (Washington, D. C.)
Colored Sheet, 68 x 56 cm
Illinois State Library, MAP I 19.81: (NO.-LTR.) (Ch-Cri)

The United States Geological Survey (USGS), which was established in 1879, is the government agency charged with mapping all areas of the United States. It was originally organized to unify and centralize four great surveys of the American West (these surveys were conducted by Clarence King, F. V. Hayden, George W. Wheeler, and J. W. Powell). Today, the mission of the USGS is "to provide geologic, topographic, and hydrologic information that contributes to the wise management of the Nation's natural resources and that promotes the health, safety, and well-being of the people."

The best known maps published by the USGS are its topographic maps; in particular, its 1:24,000-scale topographic maps, also known as 7.5-minute quadrangles. Completed in 1992, this series of maps required over 57,000 maps to cover the forty-eight contiguous states, Hawaii and the U.S. territories. This program of topographic maps has since been replaced by *The National Map*, an interactive World Wide Web service. Other types of maps published by the USGS include topographic-bathymetric maps, photoimage maps, satellite image maps, geologic maps, land use and land cover maps, hydrologic maps, and maps of the planets and moon.

The USGS map presented here shows Chicago's Loop and north side in the year 1963. Prominently featured are Lincoln Park with Belmont and Diversey Harbors, the lakeside water filtration plant, and Navy Pier, which at the time housed the University of Illinois at Chicago Circle (now the University of Illinois at Chicago). Also shown is Goose Island in the north branch of the river. The story of Goose Island begins in 1853 when the Chicago Land Company, under the direction of William Ogden, bought land along the east side of the north branch of the river. It had occurred to Ogden and other trustees of the company that a shortcut up the North Branch could be made here—by, in effect, "straightening" the bow-shaped bend in the river at this point. In 1857, company workers began excavating a canal, using the clay they dug out for the making of bricks. They were finished within a decade, and the shortcut became known as the North Branch Canal, or Ogden's Canal. The completed channel created Goose Island, which is nearly one-and-one-half-miles long and one-half mile wide at its widest.

CHICAGO FROM ABOVE

The SPOT Metroview

Title: Satellite Image of Chicago
Date Issued: 2001
Cartographer: SPOT Image Corporation
SPOT Satellite Image: © CNES 2005

Chicago in Maps is the fifth in Rizzoli's series of map books, being preceded by *Manhattan in Maps*, *Washington in Maps*, *Holy Land in Maps*, and *Mapping the West*. The first two both conclude with a satellite image of their respective urban landscapes that was provided by the SPOT Image Corporation. The tradition continues here, with this striking satellite view of Chicagoland.

This image, unlike its predecessors, is presented in natural color. The high resolution satellite cameras that took these "metroviews" use light in the infrared part of the spectrum, which distorts the natural colors of the objects being photographed. Water, for example, absorbs most of the infrared spectrum, and thus appears somewhat black in an unprocessed image. Green objects (such as vegetation) appear as red. Thus, we have the "false color" in the images of Manhattan and Washington. The image here has been reworked so that water appears blue, and vegetation green.

Clearly evident in this image are the geographical elements that shaped the formation of Chicago. The city lies on the southwestern shore of Lake Michigan, the great lake that provided its early portal to the East and the North. The Chicago River intersects the heart of the city, connecting the lake to its north and south branches. To the west, the Des Plaines River winds its way southward to the Illinois River. Note too, the flat plain on which Chicago is situated, a feature—as can be seen here—ideal for the development of a sprawling conurbation.

Over what was once a portage trail, the Chicago Sanitary and Ship Canal is clearly visible, connecting the South Branch of the Chicago River with the Illinois River. Alongside and a bit to the south of this channel runs the Illinois and Michigan Canal, the impetus for the founding of Chicago. These canals, along with several major highways and railways, cut through the northern arm of the Chicago Outlet—the original "Chicago Portage" through which traveled Marquette and Joliet. To the south, the Calumet Sag Channel is also clearly visible. This canal, built between the years 1911–22, passes through the southern arm of the Chicago Outlet (the Sag Valley). This canal was used to

reverse the flow of the Calumet River, and it connects Calumet Harbor, which now handles the bulk of Chicago's shipping traffic, to the Sanitary and Ship Canal. Both canals are part of the Illinois Waterway, which connect Lake Michigan, via the Illinois River, to the Mississippi. In turn, the Illinois Waterway is part of the Great Lakes to Gulf Waterway, which provides Chicago with direct water transportation to the Gulf of Mexico.

The Great Lakes-St. Lawrence Seaway system, the major inland waterway in North America, permits lake freighters and oceangoing vessels to reach Chicago, which remains one of America's leading ports. Chicago also continues to be the center of the nation's transportation and distribution network: it is the nation's most important rail and trucking center, and is home to the nation's busiest airport, Chicago-O'Hare International Airport (seen in the upper left-hand corner of this image).

The beaches, parks, and museums along Chicago's lakefront, one of the world's most beautiful, are also visible in this satellite view. Just to the north of the Loop, one can also see Navy Pier and the Jardine Water Filtration Plant jutting into the lake. To the south of Grant Park, Northerly Island extends parallel to the lakeshore.

SELECTED BIBLIOGRAPHY

Andreas, Alfred Theodore. *History of Chicago: From the Earliest Period to the Present Time*, 3 vols. (Chicago, 1884–1888).

Beers, J. S. & Co., pub. *History of the Great Lakes*, 2 vols. (Chicago, 1899).

Black, Glenn A. Laboratory of Archaeology. *Miami Indians Ethnohistory Archives* (http://www.gbl.indiana.edu/archives).

Bressani, Francesco. *Breve relation d'alcune missioni de' pp. dela Compagnia di Giesú nella Nuovia Francia* (Macerata, 1653).

Buisseret, David. *Historic Illinois from the Air* (Chicago, 1990).

___. *Mapping of the French Empire in North America* (Chicago, 1991).

Burden, Philip D. *The Mapping of North America* (Rickmansworth, Herts, England, 1996).

Burnham, Daniel H., and Edward H. Bennett. *Plan of Chicago* (Chicago, 1909).

Champlain, Samuel de. *Les Voyages du Sieur du Champlain Xainctongeois* (Paris, 1613).

___. *Les Voyages de la Nouvelle France Occidentale, dicte Canada, faits par le Sieur de Champlain Xainctongeois, depuis l'an 1603 jusques en l'annee 1629* (Paris, 1632).

Charlevoix, Pierre François Xavier de. *Histoire et description generale de la Nouvelle France, avec le Journal historique d'un Voyage fait par ordre du Roi dans l'Amerique Septentrionale*, 3 vols. (Paris, 1744).

Chicago Plan Commission. *Report of the Chicago land use survey, directed by the Chicago Plan commission and conducted by the Work projects administration*, 2 vols. (Chicago, 1942–1943).

Conzen, Michael P., ed. *Chicago Mapmakers, Essays on the Rise of the City's Map Trade* (Chicago, 1984).

Coronelli, Vincenzo. *Atlante Veneto* (Venice, 1690).

___. *Isolario de' Atlante Veneto* (Venice, 1696).

Cronon, William. *Nature's Metropolis: Chicago and the Great West* (New York, 1991).

Danckers, Ulrich Friedrich, and Jane Meredith. *A Compendium of the Early History of Chicago to the Year 1835 when the Indians left* (River Forest, Ill., 2000).

Danzer, Gerald. "Chicago's First Maps," in Michael P. Conzen, *Chicago Mapmakers, Essays on the Rise of the City's Map Trade*, pp. 12-22.

Delanglez, Jean. "Franquelin: Mapmaker" *Mid-America* 25 (1943).

___. "The 1674 Account of the Discovery of the Mississippi" *Mid-America* 26 (1944).

___. "Marquette's Autograph Map of the Mississippi River" *Mid-America* 27 (1945).

___. "The Joliet Lost Map of the Mississippi" *Mid-America* 28 (1946).

Drake, Benjamin. *Life and Adventures of Black Hawk: with Sketches of Keokuk, the Sac and Fox Indians, and the Late Black Hawk War* (Cincinnati, 1838, 1841, 1849).

Fite, Emerson D. & Archibald Freeman, eds. *A book of old maps delineating American history from the earliest days down to the close of the Revolutionary War* (Cambridge, Mass., 1926).

Greenberg, Joel. *A Natural History of the Chicago Region* (Chicago and London, 2002).

Griffin, Appleton P. G. *The Discovery of the Mississippi: A Bibliographical Account with a Fac-simile of the Map of Louis Joliet, 1674* (New York, 1883).

Grossman, James R., Ann Durkin Keating, and Janice L. Reiff. *The Encyclopedia of Chicago* (Chicago, 2004).

Hanson, Philip C. *Early Chicagoland* (Chicago, 1976).

___. *Geology of Chicago* (Chicago, 1978).

Heidenreich, Conrad E. "An Analysis of the 17th Century Map 'Nouvelle France'" *Cartographia* 25 (1988).

Heidenreich, Conrad E., and Edward H. Dahl. "The French Mapping of North America, 1600-1760" *The Map Collector* (1982).

Hill, Libby. *Chicago River: A Natural and Unnatural History* (Chicago, 2000).

Howe, Walter A. *Documentary History of the Illinois and Michigan Canal* (Springfield, 1956).

Hubbard, Gurdon Saltonstall. *The Autobiography of Gurdon Saltonstall Hubbard: Pa-pa-ma-ta-be, "The Swift Walker"* (Chicago, 1911).

Hull House, Residents of. *Hull-House Maps and Papers: A Presentation of Nationalities and Wages in a Congested District of Chicago, Together with Comments and Essays on Problems Growing Out of the Social Conditions* (New York, 1895).

Karpinski, Louis C. *Bibliography of Printed Maps of Michigan 1804–1880 with a series of over one hundred Reproductions of maps constituting an historical atlas of the Great Lakes and Michigan* (Lansing, 1931).

Karrow, Robert W., Jr. *Checklist of printed maps of the Middle West to 1900* (Boston, 1981).

Karrow, Robert W., Jr., and David Buisseret. *Gardens of Delight: Maps and Travel Accounts of Illinois and the Great Lakes from the Collection of Hermon Dunlap Smith* (Chicago, 1984).

Kaufman, Kevin, ed. *The Mapping of the Great Lakes in the Seventeenth Century* (Providence, R. I., 1989).

Kinzie, Mrs. John H. "Narrative of the Massacre at Chicago, Saturday, August 15, 1812, and of some Preceding Events" *Fergus Historical Series* 30 (1844).

___. *Wau-Bun: The "Early Days" in the North-West* (Chicago, 1856).

Kirkland, Caroline. *Chicago Yesterdays, A Sheaf of Reminiscences* (Chicago, 1919).

Knight, Robert, and Lucius H. Zeuch, M. D. *The Location of the Chicago Portage Route of the Seventeenth Century* (Chicago, 1928).

Lahontan, Louis Armand de Lom d'Arce, baron de. *Nouveaux voyages de Mr. le baron de Lahontan dans l'Amerique Septentrionale . . .* 2 vols. (La Haye, 1703).

___. *Dialogues de Monsieur le baron de Lahontan et d'un sauvage, dans l'Amerique . . .* (Amsterdam, 1704).

Larson, John. *Those Army Engineers* (Chicago, 1979).

Margry, M. Pierre, ed. *Découvertes et établissements des Français dans l'ouest et le sud de l'Amerique Septentrionale (1614–1754)*, 6 vols. (Paris, 1879–86).

Mayer, Harold M., and Richard C. Wade. *Chicago: Growth of a Metropolis* (Chicago, 1969).

Meehan, Thomas. "Jean Baptiste Point du Sable, the First Chicagoan." *Journal of the Illinois State Historical Society* 56 (1963).

Miller, Donald L. *City of the Century: The Epic of Chicago and the Making of America* (New York, 1996).

Paul Eduard Miller, ed. *Esquire's 1946 Jazz Book* (New York, 1946).

Moffat, Bruce. *Forty Feet Below: The Story of Chicago's Freight Tunnels* (Glendale, Calif., 1982).

___. *The "L": The Development Of Chicago's Rapid Transit System, 1888–1932* (Chicago, 1995).

Quaife, Milo Milton. *Chicago and the Old Northwest, 1673–1835: A Study of the Evolution of the Northwestern Frontier, together with a History of Fort Dearborn* (Chicago, 1913).

___. *Chicago Highways, Old and New, from Indian Trail to Motor Road* (Chicago, 1923).

___. *Checagou: From Indian Wigwam to Modern City, 1637–1835* (Chicago, 1933).

Schwartz, Seymour I., and Ralph E. Ehrenberg. *The Mapping of America* (New York, 1980).

Stead, William T. *If Christ Came to Chicago!* (Chicago, 1894).

Swenson, John F. "Chicagoua/Chicago: The Origin, Meaning, and Etymology of a Place Name" *Illinois Historical Journal* 84 (1991).

Thévenot, Melchisédech. *Recueil de Voyages de Mr Thévenot* (Paris, 1681).

Thwaites, Reuben Gold, ed. *The Jesuit Relations and Allied Documents—Travels and Explorations of the Jesuit Missionaries in New France, 1610–1791*, 73 vols. (Cleveland, 1896–1901).

Tooley, R.V. *Maps and Mapmakers* (New York, 1987).

Toronto, University of, Université Laval, and the National Archives of Canada. *Dictionary of Canadian Biography Online* (www. biographi.ca).

Wing, J. M. & Co., pub. *The Tunnels and Water System of Chicago: Under the Lake and Under the River* (Chicago, 1874).

INDEX